APOSTLE OF FREEDOM

APOSTLE
OF
FREEDOM

BY D. RAY LINDLEY

THE BETHANY PRESS
St. Louis, Mo.

CONTENTS

PREFACE

The purpose of this book is to present Alexander Campbell's conception of the structure and function of the church as revealed in his extant writings.

The study basically is concerned with the local congregation, and particularly with the educational principles involved in the organizational pattern which Campbell advocated for the local church. Other studies have dealt with Campbell's plea for Christian union. This work concerns itself neither with his advocacy of Christian union, with his total world view of the church, nor with any theology he might have held about the church, except as those areas of his thought shed light on his conception of the functioning of the local congregation as an organized body of Christians, and the way in which the aggregate of local congregations was organically and functionally related to one another.

The natural divisions of the study are: Alexander Campbell's rejection of and opposition to all forms of ecclesiastical control of the local congregation; his conception of the "Lordship of Christ" and the "priesthood of the believer" fusing to bring the church under a "Christocracy"; his understanding of the nature and offices of the Christian ministry, including the call and ordination to those offices; the internal structure of the local congregation as he believed it to center around the "minds of the brethren"; the principle of co-operation by which he urged that the aggregate of local congregations be related to one another in doing all good throughout the world; and finally, his conception of the function of the church, together with a consideration of the implications of his thought for religious education and for that body of Christians known as Disciples of Christ.

Alexander Campbell (1788-1866) was born in County Antrim, Ireland, on September 12, 1788, the son of Thomas Campbell (1763-1854), an ordained minister of the Seceder branch of the Presbyterian church in Northern Ireland, and an honor graduate of the University of Glasgow. Coming from the direct line of the Duke of Argyle, his religious convictions nurtured by such Scotch Independents as Greville Ewing, Robert Haldane, Rowland Hill, Alexander Carson, and Robert Sandeman, and his mind steeped in the writings of John Locke, Francis Bacon, Isaac Newton, David Hume, William Godwin, Thomas Reid, and Rousseau, Alexander Campbell came to America in the year 1809.[1] On account of ill health Thomas Campbell had preceded his family to this country two years previously.

In America, Alexander Campbell launched upon a career which lasted for fifty-seven years, and which projected him into increasing prominence until the day of his death in the year 1866. During those years he was gentleman farmer, Virginia legislator, political theorist, educational philosopher, lecturer, debater, preacher, and religious journalist. But he is known chiefly as the central figure giving stimulus to the origin and early development of that religious communion which developed along the frontier of nineteenth-century America, and which is variously known as "Disciples of Christ," the "Churches of Christ," and "Christians."[2] To date this communion is the largest indigenous religious body hav-

---

[1] A number of biographies of Alexander Campbell's life have been written. These are catalogued in the bibliographical section of this book. *Infra.*, pp. 257ff. Too much work has been done in this connection to justify an extensive treatment here.

[2] For the sake of convenience, we shall henceforth employ the title "Disciples of Christ."

ing its inception in America, and is the fifth largest Protestant body in this country.

Having had their origin along the American frontier, having come to be the largest indigenous denomination in America, and having centered their work and growth in the United States, Disciples of Christ may be considered to be a phenomenon of Christianity adapted to American culture. In a day in which there is a rethinking of democracy as a way of life, of the educational possibilities in a process of group thought and action, and of the church as a seedbed of democracy, a study of the thought of the central figure in a religious movement so peculiarly American in its setting is in order, particularly as that thought relates itself to the organizational structure and function of the church.

This study is based on an objective, critical, and detailed examination of the writings of Alexander Campbell. These include the seven volumes of the *Christian Baptist,* the thirty-five volumes of the *Millennial Harbinger,* the published records of his many debates, the *Christian System,* and the numerous other books which he published during his lifetime.[3] Since the religious journals which he edited and published give continuity to his writings over a period of forty-two years, they are invaluable as a source of his thought. None of his available writings, however, has been omitted from this study.

---

[3]Alexander Campbell owned, edited, and published the *Christian Baptist* (1823-1829) and the *Millennial Harbinger* (1830-1864), both of which were monthly religious journals. In addition to the regular issues, there was an occasional "Extra."

CHAPTER ONE

CAMPBELL'S DEFIANCE
OF ECCLESIASTICAL CONTROL

The present is a momentous crisis. All sects are shaking. The religious world is convulsed. Atheism has opened her batteries and unsheathed her sword. Scepticism is big with hopes. Catholic and protestant Popery are plodding and plotting for the supremacy. The little and the great Popes are on tiptoe. Saints are praying for the Millennium; myriads are laboring for its introduction. The bible and the creeds are at war. There is no truce. Such is the present, and such has been the past.[1]

The tinkle of a token on the communion plate in the Seceder church at Glasgow in the year 1809 had echoed with such crescendo that by the year 1823 it had become the clarion call to a religious crusade in America. It was in the former year that young Alexander Campbell had symbolically broken with the existing order. It was in the latter year that he literally declared war upon it. His infant faith having been cradled in the arms of a religious freethinker, his adolescent thought having been nurtured with the philosophy of John Locke[2] and the preaching of the Scotch Independents,[3] young Campbell

---

[1]Campbell, Alexander. *Christian Baptist*, 1828, VI, 541.

[2]The influence of Locke on Campbell is so well recognized and so undeniable, that there would be little gained by treating of it here.

[3]These included such men as Robert and James Haldane, Greville Ewing, Robert Sandeman, Alexander Carson, John Walker, Rowland Hill, and Dr. Wardlaw. The influence of these men on Campbell has been sufficiently treated by Richardson, Moore, Smith, Athearn, West et al.

11

had approached the semiannual communion service at Glasgow with some misgivings. He had begun to entertain such doubts of his right to continue in the fellowship of the Seceder church that he debated with himself as to whether he should share in the communion service. The church had adopted a rule that all who were entitled to a place at the Lord's Supper should be supplied with a metallic token thus excluding those who were considered unworthy of the holy fellowship. Campbell finally applied for a token, and passed the examination which conditioned its being granted, but when the time came for communion, instead of partaking, he cast the token into the communion plate. Commenting on the incident, Grafton says:

The ring of that token, as it fell from his hands, like the ring of Martin Luther's hammer on the door of the Wittenberg cathedral, announced his renunciation of the old church ties, and marks the moment at which he forever ceased to recognize the claims or authority of a human creed to bind upon men the conditions of their acceptance with God.[4]

But it was a far cry from the Campbell filled with adolescent doubts at Glasgow to the man whom Smith calls "the iconoclast—the image-breaker" of the third decade of the 19th century. It was in the year 1823 that Campbell, declaring that "the present popular exhibition of the christian religion is a compound of judaism, heathen philosophy and christianity," began to edit and publish the *Christian Baptist* with the avowed intention of restoring primitive Christianity. In the closing volume of this, his first editorial venture, Campbell succinctly sets forth his moving objectives:

To the co-operation of a few friends, under the divine government, is to be ascribed the success which has accompanied this first effort to restore a pure speech to the people of God—to

---

[4]Grafton, Thomas. *Alexander Campbell* (St. Louis: Christian Board of Publication, 1897), p. 41.

restore the ancient order of things in the christian kingdom—
to emancipate the conscience from the dominion of human
authority in matters of religion, and to lay a foundation, an
imperishable foundation, for the union of all christians, and for
their co-operation in spreading the glorious gospel throughout
the world.[5]

It is all very well to delve into the Irish and Scotch
milieu of Campbell's training, to call attention to the
many scholars to whom he inclined his head, to point out
that he sprang out of the matrix of a culture which had
begun to seethe with the spirit of freedom. These were
factors which helped to make him a product of his age.
But it took more than these to make him the reformer,
the crusader. Something had happened between the
years of 1809 and 1823 to cause him to want to consume
and destroy all forms of what he conceived to be religious
tyrannies.

If we are to seek the answer to what had happened,
we find our clues partly in the record of those years
and partly in Campbell's own peculiar mental traits.
There were two aspects of his mental make-up which are
essential to any satisfactory understanding of Campbell.
The first has been pointed out by Fred West:

When he was interested chiefly in physical endeavors, he won
the reputation of being able to hurl the *biggest* snowballs of
all those by his playmates. Moreover, Alexander Campbell
wanted to roll the *largest snowballs!* When he was laboring
on the farm, he got interested in it enough to delight in the *art*
of being the *best* sower of grain. He achieved the reputation
by his associates of being an *expert* hunter, and an *expert*
fisherman.

Now, how does this apply to his intellectual world? The
answer is simple; as put in his own words, he aspired to be
"one of the best scholars in the kingdom."[6]

[5]*Christian Baptist*, VII, 661.

[6]West, Fred. *Alexander Campbell and Natural Religion.* Sterling Library, Yale University, New Haven, Conn. An unpublished dissertation, pp. vi-vii.

This was the aspect of his nature which did much to make of him a crusader. The historical incident which did most to arouse his competitive spirit was his debate with John Walker on the subject of Christian baptism. He experienced such keen joy in the conquest which he felt he had made that from this time forth he was like a soldier roused for battle. Here for the first time he began to discover those powers of generalization and the rapierlike gift of satire which did much to shape his future career. His chief biographer, Robert Richardson, says:

It was not until after he saw the effect of the debate into which he was reluctantly drawn with Mr. Walker that he began to take new views of his position, and to cherish, for the first time, the hope that something might be done upon a more extended scale to rouse the people from their spiritual lethargy.[7]

Campbell himself attests the importance which he attached to this debate in the following passage:

. . . In the year 1820, when solicited to meet Mr. Walker on the subject of baptism, I hesitated for six months whether it were lawful thus to defend the truth. I was written to three times before I gained my own consent. I did not like controversy so well as many have since thought I did; and I was doubtful of the effects it might have upon society. These difficulties were, however, overcome, and we met. It was not until after I discovered the effects of that discussion that I began to hope that something might be done to rouse this generation from its supineness and spiritual lethargy. About two years afterwards I conceived the plan of this work, and thought I should make the experiment. I did so, and the effects are now before the public.[8]

It was thus that Campbell found a method of achieving mastery through religious controversy. But his desire to throw the largest snowballs does not explain why he

[7]Richardson, Robert. *Memoirs of Alexander Campbell*, II, 49.
[8]*Christian Baptist*, VII, 1.

took the particular stand which he did against organized Christianity as constituted at that time. Our clue to this phase of his career is found in the second distinctive quality of his mental make-up. That quality was the extreme degree to which he was aroused by what he considered to be any personal affront. Alexander Campbell changed in many things, but he never changed in these two psychological traits: desire for mastery, and sensitivity to whatever he considered to be a threat or affront to his person. Any satisfactory understanding of him must recognize the presence of these two qualities.

As to the second of the qualities mentioned, there is evidence of its existence in every issue of every magazine or book which he published. Not only is it there, but its presence is the only satisfactory explanation of contradictions which otherwise seem irreconcilable. Because of its presence he opposed every major movement among Disciples of Christ which he either did not initiate or of which he was not made the head. Because of it he could be vitriolic when attacked by an opponent, although all his associates attest to his gentle nature. Because of it he consistently denied that he ever changed his position after beginning the publication of the *Christian Baptist,* although any number of his later writings can be adduced which are greatly at variance with his earlier utterances. And because of this he launched on a lifetime crusade against all ecclesiasticisms in response to the presumption of the Presbytery of Chartiers, Washington County, Pennsylvania, in bringing charges of heresy against his father, Thomas Campbell. If the debate with Walker was the historic incident which set fire to his desire for mastery, the heresy trial of his father was the historic incident which aroused him to an undying conflict with all ecclesiasticisms.

It would be unfair to Campbell to suggest that this is the complete story. He was a man of deep personal faith and piety, he held a great reverence for the authority of the scriptures, and he never failed to be moved with an earnest spirit of inquiry and devotion to truth. Moreover, his mind and heart were prepared with a love of freedom before he came to America. But more than anything else these two mental traits and these two historical experiences helped to set him apart from other lovers of truth and liberty, and to cause him to dedicate himself to a conflict with all forms of ecclesiastical tyranny.

The trial of Thomas Campbell is often thought of as an incident, however important, in the life of Alexander Campbell. It would be better thought of as the key to his career. Coming as it did at the very time when the decision as to his lifework was being made, and being of such a nature as to outrage his sensitive spirit, it launched him on his career. The situation was as follows:

Thomas Campbell, after gentle attempts at reform as a minister of the Seceder Presbyterian church of Scotland, embarked for America in pursuit of better health, leaving his family in Scotland. Alexander, as the eldest son, shouldered many of the responsibilities of the family, and in the year 1808 at the bidding of his father, he set sail with them for America. Because of a shipwreck, the family was delayed for about a year, during which time they removed to Glasgow where Alexander entered the University. In the fall of 1809 they again set sail for America, arriving in New York on September 29. Upon the first meeting of Alexander with his father in the New World, he was greeted with the story of his father's trial for heresy. Richardson, who is our best authority for this history, details the story of the trial:

. . . It happened that, about this time, he was deputed to visit a few scattered members of the flock who were living some distance up the Alleghany above Pittsburg, and to hold amongst them, in conjunction with a young minister, a Mr. Wilson, who accompanied him, a communion, or, as it was termed, a "sacramental" celebration. This part of the country was then thinly settled, and it was seldom that ministerial services were enjoyed by the various fragments of religious parties, which, having floated off from the Old World upon the tide of emigration, had been thrown together in the circling eddies of these new settlements. It happened that, on this occasion, Mr. Campbell's sympathies were strongly aroused in regard to the destitute condition of some in the vicinity who belonged to other branches of the Presbyterian family, and who had not, for a long time, had an opportunity of partaking of the Lord's Supper, and he felt it his duty, in the preparation sermon, to lament the existing divisions, and to suggest that all his pious hearers, who felt so disposed and duly prepared, should, without respect to party differences, enjoy the benefits of the communion season then providentially afforded them. Mr. Wilson did not, at that time, publicly oppose these overtures, but finding, from these proceedings and from his conversations and discussions with Mr. Campbell, that the latter had but little respect for the division walls which the different parties had built up with so much pains, his sectarian prejudices became fully aroused. He felt it his duty, therefore, at the next meeting of the Presbytery, to lay the case before it in the usual form of "libel," containing various formal and specified charges, the chief of which were that Mr. Campbell had failed to inculcate strict adherence to the Church standard and usages, and had even expressed his disapproval of some things in said standard and of the uses made of them.[9]

Thomas Campbell made a strong defense, appealing to the Bible and pleading for Christian liberty and fraternity. He was not dismissed from the Presbytery, but was censured for not adhering to the "Secession Testimony."

The result was the preparation of the famous *Declaration and Address,* which was delivered before the Associate Synod of North America, and which led directly to his withdrawal from the Synod and the clustering around

---

[9]Richardson, *op. cit.,* I, 224-225.

him of many friends of independence. To all the principles of this document Alexander gave his unswerving allegiance. From this date the lines were gradual in forming, but the die was cast. A voice was in training to be raised against religious tyrannies. It cried out in many directions. In its course it was to condemn all existing religious sects, ecclesiasticisms, courts, synods, associations, creeds, orders of succession, and systems of priesthood. Basic to Campbell's whole position was the assumption that the Church of Rome was a major heresy, and that the reformation begun by Luther had retained most of its errors. The Roman Catholic Church was the "Mother of Harlots," and the Protestant sects were its offspring. The remainder of this chapter will be devoted to dealing in order with Campbell's attitude toward the various phases of 19th-century Christianity which he believed contained the seeds of religious tyranny.

I. *The Roman Church and Her Progeny*

Campbell possessed a sensitive nature, but he was also endowed with a coldly logical mind. Benjamin Lyon Smith says of him: "No one can have a proper understanding of his peculiar cast of mind and action who does not perceive him as unemotional and coldly intellectual." He possessed great powers of generalization, and his success in debate was due largely to the fact that he proceeded from his premises in an airtight, logical fashion. To defeat him it was essential to refute his major assumptions. In his campaign against ecclesiasticism, his whole position rested upon a few major assumptions:

(1) The supreme authority of the scriptures.
(2) The absolute lordship of Christ.
(3) The priesthood of every believer.
(4) That the church is essentially, intentionally, constitutionally one.

(5) The autonomy of the local congregation.
(6) That the Roman heirarchy is Antichrist, the Mother of Harlots, and has usurped the inalienable rights of believers.
(7) That 19th-century Protestantism contained all the seeds of the various forms of Roman tyranny and represented a hierarchy of descent from the Mother.
(8) That Christianity is under an imperative to restore the primitive church in its pure form.

Since large groups of Protestants were ready to endorse the first four of these premises, Campbell devoted considerable attention to the fifth, sixth, and seventh. By establishing the sixth and seventh propositions he felt that he could shatter all forms of religious tyranny with one grand stroke. The realization of the eighth proposition would then be a matter of course.

A. *"The Mother of Harlots"*

Campbell's various criticisms of the Roman Catholic church may be grouped under four general headings: 1. It is without scriptural warrant. 2. It embodies religious tyranny, denying the priesthood of the believer. 3. It aims at political tyranny, seeking union with the state, and dominance over the state. 4. It thwarts the true basis of culture by withholding the Bible as a textbook from the masses.

Campbell approached his conflict with Roman Catholicism as himself a Protestant. As such, his appeal was to the scriptures.

1. *The Roman Catholic Church Is Without Scriptural Warrant*

The first and characteristic difference between the Protestant and the Roman Catholic, said Campbell, is that the former relies on the scriptures first and the church afterward. The Roman Catholic does contrari-

wise. The Protestant rule of faith is superior to the
Roman Catholic on seven grounds. These grounds are
that it is inspired, it is authoritative, it is intelligible, it
is moral, it is perpetual, it is catholic, it is perfect.

Not only does Roman Catholicism fail to appeal to
the scriptures. It is contrary to the scriptures:

> . . . The Douay catechism, in answer to the question—''What
> are the essential parts of the church?'' teaches ''A Pope, or
> supreme head, bishops, pastors, and laity.'' p. 20.

These, then, are the four constituent and essential elements
of the Roman Catholic church. The first is the pope, or head.
It will be confessed by all, that, of these, the most essential is
the head. But should we take away any one of these, she loses
her identity, and ceases to be what she assumes. My first
effort then shall be to prove that, for hundreds of years after
Christ, she was without such a head; the most indispensable of
these elements; and consequently, this being essential to her
existence, she was not from the beginning. Because no body
can exist before its head. . . .

I affirm then, that not one of the offices, I have enumerated,
as belonging to the Roman Catholic church, was known in the
days of the apostles, or is found in the New Testament. On the
contrary, the very notion of a vicar of Christ, of a prince of
the apostles, or of a universal head, and government in the
Christian church is repugnant to the genius and spirit of the
religion. We shall read a few passages of scripture, from the
Roman version, to prove that the very idea of an earthly head
is unscriptural and anti-scriptural.[10]

In line with his strategy of striking at the head, Campbell set out to establish that the whole concept of a
''pope'' was without foundation. Peter could never
have been bishop at Rome because his commission as an
apostle precluded it. Every office is specific, and the
offices of apostle and bishop are incompatible. The
commission of an apostle is universal, a bishop watches
over a particular diocese. One might as well try to make

---

[10]*Campbell-Purcell Debate*, p. 13.

the President of the United States mayor of Cincinnati.
The entire attempt to establish papal succession through
Peter rests on a gross misinterpretation of Matthew 16.
Campbell's interpretation of this passage is best given
in his debate with Bishop Purcell:

... There are, indeed, but three cardinal ideas in all Christian
doctrine; for there can be but three cardinal ideas about any
being. Two of these are distinctly embodied in Peter's confession of faith. The whole three are, 1st the person, 2nd the
office, and 3rd the character of Christ. Beyond these—*person,
office,* and *character,* what conception can mortals have of our
Redeemer? Peter mouthed of these, the two which gave value
to the third—the *person* and the *mission* of Jesus. He was the
first mortal who, distinctly and intelligibly avowed the faith,
in the person and mission of Jesus the Nazarene, upon which the
empire of the ransomed race shall stand forever. This is the
good confession spoken by Jesus himself at the hazard of his
life, before Pontius Pilate, of which Paul speaks in the highest
terms of admiration.

Now, because Peter was the first to utter it, Jesus says to him:
"I will give to you the keys of the kingdom of heaven."

What a controversy there has been about these keys. Jesus
gave them to Peter alone—not to him, his heirs, and successors
forever! ... The gates of heaven have not since been locked.
There is no more use for the keys. Peter has them yet. He
took them to heaven with him. He did not will them to any
heir or successor. The popes are fighting for shadows. Heaven
never trusted such gentry with the keys. They might take into
their heads to lock the heretics out.[11]

Not only is there no supremacy, there is no succession of church office. The idea of apostolic succession
rests upon a failure to understand the apostolic office.
If the apostles had successors, they would be apostles,
too. But the office of apostle was a special office to continue for only a limited time. Apostles were supernatural characters, designed for a special object. This

---

[11]*Ibid.,* pp. 84-85.

object was the erection of the church, after which a regular and permanent type of office was to be created. If there had ever been any such thing as apostolic succession, the church of Rome could lay no claim to it, for there have been so many "leaky" prelates that no man living could swear that the hands laid upon his head had any more connection with Peter or any of the apostles than with Aaron or Melchizedek.

That Campbell felt that he had sufficiently established his position is seen in the following passage:

. . . To adopt the positive and dogmatic style of my learned opponent, may I not say that *I have fully proved*—

1. That the office of pope, or supreme head on earth, has no scripture warrant or authority whatever. Indeed, that the whole *beau ideal* of a church of nations, with a monarchical head . . . is as gratuitous an assumption as ever graced a *romance*, ancient or modern.

2. That it cannot be ascertained that Peter was ever bishop of Rome—nay, it has been shown that it is wholly contrary to the New Testament history, and incompatible with his office.

3. That Christ gave no law of succession.

4. That if he had, that succession has been destroyed by a long continuance of the greatest monsters of crime that ever lived; and by cabals, intrigues, violence, envy, lust, and schisms, so that no man can believe that one drop of apostolic grace is either in person or office of Gregory XVI, the present nominal incumbent of Peter's chair![12]

2. *The Roman Catholic Church Embodies Religious Tyranny, Denying the Priesthood of the Believer*

Christians, *true Christians*, never persecuted. They never erected tribunals for orthodoxy; they never proscribed men for matters of opinion; and they who call themselves Christians, and mimic the Mother of Harlots, had better pause and examine their title to the denomination *Christian*.[13]

---

[12]*Ibid.*, pp. 139-140.
[13]*Millennial Harbinger*, 1830, p. 435.

The mightiest tools of the Church of Rome have been "the lightning and thunder of the Vatican, the racks, and wheels, and screws, and fires of the Inquisition." The laws of Christ are too mild and simple for Antichrist, they leave no penalties that man can apply. Therefore, Rome made laws which can be brought to bear upon earth, such as dungeons, fires, and excommunications for the purging of the church of Christ.

In order to aid the despotism of popery the church must needs have its ecclesiasticisms, its few general councils, its definitions, and must use as much Latin as possible in its modes of worship. In fact, its great objective is to abolish thinking altogether:

It is as contrary to reason as to religion. To make men think infallibly by infallible definitions is the perfection of folly. And to place virtue and vice in not thinking at all, or in thinking from necessity, by statute and penalty, is abhorrent to religion—all the world, but Roman Catholics, being judges.[14]

It is ridiculous for the Roman Catholic to believe that there is more authority and reason in church councils than in his own opinion, for does he not follow his own opinion when he follows the decision of the general council or when he holds that the pope is infallible? All church tribunals which substitute their own reasonings for the authority of the scriptures and then enact that men should not rely upon their own conclusions are guilty of a palpable sophistry.

Tyranny is not dependent upon any particular individual in the Roman church, but upon the very nature of the system itself:

Popery is naturally, necessarily, and essentially despotic, cruel, and implacable. It constitutionally claims a sovereignty over not only the secular sword, but over everything on earth—thought, language, action, spirit, soul, body, and estate. It regards itself as the heir of all earthly things, and by a right

---

[14]*Ibid.*, 1834, p. 264.

divine and irrevocable, the only earthly King of Kings and
Lord of Lords. Its motto is, The empire of the globe, or nothing.
The law of gravity will cease to act sooner than this superstition
sleep on this side of absolute dominion.

. . . .

. . . While Popery lives, it must reign.[15]

3. *The Roman Catholic Church Aims at Tyranny, Seeking Union with the State, and Dominance over the State*

But the presumptions of the papacy do not end with
despotism in the realm of religion. They extend to the
state itself. Next to the institution of slavery, Campbell feared the rapid growth of the popish empire as a
threat to American freedom. To thwart this he called
upon all Protestant sects to join in a mutual association:

I am no friend to Protestant Popery any more than to Papal
Popery; but the Protestant Popes are pigmies compared with
his Roman Holiness, and they will hold each other in check
until the people will be able to repudiate them all. And,
therefore, I say, let all the Protestant Popes unite and bear
their united testimony against the Grand Papa, and then they
will be the more willing and able to recede from their unequal
assumptions.[16]

Campbell held that it is in the very nature of political
religious establishment to extend its proscriptions from
the religious to the civil life, that whenever Christianity
(so called) mounts the throne, it begins to hurl its
anathemas against those who dissent from the popular
opinions. When Christianity gains the throne, Jesus
Christ will place it there himself, but that shall not be
until the millennium.

Campbell was not content simply to oppose the control of the state by any kind of ecclesiasticism, or the

---

[15]*Ibid.*, 1835, p. 114.
[16]*Ibid.*, 1843, p. 352.

union of Church and State. He went further and opposed any form of court religion. At this point, the Church of England as well as that of Rome came under his axe:

I must distinctly state the capital error in the Magna Charta of Great Britain, so pregnant with evil to the government and to the nation. But you anticipate me and point to that article which says, "The King of England joins to the dignity of Supreme Magistrate that of Head of the Church." Thus being constituted HEAD OF THE CHURCH "gives him power to convoke national and provincial Synods, who, under his approbation, *establish dogmas and discipline*," and also authorizes him to appoint the chief ecclesiastical dignitaries. Thus the King or Queen Monarch of Great Britain is, in fact, made the visible and efficient Head of the Church of England, presumed to be the Church of Christ. He is, therefore, as much a spiritual as a civil Monarch. This assumption constitutes him a Protestant Pope—as true and real as he of Rome, though with a jurisdiction more limited in territory and in spiritual supervision. He does not, indeed, profess to be infallible; but only acts as though he was.[17]

The influence of Romanism was like a termite undermining the spirit of liberty, for even though in America it did not control the state, its benumbing and paralyzing influence disqualified a person for the relish and enjoyment of political liberty. For civil liberty always follows in the wake of religious liberty; religious liberty is the cause, and political liberty the effect of that cause, without which it has never been found.

The idea of a national church must be rejected, not only because it leads to tyranny and oppression, but because it leads to the degeneracy of the church itself:

I will go farther and affirm the deep and heart-felt conviction, that none of the national churches has ever been converted to God. "They are Pagan in heart." There are Christians in them all; but none of them are Christian. Christianity must be

---

[17]*Ibid.*, 1848, p. 661.

greatly corrupted before it could be established by any nation—even Scotland itself. Whatever creed has been national is not Christian, no matter how much sound doctrine is in it. Whatever will please a king and his court, or the majority of Scotland, England, or France, is not according to the New Testament.[18]

4. The Roman Catholic Church Thwarts the True Basis of Culture by Withholding From the Masses the Bible as a Textbook

Perhaps the greatest of all indictments Campbell made against the Roman church was his accusation of what it did to the principle of growth. It is at this point that he gave evidence of faith in democracy not simply as a principle of control, as an expedient of government, but as a way of life:

Roman Catholicism enervates, while Protestantism energizes and invigorates the minds of people. Free discussion, free thinking, free reading, and most of all, freedom of action, expand and corroborate the human mind. Popery dethrones reason, inhibits inquisitiveness, anathematizes thinking for oneself, denounces the Protestant Reformation and condemns to eternal perdition, all beyond the precincts of her communion.[19]

His grand proposition for thwarting all such attempts to control the minds of men was double-barreled: universal education, and the Bible as a textbook. With regard to the first he says:

. . .The Roman hierarchy and Negro slavery, or the former by means of the latter, may, and in all probability will, dash the American ship upon a rock, and engulf us all in one common ruin.

But there is an ark of safety which might be reared, if we had one hundred and twenty years to construct it. That ark is UNIVERSAL EDUCATION—education patronized, sustained,

[18]*Ibid.*, 1844, p. 409.
[19]*Ibid.*, 1848, p. 672.

guarded, and controlled by the State.   Enlighten all, Catholic and Protestant.

Let it be the first care of every state to have all its children well educated.   Let there be state funds, state teachers, state schools, and state laws compelling all to be enlightened.   Let no uneducated youth, whether 21 or 22 years old, be considered his own master unless he be well educated in all the branches of a good English education. . . .

. . . An enlightened community cannot be enslaved—an ignorant and an uneducated community cannot be free.[20]

This was a theme which occupied Campbell's attention throughout his career. He wrote thousands of pages upon the subject. But he always made it clear that while education is the task of the state, no education is complete without the Bible as a part of the curriculum. When he was challenged to reconcile this position with his stand against a court religion, he asserted the following:

In all nations, as well as in our own, there is a by law established religion. What, say some American citizens, have *we* a *by law* established religion? Yes, fellow-citizens, we have a by law established religion. I do not affirm that we have a *by law established* Jewish, Christian, or Pagan religion, in the specific terms of a Jewish, a Christian, a Roman, or an English hierarchy. Still, we have a *by law established religion;* not, indeed, in any specific form of worship, but in the rights of conscience, in the administration of oaths, or appeals to God, on the part of all the organs of civil government, from the President of the United States down to a common magistrate, and in the administration of oaths to all witnesses, according to the conscience. In these we have a solemn recognition of the being and perfections of God, of a day of judgment, of future and eternal rewards and punishments. We have, moreover, a still more specific recognition, though not an exclusive recognition, of the Christian religion, in the observance of the ordinances of Christian worship, in the cessation of all secular and legal business on the "Christian Sabbath,". . . or Lord's day, . . . and in

---

[20]*Ibid.*, 1835, pp. 66-67.

a perfect freedom to swear and to worship God according to the dictates of every citizen's own conscience. . . .

Religion, in its essence and spirit, can never be compulsory, as in the Papal states and territories; but it can, and of political right and immunity ought to be, left to the free choice and the spontaneous action of every human being.[21]

Building upon this premise, Campbell pleaded that the people be given the Bible without creeds. Even though the governors be atheists, as a political defense against papal tyranny, let them decree that the Bible be read and taught in the schools by the same authority which administers oaths before civil tribunals. "In one word, let no squeamishness on the subject of a state religion, prevent the reading and teaching of the Bible; the Bible is the shield of the nation."

B. *The Daughters of "The Mother of Harlots"*

The old scriptural adage, "Who can bring a clean thing out of an unclean?" has caused me long since to despair of any "Protestant" sect rising above its fountain. If the mother sect was a tyrant, the daughter will ape her temper; and when of mature age and reason, she will imitate her practice.[22]

Campbell approached his conflict with Roman Catholicism as a Protestant, appealing to the Protestant "rule of faith and practice." But the Protestantism he defended was not a "pretended" Protestantism. It was "true, real, and unsophisticated," the Protestantism of Wyckliffe and Peter Bruys rather than that of Martin Luther or John Calvin. It was that Protestantism which was

. . . A solemn negation of all human dictation and usurpation over man's understanding, conscience and affections; over his personal liberty of thought, of speech, and of action, in reference to each and every thing pertaining to himself, his fellows, his God, and his Redeemer.

[21]*Ibid.*, 1854, pp. 67-68.
[22]*Ibid.*, 1833, pp. 469-470.

Education, religion, morals and politics, are, therefore, the fields and realms over which Protestantism, *de jure Divino*, presides.[23]

The Protestantism which had bred the competing sects of 19th-century Christianity was of an entirely different sort. "The reformations most celebrated in the world are those which have departed least from the systems which they professed to reform."[24] The Protestant reformation under Luther was held to have been more political than religious, the well-meant efforts of Luther having been frustrated by both the friends of reformation and the schemes of statesmen. Even the attempt to go back to the Bible had been frustrated by the adoption by the friends of Luther of the rules of interpretation of the papistical doctors.

The tragedy of the reformation was in the fact that it had bred a multitude of Popes in the place of one:

. . . It has happened to some of them as it happened to those called Reformers from Popery. They disliked the Pope in Rome, but had no objections to a Pope in Geneva or at Wirtemberg. They disliked the incumbent rather than the incumbency; and each sect in setting up for itself, had either an effigy of the Pope's chair, or a few of the relics of an old one set up in their little *Sancta Sanctorum*.[25]

Campbell entered the conflict against what he conceived to be Protestant tyranny not as a Protestant, but as an iconoclast. He chose the path not of reformation but of restoration. The only solution was a "Restoration of the Ancient Order of Things," a theme on which he wrote some thirty-odd editorials. In the very first of these he said:

All the famous reformations in history have rather been reformations of creeds and of clergy, than of religion. Since the

[23]*Ibid.*, 1852, p. 454.
[24]*Christian Baptist*, II, 127.
[25]*Ibid.*, V, 442.

New Testament was finished, it is fairly to be presumed that there cannot be any reformation of religion, properly so called. Though called reformations of religion, they have always left religion where it was. . . .

Human creeds may be reformed and re-reformed, and be erroneous still, like their authors; but the inspired creed needs no reformation, being like its author, infallible. The clergy, too, may be reformed from papistical opinions, grimaces, tricks, and dresses, to protestant opinions and ceremonies; protestant clergy may be reformed from protestant to presbyterial metaphysics and forms; and presbyterian clergy may be reformed to independency, and yet the Pope remain in their heart. They are clergy still—and still in need of reformation. . . .

A restoration of the ancient order of things is all that is necessary to the happiness and usefulness of christians.[26]

In his insistence on the similarity between Roman Catholic and Protestant forms and systems Campbell's art of satire was most dexterous, and his contemporary opponents felt its sting. The following passage is illustrative of any number of similar vein:

. . . Archbishop Laud and Lawrence Greatrake are both clergymen, though of different dimensions. The spirit of the latter is as lordly and pontifical as that of the former, though his arm and his gown are shorter. The moschetto is an animal of the same genus with the hornet, though the bite of the former is not so powerful as the sting of the latter. A creed, too, that is formed in Geneva or in London, is as human as one formed in Constantinople. They have all given employment to tax gatherers, jail-keepers, and grave diggers.[27]

Campbell anticipated Pearl Buck by more than a hundred years in feeling that this tendency toward dictatorship in the sects of Christianity represented the totalitarian movement in America. In fact, political democracy in America seemed to be the only factor holding them in check:

---

[26]*Ibid.*, II, 127-128.
[27]*Ibid.*, II, 128.

. . . The Catholic, Episcopalian, and Presbyterian in America, are the same as in Rome, England, and Scotland, only under the control of different circumstances.   Assimilate the circumstances here to the circumstances there, and no law of nature will be more consistent with itself than the spirit of these sects.   They would be on the throne here, as certainly as the smoke ascends upwards. . . .

. . . The creed must be changed, and its spirit cast out, before I dare trust my civil liberties in the hands of the best members of any one of these three royal sects.   Each of them has its children too; and, as nature never errs, the third generation is to be suspected as well as its progenitors.[28]

Campbell was careful to remind American citizens that preachers "at home and abroad . . . opposed the American revolution."   On the contrary, it seemed to be his goal to help usher in a religious freedom commensurate with the political freedom which he enjoyed in America, and for which he never ceased to be grateful.   In one of his letters to his daughter, Clarinda, written from England, he says:

We can desire for ourselves no better political or temporal birthrights or inheritance than we now possess, and we can pray for no greater honors and privileges of this world for any living people greater or better than those guarantied by our institutions to every American citizen.   May we act worthily of them! May they be long continued as the inheritance of our posterity, and may they soon be bestowed on all kindreds, tongues, and people of earth, until there shall ascend from every dwelling on the spacious earth one grateful song of praise to Him that hath redeemed man from the tyranny of man, and invested the human race with equal laws, equal institutions, and equal national and political birthrights, leaving it to every human being under the government and providence of God to be the architect of his own fortune—the creator of his own personal rank, dignity, and honor.[29]

---

[28]*Millennial Harbinger,* 1833, pp. 469-470.
[29]*Ibid.,* 1848, p. 678.

But if civil liberty had been achieved in America, religious liberty was still only a dream, the realization of which awaited the "restoration of the ancient order of things." Throughout the years from Campbell's arrival in America until the early days of the publication of the *Millennial Harbinger,* which was founded in the year 1830, his cry against sectarianism was the cry of a hurt thing, an injured soul. The heresy trial of his father was succeeded in the third decade of the 19th century by charges of heresy brought against himself and his followers by the Redstone Baptist Association, with which they had identified themselves. Later, when his leadership threatened to disrupt the entire Baptist movement in America, there were wholesale ejections of his followers from various Baptist associations. To understand him during this period, his extreme sensitiveness to what he considered any kind of personal affront, as well as his own natural love of freedom and his respect for individual personality, must be kept in mind. He was more than an apostle of religious liberty, he was a wounded spirit, personally bearing in his body any slight against any of his followers. His publications were filled with protestations against such proscriptions, even though in some cases he did not even know the injured parties.

His movement was frankly of a proselyting nature. Although the first intentions of Thomas Campbell had been anything but the creation of a new religious movement, and Alexander Campbell had distinctly disavowed any such intentions on numerous occasions, his position had led him to the point where the favorite battle cry of himself and his associates was "come out from among them." His two grand indictments of Roman Catholicism as Antichrist and Protestantism as its offspring could have entailed nothing else.

In his excoriation of sectarianism, no denomination escaped. He was, however, more friendly to some than to others. In a way, he never ceased to woo the Baptists, though stung to some of his most bitter remarks by their spurning of his courtship. The Congregationalists, too, came in for only minor thrusts, and that because of their tendency toward state religion in New England. On the whole, Protestantism was divided into two camps, the daughters and the granddaughters of the old Mother. In the first group were those which had either adopted an Episcopal form of government or had been wedded to the state—the Episcopal, Presbyterian, and Methodist churches. In the second group were the Independents —the Baptists and the Congregationalists. Other groups yet, such as the Quakers, came in occasionally for consideration, but the man "who liked to throw the biggest snowballs" wasted little time on lesser adversaries. As in the case of his debate with Robert Owen, only the biggest infidel of them all merited his attention.

1. *The Daughters Who Most Resembled the Mother*

. . . there is but a paper wall between England and Rome. The church of England, with king Henry or George IV. as her head, though a celebrated reformation, has made but a few and very short strides from her mother, the church of Rome, with the pope at her head. . . . The reformation of the church of England, effected by Mr. Wesley, . . . has entailed the same clerical dominion over that zealous people, which their forefathers complained of in the hierarchies of England and of Rome.[30]

a) *The Church of England*

The only real differences distinguishing one state religion from another, Campbell held, were differences in nomenclature and locus. Time and again he mentioned both the Church of England and the Church of Scotland in the same breath with the Church of Rome, and brought against them the same indictments. They were possessed of the same presumptions for power, and made

---

[30]*Christian Baptist*, II, 127.

use of the same weapons in their efforts to enslave the minds of men. The Church of England still retained the rituals and the ecclesiasticisms of Rome, and the two actually "sympathize with one another in their notions of sacerdotal lineage and the authority of human heads, on which a Roman prelate has laid his blood-stained hands." In a way, the Church of England was the loser in the exchange, for it had actually gained little or nothing in its reformation, while retaining the errors of Rome. "I do not think that King Harry was a whit more religious when he proclaimed himself head of the church of England, than when writing against Luther on the seven sacraments, as a true son of the church of Rome."[31] As a matter of fact, it had weakened its position, for at least the Roman Catholics were more consistent when it came to the doctrine of infallibility:

. . . Until . . . you can find a synod partly composed of such characters as are competent to enact decrees under the infallible guidance of the Holy Spirit . . . it is vain to plead . . . for ecclesiastical courts, or to talk of enacting authoritative rules of faith and manners for the disciples of Christ. The claims of the court of Rome, on this score, have some degree of consistency with them. It at once sets up for infallibility, and his Holiness tells you plainly, that he is the successor of Peter, and derives his authority immediately from Jesus Christ, whose vicar he is upon earth, but there are ecclesiastical courts claiming a right, authoritatively, to enact laws for the people of God; to determine articles of faith, and resolve cases of conscience, and that, at the very time they are disclaiming every thing like infallibility.[32]

The Roman Catholics also had the advantage when it came to the doctrine of apostolic succession, the essential difference being priority of title, the "keys of the kingdom" being very rusty indeed when attached by act of Parliament. In fact, the only way in which either

[32]*Ibid.*, IV, 317.
[31]*Ibid.*, II, 128.

Episcopalians or Presbyterians could hope successfully to withstand the position of Roman Catholicism would be by an abandonment of their own creed, as they could not hope to wage a successful war on the Mother Church while holding fast the traditions which they had received from her.

b) The Presbyterian Church

". . . The appelation *church*, from designating a few disciples associated together to sing praises to Jesus Christ" (and commemorate his death), "has come to signify a large and respectable body or sect of professing christians, once a year represented in general assembly, or in its convocation of bishops, usually convened to make laws to bind the consciences of their careless and submissive adherents. Accordingly, we have the Romish church, the Episcopal church, The Presbyterian church."[33]

Here was a tender spot indeed! Campbell not only could bring all the charges against the Presbyterians which he brought against the Romans and Anglicans, he had a few choice grievances of his own. It was the church of his childhood, of his first communion. And it was the church which had dared to bring heresy charges against his father!

Campbell was never more bitter against tyranny than when it was found in supposedly democratic institutions:

Our pious forefathers hated persecution while they were its unfortunate victims; but soon as their wounds were healed under the genial influence of an American sun, they thought of erecting to themselves temples and tribunals after the manner of England and Scotland, of France and Italy, only without that imp of horror, a Lord Inquisitor. A few lashes, indeed, at least skin deep, they thought might be good for the soul, and accordingly they made for themselves a few scourges for the spiritual good of their much beloved neighbors and brethren, the Quakers and Baptists; thus showing, that, in their judgment, a few gentle strokes, dealt out by *Protestant* hands, could

---

[33]*Ibid.*, IV, 315.

have no bad effect when judiciously administered to bodies not their own.[34]

It was the intolerant spirit of Presbyterianism to which Campbell attributed the beginning of his career. Even in the face of what he considered the errors of the Presbyterians he had not separated from them, but they had separated from him.

He insisted that American Presbyterianism was guilty of seeking court favors, of surreptitiously courting favors from the state. "They too much resemble the royalist, who, in drinking a toast to the protector Cromwell, would by a glance of his eye, show that Charles was in his heart."[35] On two different occasions Campbell called them to task on the grounds of seeking national favor. The first was in connection with an attempt by the Synod of Kentucky to get a bill passed through the state legislature in 1824 for the establishment of a university at Danville, permanently vesting its government and control in the hands of the Synod. This became the occasion for another satirical outburst:

. . . If the legislature incorporate a University for creating priests, let all the religious sects in Kentucky, who desire to have priests manufactured in modern style, have a fair, that is, an equal chance of participating in its advantages. . . . But, perhaps, it may be thought expedient to have a few high priests in the state; if so, then do not give the control of the University to the Presbyterian synod, for they stand in the least need of it, inasmuch as they are pretty generally high priests already.

. . . .

What sort of a spirit do they exhibit in this effort? What moved them to solicit such a favor for themselves, to the exclusion of all other christian sects? I see in them the spirit of the two sons of Zebedee . . . we are up, we wish to be higher, and to see our brethren among the vulgus. We want the throne

[34]*Millennial Harbinger*, 1833, p. 468.
[35]*Ibid.*, 1833, p. 468.

—we know how to wield the sceptre; for we were born to rule, and other religious sectaries to obey. We are no friends to equal rights and immunities—we would rather have peculiar rights and privileges ourselves.[36]

A second protest was occasioned by the General Assembly of the Presbyterian Church entertaining a motion to return thanks to Congress for its decision in a certain matter. This Campbell regarded as a jesuitical stroke of policy to gain power. "If the authority of the General Assembly is to be felt in Congress, in the way of benediction, it is to be presumed that it would soon expect to be felt in the way of malediction."[37]

c) The Methodist Episcopal Church

. . . The Methodist people never made any part of their government, any more than the present Catholics living in Louisiana, made the present pope of Rome.

. . . .

America has no men standing upon its soil, who possess so great and so varied authority, as the present dynasty of the Methodist Episcopal church.[38]

Campbell affirmed that there was not a more concentrated despotism on earth, outside of the city of Rome, than that which Methodist Episcopacy exerted over the conscience, persons, and property of its religious communities. John Wesley's reformation of Protestant Episcopacy had ended in a five-headed priesthood. In the place of Metropolitan Bishops and Archbishops had sprung up diocesan prelates, presiding elders, circuit riders, local preachers, and class leaders. There was a question whether a conference of Methodistic clergy, with its bishop in its chair, and laity at home, was any reformation at all from a conclave of English prelates.

---

[36]*Christian Baptist,* II, 128-219.
[37]*Millennial Harbinger,* 1833, p. 469.
[38]*Ibid.,* 1834, p. 497.

Campbell wrote a series of editorials on "Methodistic Episcopacy" in the year 1835, in one of which he held that in some respects the power of Methodist bishops in America exceeded that of Episcopalian bishops:

To atone for the want of a seat in the house of Lords, the Methodist bishops have the supervision of the temporal affairs of the whole Methodist Episcopal church, and are invested with more power than the Episcopalian bishops in America; and, indeed, though inferior in dignity, not having patents from the king, nor a seat in the house of Lords temporal, they are superior in ecclesiastical authority to the twenty-four bishops of Old England, and are more on a footing with the Archbishops of York and Canterbury; for when John Wesley commissioned *"two general superintendents"* over all the American Methodists, he modeled much more after these two general superintendents of the Sees of York and Canterbury, than after the ordinary diocesan prelates of England.[39]

Summing up what he called the powers of the bishop, Campbell concluded by claiming that the editor of the *Millennial Harbinger* had as much power to choose a pastor and ruler of a local Methodist church as one of its own members had.

2. *The Daughters of Less Striking Resemblance—The Independents*

. . . When a tyrant is dethroned, and his vassals liberated, he finds his quietus in a guillotine, and they convert his palaces into towers and strong holds for each other in rotation. So in the church. They who call the Pope Anti-christ, and renounce any successor of St. Peter, set themselves up as Popes, and thus a whole congregation of protestors became a college of cardinals, and they will have no Pope because each one wishes to be Pope himself. Democrats in politics, and Independents in religion, are not unfrequently the greatest tyrants in the world.[40]

---

[39]*Ibid.*, 1834, p. 496.
[40]*Christian Baptist*, III, 198.

a) *The Congregationalists*

It had been the Independents of Scotland who had stirred in Campbell a love of religious freedom. To the Haldanes, Robert Sandeman, and Greville Ewing, he was indebted for many of the ideas which he later advocated, some of which were only very remotely connected with the principle of religious freedom, such as the weekly observance of the Lord's Supper. Had Campbell not come to the conclusions he did about Christian baptism, it is interesting to conjecture what overtures he might have made, if any, toward the Congregationalists. In any case, Campbell dealt with them far more lightly than with any other numerous religious group in America. He occasionally included them, simply by name, in his castigation of the "sects." It is possible that he steered clear of them for the most part because of his refusal to get into the unitarian-trinitarian controversy which raged during his lifetime. His chief score against American Congregationalism was its history as a court, or state, religion in early New England:

. . . A *national church,* if we could only agree about what it ought to be, would be a glorious disideratum; and then *a tax to support it would not be amiss.* Did you ever, my dear sir, discover the policy of the General Assembly admitting into its deliberations commissioners every year from the Congregational Associations of *New England?* This union will always further the prospects of all the sons of hierarchy in the land; and should the happy day arrive that the old leaven will leaven the whole mass, the world will, in the bosom of the church, be astonished how gently it got into its kind embraces.

. . . .

A church of this world, controlling the literature of the country, and founding great theological and ecclesiastical establishments, boasting of wealth and learning, and gathering under its control all the children of the flesh, exhibits the boldest traits of the proudest hierarchies of the old world; and it would be a new thing under the sun if such an institution would not assume a menacing attitude when fast rising into power.[41]

b) *The Baptists*

. . . I and the church with which I am connected are in "full communion" with the Mahoning Baptist Association, Ohio; and, through them, with the whole Baptist society in the United States, and I do intend to continue in connexion with this people so long as they will permit me to say what I believe, to teach what I am assured of, and to censure what is amiss in their views or practices. I have no idea of adding to the catalogue of new sects. This game has been played too long.[42]

The above quotation represented Campbell's attitude toward the Baptists during the first period of his relations with them. This was the period of courtship. But like the suitor who seeks to make his beloved over in the process of suit, Campbell was seeking at this time to work a reformation "from within" the group which he felt to be nearest the New Testament pattern.

The situation had developed in the following manner: Subsequent to the "Declaration and Address" by Thomas Campbell, a group of independents had constituted themselves into the Brush Run church. Intent on using only the Bible as their "rule of faith and practice" they in time arrived at the conclusion that immersion was the New Testament mode of baptism. Alexander Campbell took the lead in this, with some difficulty persuading his father to an acceptance of his views. Following the adoption of the practice of immersion by the group, they began to be looked upon with favor by members of the Redstone Baptist Association, which was situated along the Allegheny mountain range south of Pittsburgh. Ultimately in the year 1813, they were persuaded to apply for, and were granted, fellowship in this Association.

[41]*Millennial Harbinger*, 1833, p. 469.
[42]*Christian Baptist*, III, 217.

In addition to the matter of immersion, the Baptists had much to commend themselves to Campbell. Their theory was that of local church autonomy; for the most part they repudiated the idea of apostolic succession; and while they did have a "Philadelphia Confession of Faith," it was not generally accepted in the sense of a written creed.

But in other respects Campbell felt that his Baptist brethren needed enlightening. While they repudiated "apostolic succession," they believed in a "special call"; they had a doctrine regarding the influence of the Spirit in conversion which he felt militated against the idea of human freedom; and their "Associations" would sometimes decide upon matters which he believed were purely in the province of the local church.

Campbell insisted on his right to hold his own private views while in fellowship with the Baptists. But he did more than this. He insisted on publishing them, and hence on the right of seeking to correct what he felt were errors in the Baptist system:

. . . I labor to see sectarianism abolished, and all christians of every name united upon the one foundation on which the apostolic church was founded. To bring Baptists and Paido-Baptists to this is my supreme end. But to connect myself with any people who would require me to sacrifice one item of revealed truth, to subscribe any creed of human device, or to restrain me from publishing my sentiments as discretion and conscience direct, is now, and I hope ever shall be, the farthest from my desires, and the most incompatible with my views.[43]

While Campbell forever claimed the right to express his convictions, so far as the record shows he never denied that right to another. Throughout the forty-one years of publication of the *Christian Baptist* and the *Millennial Harbinger* his pages were always open to his opponents. But this complete freedom of expression

---

[43]*Ibid.,* IV, 217.

soon began to shake the Baptist fellowship like an earthquake. In an article written in 1837 in which Campbell reviewed his history, he said:

In process of time, difficulties arose, rather about human traditions and opinions, than about any thing in the Bible. . . . The particular societies which we erected met every Lord's day, celebrated both the death and resurrection of our Lord, and had their own peculiar arrangements. The other churches knew our order: we knew theirs. They did not seek to impose their rules upon us, nor did we think of making our order obligatory on them. . . . Thus things progressed for some years, till envy, jealousy, and pride began to work in some bosoms; and these passions, rather than erroneous or false doctrines dissociated us.[44]

Things came to a head in 1816 when Campbell preached his famous "Sermon on the Law." In this sermon he divided the Reign of God into three dispensations—the patriarchal, the Jewish, and the Christian—and stressed the distinction between the law of Moses and the gospel of Christ. Certain members of the Redstone Association considered the sermon heretical, and those churches in which Campbell's followers were in a majority, in order to circumvent a withdrawal of fellowship, formed a new association called the Mahoning.

As a member of the Mahoning Association, Campbell continued to seek to woo the Baptists. In 1829 he wrote "An Appeal to the Uncharitable":

. . . We will not lord our views or our sentiments over you: we will not denounce you as either traitors or rebels against him that is crowned Lord of all, because you cannot walk as fast as we; nor will we submit to have our rights and liberties wrested from us; nor any lords to reign over our faith or obedience, but the Lord of all. Do then, brethren, allow us the rights and liberties we allow you. . . . We will commune with you and welcome you to commune with us in all acts of religious worship, so long as you hold the head, and build upon the

[44]*Millennial Harbinger*, 1837, pp. 147-148.

foundation of the Apostles and Prophets; and so long as you will allow us to worship him agreeably to our own consciousness of his will.[45]

The earnestness of Campbell's attempt to continue in the Baptist fellowship, on his own terms, is seen in the following entreaty, in which he lists what he considers their common grounds:

. . . We already agree in all the grand items of christian faith. We adore the same Lord God—we worship, confide in, and supremely love the same Saviour—we all partake of the same Holy Spirit. We believe the same glorious facts, and hope for the same blissful resurrection. Why, then, bite and devour, or consume one another. Let us, then, aim at union, harmony, and love; and by our mutual prayers and endeavors, we shall come to be one in all the items of christian worship, as we are now in the one body, the one spirit, the one hope, the one Lord, the one faith, the one immersion, the one God and Father of all. We entreat you, then, to extend to us that love and respect which you would require of us and all christians towards yourselves.[46]

The landslide had started, however, and as Campbell's followers began to multiply, the churches of the Baptist fellowship began to be disrupted. There followed ejections of Disciples as schismatics. Campbell reversed the charge:

. . . in no instance has a majority in any of our churches ever cast out a minority of Baptists for any difference of opinion. But how often their majorities have cast out our minorities in the last ten years it would pain me to record. Yet we are schismatical! Is the *separatist* or the *separated* the *schismatic?* This is a new question, perhaps, to a million. It were well it was decided. If a brother says you shall neither think nor speak differently from me; and thus compels me to surrender my independence or to withdraw from him, is he or I the schismatic?[47]

[45]*Christian Baptist*, VI, 477.
[46]*Ibid.*
[47]*Millennial Harbinger*, 1837, p. 149.

As association after association began to take action against Disciples of Christ, Campbell became as bitter against them as he had ever been against the more episcopal ecclesiasticisms. In 1829 he wrote "there is no scheme of ecclesiastical policy under which tyranny and proscription appear so odious as under the Baptist system."

Particularly baneful were the "Appomattox Decrees." Not content with excluding some of his followers, the Appomattox Association had listed Campbell himself by name as a schismatic. This action Campbell condemned as more tyrannical than the church of Rome itself:

. . . All ecclesiastical councils in christendom, not even excluding the Roman Catholics themselves, give every person a trial whom they presume to condemn. The accused is allowed to make his defence before his accusers, and . . . no person is condemned upon mere rumor. The Beaver and Appomattox Associations have condemned upon rumor, and have never permitted, summoned, nor invited the accused to defend themselves. . . . How many of them know any thing about my sentiments or writings from my own lips or pens? *Not one in ten who vote on such matters.* To them it is all rumor. They are complete tools in the hands of a few designing men. . . . From such courts I view an anathema as more ridiculous, or malicious, or unjust, than a papal *bull;* and though not so potent in mischief as unchristian, being equally without the forms, as well as without the reality of impartiality and humanity.[48]

After concluding that Baptist Associations were arrogating to themselves powers which should reside in the local congregation, Campbell's next step, as might be expected, was to affirm that they were unscriptural. By 1831 the break was pretty well effected, and at this time he wrote an article denying that the Baptist sect was the scriptural church of Christ, since the scriptural church of Christ never met at night to proscribe those who take the whole New Testament as their guide. Neither did

---

[48]*Ibid.,* 1830, p. 262.

it meet by proxy, two delegates for each church, to decide upon what course the whole church ought to pursue.

While trying to woo them, Campbell had listed the points of agreement between himself and the Baptists. After he had been spurned, he wrote an article listing points of difference. This included their neglect to observe the Lord's Supper each first day of the week; the fact that they allowed one preacher the pastoral care of several churches; that they paid him for preaching the gospel; that they sanctioned covenants, creeds, and associations; that they neglected parental religious instruction, and were wanting in family piety.

II. *The Tools of Ecclesiastical Tyranny*

But Campbell was not yet done. Not only did he take as his two grand propositions that the church of Rome was the Mother of Harlots and that the Protestant sects were her daughters, he went further and charged that these ecclesiasticisms had created certain tools with which they tyrannized the human mind and restrained freedom of thought. These "tools" were: a. The kingdom of the clergy. b. Creeds, and confessions of faith. c. Theology and orthodoxy.   d. Church courts.   e. Church auxiliaries.

A. *The Kingdom of the Clergy*

. . ."Many will, from various motives, decry the clergy . . . . In opposing and exposing them and their kingdom, it is not to join in the infidel cry against priests and priestcraft; it is not to gratify the avaricious or the licentious; but it is to pull down their Babel, and to emancipate those whom they have enslaved; to free the people from their unrighteous dominion and unmerciful apoliation. We have no system of our own, or of others, to substitute in lieu of the reigning systems. We only aim at substituting the New Testament in lieu of every creed in existence."[49]

---

[49]Robinson, *op. cit.*, II, 62.

The first step in ecclesiasticism's attempt to dominate the minds of men was to create a class called the clergy, with its correlate, the laity. "God made men, the priests make laymen. Man is the creature of God, a layman the creature of priests." By the clergy he meant those who, without credentials, claimed to be the ambassadors of Christ, and set themselves upon apostolic thrones, assuming to be the sole authorized expositors of the holy oracles, while having "no new divine revelations." By their false assumptions they denied the people the right of comprehending or interpreting the scriptures for themselves, and so succeeded in exercising over men a powerful influence "largely devoted to the maintenance of their own usurpations."

While ostensibly seeking the peace and prosperity of Zion, the real goals of the clergy were clerical power, the pride of place, and material greed, "their mitres, their pulpits, and their stipends."

With regard to clerical power, Campbell charged that no class of men on earth had exercised so much influence or acquired such complete ascendancy over the human mind as the popular clergy. As if this were not enough to impede the progress of mankind, they refused to be creative in their own thought. "Not a king nor a priest smiled upon our faith until it won the day. It offered no lure to the ambitious, no reward to the avaricious." Having nullified the thought of the people, they then dictated to them what they must think, believe, and do. The very existence of priestcraft depended on keeping the people in darkness. "There are three things on earth which require an ignorant population. . . . What shall we call them? Call them monarchy, hierarchy, and slavery." The world was indebted to the clergy not only for ignorance and superstition, but for persecution. It was against the popular clergy of his day that Jesus inveighed with the greatest severity, and Campbell sought to point out the analogy between the Christian clergy of the 19th and the Jewish clergy of the 1st centuries.

Pride of place served the clergy both as ends and means. As an end, it satisfied their vanity. As a means, it helped them increase their power. Their air of sanctity and official titles, like the habiliments of the popish priest, were helpful "to make the people fear them and pay them." Professional piety occasioned another satirical outburst:

. . . His former classmates, with whom he was once so jovial, retain their former jocularity or sobriety, there is no alteration of their visage. But my young priest gradually assumes a sanctimonious air, a holy gloom overspreads his face, and a pious sedateness reigns from his eyebrows to his chin. His very tone of voice participates of the deep devotion of his soul. His words flow on with a solemn slowness, and every period ends with a heavenly cadence. There is a kind of angelic demeanor in his gait, and a seraphic sweetness in all his movements. With his sunday coat, on a sabbath morn, he puts on a mantile of deeper sanctity, and imperceptibly learns the three grand tones—the sabbath tone, the pulpit tone, and the praying tone—these are the devout, the more devout, and the most devout.[50]

The secret of Campbell's own eloquence lay not only in his reasoning powers, but in the calm poise, the quiet naturalness of his delivery, and he never ceased to ridicule anything which smacked of shamanism in the pulpit. Perhaps he reached the peak of his satire in an article entitled "Sermons to Young Preachers, No. 1," published in the last volume of the *Christian Baptist:*

Often have I seen a preacher try to get his mind abroach until he began to snuff the breeze like a whale snorting in the North Atlantic ocean. It is more easy to bring a seventy-four gun ship into action in a gale of wind, than to get the mind to bear upon the text, until the nostrils catch the corner of a volume of air, and sneeze it out like a leviathan in the deep. I

---

[50] *Christian Baptist*, I, 35.

have seen other preachers who can strike fire no other way than
by the friction of their hands, and an occasional clap, resembling
a peal of distant thunder. In this holy paroxysm of clapping,
rubbing, sneezing, and roaring, the mind is fairly on the way,
and the tongue in full gallop, which, like a race horse, runs the
swifter the less weight it carries. The farther from nature the
nearer the skies, some preachers seem to think. But so it is
whenever they acquire this habit it is almost incurable. They
can neither speak to God nor man in the pulpit to purpose, as
they think, unless when, like the boiler of a steam boat, they
are almost ready to burst. This is one extreme. There are
various degrees marked on the scale before we arrive at this
dreadful heat. There is a certain pitch of voice which is at
least ten degrees above a natural key. To this most preachers
have to come before their ideas get adrift. Their inspiration is
kindled from the noise they create. I have seen children cry
who began quite moderately, but when they heard the melody
of their own voice their cries rose in a few seconds to screams.
No person can tell how much is to be ascribed to these factitious
influences in giving play to the imagination and wings to our
ideas. Some people have to milk all their sermons from their
watch chains. . . . and others from the buttons on their coats.

. . . .

These prophets of Baal are the worst models for young preachers; and I trust none of you, my friends, will, from this time
forth, ever follow so scandalous an example.[51]

In the scramble after pride of place the clergy had
developed a class system which included an almost endless array—divines, clergymen, elders, circuit preachers,
class leaders, licentiates, presiding elders, bishops,
priests, deans, archdeacons, archbishops, friars, priors,
abbots, cardinals, and popes. Rummaging the New
Testament for scriptural names for them and finding
only such offices as those of deacon, bishop, pastor, evangelist, and Antichrists, Campbell decided that the latter
term applied to most of the modern divines. Consist-

[51]*Ibid.*, VII, 585.

ently rejecting all official titles and honorary degrees, he derided those who accepted them.

The third advantage sought by the priesthood was that of material gain. "From this dominion over the feelings and consciences of mankind, it was not difficult to slide the hand into the pockets of the superstitious." Priestcraft was thus the craftiest of all crafts. It was "so crafty that it obtained by its craft the means to make craftsmen, and then it made the deluded support them."

Campbell boasted that he had never accepted a single dollar in remuneration for his preaching. When some of his opponents attributed this practice to the fact that he had no need of it, he retorted that it rooted back in a disgust at the popular schemes, imbided when he was a student in the University of Glasgow, and had been adopted when he arrived in this country with no other property than his education. He had followed the avocation of a husbandman, and insisted that his circumstances were not as good as some of theirs: "I know some of the neighboring clergy who are in better circumstances than I am, that complain of great difficulties in 'getting along,' who receive as good as $500 or $1000 a year."[52]

It would be an unfair picture to paint Campbell as meaning his words to be taken categorically, but he had such an extreme method of expressing himself that great care must be exercised in making the line of demarcation between the clergy which he indicated and the total ministry as a group. In later life he pled for the church's support of the ministry, and denied that he had ever stood for anything else. Richardson supports him in this position:

It should be remembered . . . that Mr. Campbell regarded the Church and the clergy from a point of view very different

---

[52]*Ibid.*, I, 72.

from the popular one, and did not consider all ministers as
"clergy" in the sense he condemned. Hence care is to be exercised in giving to his censures an application no more extensive
than he designed.[53]

There is some ground for Richardson's caution, since
Campbell frequently qualified his censure of the clergy
by the term "popular" clergy, and since he did not include the Baptists and Independents in his censures,
except in regard to their love of honorary degrees. But
there is other evidence which seems to be basically contradictory. Certainly, during the early days of his violent antiecclesiasticism, Campbell definitely opposed a
regular salary for the ministry:

A hireling is one who prepares himself for the office of a
"preacher" or "minister," as a mechanic learns a trade, and
who obtains a license from a congregation, convention, presbytery, pope, or diocesan bishop, as a preacher or a minister, and
agrees by the day, or sermon, month or year, for a stipulated
reward.[54]

On the other hand, the true minister was one who was
sought by the congregation from among themselves, and
remunerated by them "as his circumstances required,"
and that, not for preaching the gospel, for that was the
duty of every member, but for "watching over them,
visiting them in all their afflictions, and in guarding them
against seduction."

If the kingdom of the clergy was motivated by the
three goals of clerical power, pride of place, and material
gain, the means by which it sought to attain them were
two: the claim of a special call from God, and the consociation of these called ones together in ecclesiastical
groups for the alleged "interests of the church."

The first of these "props" for the priesthood was attended by even greater authority if it was conjoined

[53]Richardson, op. cit., II, 60.
[54]Christian Baptist, III, 233.

with the doctrine of apostolic succession. But some of the clergy, confronted with too great difficulty in seeking to maintain the unbroken line, were content to assert their priority by virtue of a "direct call of the Holy Spirit." Campbell, not content with his attempt to disjoint the various lines of succession, undauntedly set out to shatter the idea of a "special call."

. . . Although I feel myself as able to demonstrate and prove that both the one and the other of these positions is false, as I am to prove that there is a God, the Creator of Heaven and Earth; yet I cheerfully admit that there are now, and there were formerly, many good men who have advocated the necessity, and expatiated on the importance, of a special call of the Holy Spirit to the work of teaching the christian religion.[55]

This "special call" was enhanced not only by the doctrine of apostolic succession, but by the cultivation of a "holy grace" as well. Campbell hints of a profound conception of the nature of spiritual grace when he suggests that it does not come by being overtly sought for its own sake:

There are some who think that there is some kind of an almost inseparable connexion between clerical acquisitions and the grace of God—that none can be eminently possessed of the former, that does not possess a competent portion of the latter. How can this be? If a parent who has three sons, A, B, and C, educates A for a divine, B for a carpenter, and C for a doctor of medicine; why should A possess the grace of God or the faith of the gospel rather than B or C? . . . . Is there any reason in the nature of things, that the training of A, B, and C, will secure grace to A rather than to B or C? If so, then there is a connexion between Latin and Grecian languages, mythology, science, and the grace of God that does not exist between the education of a carpenter or a medical doctor and that grace. If the education of A secures the boon of heaven, then it becomes the imperious duty of every father thus to educate his

[55]*Ibid.*, I, 19.

sons. But this is impossible. He has not the means. Then the grace of God is purchased with money!!![56]

As to the second "prop" of the clergy, Campbell charges that their consociation together in federations, synods, etc., is for a more personal motive than the "interest of the churches":

. . . Many sermons have been delivered on the necessity and importance of a special call to the ministry; on the necessity and importance of the confederation of the ministry, in the form of general councils, synods, assemblies, associations, and conferences; in order to their securing the interests of religion, which seem so completely identified with the interests of the clergy, that many have been tempted to think that the phrase "the interests of religion," means, the interests of the clergy.[57]

The priests allied themselves not only with other priests, but with kings. Here was the ever-present threat of the union of church and state. This alliance was ever a boon to the spread of infidelity, whose spread might even serve the purposes of God by breaking it.

The attempts to attribute to Campbell a simple solution of the problem of the clergy on the one hand, or to absolve him from an absolutist position toward the clergy on the other hand, seem equally difficult to maintain. The best that can be said is that here is one of the contradictions which Campbell had not as yet resolved in his mind. At times he wrote as if what he sought was simply "a diminishing of the power of the clergy." At others he wrote as if his object was their destruction. The two following passages, both selected from the *Christian Baptist,* and both published in the same year of 1823, are illustrative:

. . . I would say, Let us have no clergy at all, learned or unlearned—let us have bishops and deacons such as Paul appoints, such as he has described in 1st Tim. 3:1-14. Titus 1:5-9.[58]

---

[56]*Ibid.,* I, 35.
[57]*Ibid.,* I, 19.
[58]*Ibid.,* I, 36.

What are the most effectual means to diminish the power and dominion of the popular clergy?

Ans. The same means which the Lord and his apostles used in their day against those of that time: chiefly to persuade the people to hold fast the holy commandments of the apostles, and to build themselves up in the christian faith.[59]

It is undeniable that Campbell would have completely eliminated the distinction between "laity" and "clergy." But he would have done this by making preachers of all disciples:

. . . To be more explicit in expressing my views of the means which the church is to use for the salvation of the world, I would remark, that having the record, or testimony of God in it, and every member professing it, it becomes the duty and high privilege of every member of it to be a preacher of the gospel, in the only sense in which any person can now be called a preacher.[60]

Nevertheless, from among the bishops (of whom there must be a plurality in each local congregation, and who were never to have supervision of *more* than one congregation) there was chosen one who would have oversight of the congregation, instruct it, and be compensated by it for his labors. From the earliest days Campbell's colaborers, those who helped build up his following, were such men, and among Disciples of Christ to this day, the minister, or pastor, of the local congregation, officially, is still one of the elders, or "bishops" of the congregation. Thus, while it contradicts some of his more extreme expressions, Campbell's position, even his early position, seems to justify Richardson's assertion that such ministers

. . . being appointed by the churches, and acting as elders and preachers of the gospel in subordination to just scriptural authority, he constantly recognized as a lawful ministry in the Church, for the accomplishment of the purposes for which it was established on the earth.[61]

---

[59]*Ibid.*, I, 46.
[60]*Ibid.*, I, 70.
[61]Richardson, *op. cit.*, II, 61.

B. *Creeds and Confessions of Faith*

I do attribute to creeds, in the proper acceptation of the term, all the divisions and strifes, partyism, and sectarian feeling, of the present day; all the persecutions and proscription, all the havoc of human life, and all the horrors of the inquisition in the cause of religion, during many centuries before we were born.[62]

It was not the content of any human creed which constituted the foundation of Campbell's objection, although he usually found something in the content to which to object. It was the *fact* of them which he considered evil. He called the principle which led him to reject all human creeds the "pole-star" of his course of religious inquiry. Any understanding of Campbell must ever recognize that principle:

. . . My faith in creeds and confessions of human device was considerably shaken while in Scotland, and I commenced my career in this country under the conviction that nothing that was not as old as the New Testament should be made an article of faith, a rule of practice, or a term of communion amongst christians. In a word, that the whole of the christian religion exhibited in prophecy and type in the Old Testament, was presented in the fullest, clearest, and most perfect manner in the New Testament, by the Spirit of wisdom and revelation.[63]

No statement which Campbell ever made provided a better clue to his career than this one. The first sentence expressed an attitude which he ever sought earnestly to maintain. The second expressed a presupposition which he never thought to question, and upon which his entire faith was posited.

The first, and fundamental, objection which he had to creeds, therefore, was that they were an addendum to the scriptures, and as such, implied their inadequacy:

. . . If they are necessary to the unity of the church, then the New Testament is defective; for if the New Testament was

---

[62]*Christian Baptist*, V, 361.
[63]*Ibid.*, II, 92.

sufficient to the unity of the church, then human creeds would not be necessary. If any man, therefore, contend that human creeds are necessary to the unity of the church, he at the same time and by all the same arguments, contends that the scriptures of the Holy Spirit are insufficient—that is, imperfect or defective. Every human creed is based upon the inadequacy, that is, the imperfection of the Holy Scriptures.[64]

But he also had many other objections. One of the major theses which he sought to prove in his debate with N. L. Rice was the charge that creeds were the cause of all the divisions of Christendom. "No human creed in Protestant christendom can be found, that has not made a division for every generation of its existence." They not only serve to originate the sects, they serve to perpetuate them. They are not only divisive, they are futile, never having served to bring a single sinner to repentance. They are cunning devices of ecclesiasticisms and the clergy for the purpose of enslaving the minds of men, and thwarting the spirit of freedom and inquiry. Not content with tyrannizing the minds of men, they arrogate to themselves the right of veto over God himself:

To attempt to unite the professing disciples by any other means than the word of the apostles, by the Westminster, or any other creed, is, then, an attempt to overrule the will of heaven, to subvert the throne of the Great King, to frustrate the prayers of the Son of the Blessed.[65]

But the objection which touched off Campbell's severest anathemas was the one which was rooted in the deep affront to his dignity sustained in the heresy trial of his father. They were the instruments of *exclusion*. They shut men out, when Christ would take them in:

. . . We . . . have opposed creeds *because they were creeds,* irrespective of the doctrine contained in them; not, indeed, because they exhibited a system of faith or of sound doctrine, but

---

[64]*Ibid.,* II, 134.
[65]*Ibid.,* II, 135.

because they were made indispensable and authoritative terms
of communion, or justifiable and valid grounds of exclusion.[66]

In this connection, there is gained an interesting insight into a basic struggle within Campbell which was
abiding, and yet of which he never seemed to be aware.
That was the struggle between his authoritarian presuppositions and his inherent spirit of inquiry, love of
truth, and reliance on reason. Here is the explanation of
many of his apparent contradictions, and here was the
ground of his difficulty in his long struggle toward a satisfactory and creative conception of church organization. What he considered to be the perfect and complete revelation of the divine will could never be questioned. Yet the spirit of inquiry within him demanded
that the human issues and emergent problems be met.
Time and again, in his opposition to what he considered
to be some evil, he would approach it at one time as the
Christian apologist, and confront it from the standpoint
of the divine fiat. But at another he would approach
it as the rationalist, the reasoning man confronted with
practical issues. This explains why, at one time, he
would abolish the clergy, and at another, aware of its
practical desirability in order to meet certain functions,
he would only reform it. It explains, too, why, after
indicting creeds and confessions of faith on what he considered to be all the scriptural grounds, he could suddenly brush aside all these objections, providing only
that the creeds not be used as tests of fellowship, as
grounds for communion or exclusion. When it came
down to the inner impulses of the man this formed the
basis of his objection which gave no quarter. The following illustrates the case in point:

. . . Keep your Covenant, all who like it, but do not impose it
upon those who do not like it. Here is a church of one hundred
members: they have a Covenant: sixty approve the Covenant,

⁶⁶*Millennial Harbinger,* 1846, p. 566.

and forty do not. What is to be done? Exclude the forty! By whose authority? Not by Jesus Christ's authority. If you presume to cut off forty of his members because of your human contrivance, he will fight against you with the sword which proceeds out of his mouth. If you do, you are the schismatics, the heretics. You being sixty, and they being forty, alters not the case. "But the forty will not commune with us while we hold the Covenant." In this they may be wrong. If the Covenant be all that is in the way, if your behavior be as becomes the gospel, they ought to bear with your Covenant. I would sit and let you read your Covenant till you got tired, if you will cut off its horns; or, if it happen to be a *muley,* you may turn it loose every day in the year, *Sundays only excepted,* and let it *butt* whom it may, so long as it cannot *gore.*

. . . .

We will bear all things, only let us have the liberty you claim for yourselves—the liberty of worshipping our Father and our God according to our own consciences. In this tolerant and charitable way we will all come together who are friends of Jesus Christ.[67]

When writing in this vein, Campbell seemed to be willing for any man or every man to have a creed, so long as that creed be for his own use, and not be made a test of fellowship with others, or binding on others. To pretend to bind it on others would be to presume infallibility for himself:

. . . if a *human* system must be fashioned out of this *Divine* system, every man must make one for himself; for unless he proves himself infallible, he cannot pretend to bind it on any other than himself. Moreover, he would have learned from a very little reflection or observation, that *"this little harmless thing,"* . . . when bound upon the consciences of men, has been the cause of the shedding of every drop of *Protestant* blood for 2000 years.[68]

. . . I never did object to creeds because they were not in the Bible. . . . I object to creeds and confessions because made

---

[67]*Ibid.,* 1830, p. 246.
[68]*Ibid.,* 1831, pp. 379-380.

authoritative "tests of religious character and terms of christian communion."

. . . .

I cared not how many creeds were published, or would not object to publishing a creed every year, provided that it was only to inform the world what I or those in union with me held.[69]

As a term of communion, Campbell professed to recognize only one creed, and insisted that none other should ever be made binding. That creed was the biblical confession of faith in Christ as made by Peter in Matthew 16:16. When N. L. Rice, in debate, charged that position with being too broad, too liberal, and making for too great laxity, Campbell responded with an amazingly ecumenical outlook:

The gentleman complains that our foundation is too broad—too liberal. It is indeed broad, liberal, and strong. If it were not so, it would not be a christian foundation. Christianity is a liberal institution.

. . . .

But how often have you heard the saying quoted by Mr. Rice, that "all sorts of doctrine, by all sorts of men, are preached amongst us.". . . Well, it is not exactly quoted. There is one word of much limitation left out, "*almost* all sorts of men." In saying this, I follow an illustrious example. Paul, in his day, was just thus plain and candid. He gave specifications of almost all sorts of doctrine, preached even while he yet lived. Some preached that the resurrection was actually passed, and had overthrown the faith of some. Some were, for the faith of filthy lucre, preaching what they ought not. Some preached that the world was immediately coming to an end; some said that the law of Moses and circumcision should be observed by gentile converts & c.; and *Paul sent it all over the world, and for all ages too*. We are then a good deal like our great apostle, and a little like the primitive church, too, in this particular!

[69]*Christian Baptist*, V, 370.

Mr. R. could not, were he and I both to try, find as great a variety amongst us, of character, preachers, and doctrine, as I can find in the New Testament, complained of by Paul and his associates. So that the argument is as strong against Paul and the primitive church, as against myself and my brethren.

. . . .

The question, for example, would you receive a Universalist —a Unitarian? We respond, not *as such*. With the New Testament in our hands, we know nothing of Calvinist, Arminian, Unitarian, Arian & c. We ask the question, do you believe that Jesus of Nazareth is the Messiah, the Son of God? If any man cordially respond—yes, we baptize him.

. . . .

We can neither justify nor condemn a man for his unfortunate education, for his peculiar organization, or his eccentric opinions. Treat him rationally, treat him humanely, and in a christian-like manner, and all these opinions will evaporate or die within him. Receive him not as a Calvinist, a Papist, a Baptist, or a Universalist; receive him as a *man* and as a *christian*. Show him that you receive him in the name of the Lord, upon his faith, his hope, and love, and you will soon allure him from his false opinions, if he have any. But repudiate and excommunicate him for an opinion, you wed him to it.[70]

Here was Campbell as an ecumenical Christian statesman at his best. When it is recalled that among those whom he would include in his fellowship were advocates of doctrines which were considered to be the great heresies in a day of heresy hunting, a picture of the spirit of inquiry and love of freedom rising in the man presents itself.

But again, this was one side of the picture. On the other side was the devotee of the divine fiat who never thought to question his presuppositions. Strangely enough, after charging Campbell with a breadth which took in all sorts of heretics, Rice charged him, in al-

---

[70]*Campbell-Rice Debate,* pp. 808-811.

most the next breath, with erecting an unwritten creed which shut men out. This was a charge which dogged Campbell to the end. Whatever justification there was in the charge was lodged in the insoluble conflict between his legalistic presuppositions and his opposition to all legalisms represented in his progressive spirit of inquiry. The crux of the issue largely settled down to the conviction which came to him that immersion was the formal act by which the divine will had decreed that the believer should be incorporated into the body of Christ.

It is the divine formula of putting on, or receiving, Christ in his personal glory and official fulness. Hence God is pleased to make it and regard it as the actual reception of the gospel, on which he formally and actually remits all our past sins.

There is just as much wisdom and propriety in making an actual conformity to the death, burial and resurrection of Christ, in baptism the act of receiving Christ, and of pardon for all past sins as could be shown by human wisdom in any other act which imagination could prescribe. The efficacy still is in the faith confessed, and not in the water.[71]

The editors of the *Baptist Recorder* had sought to maintain that Campbell's writings were themselves an unofficial creed. Campbell had little difficulty in disposing of this accusation, for in all fairness, he earnestly endeavored to distinguish between his written beliefs and a creed: "You call my whole writings my creed. . . . I am making not a creed for myself or others, no test of religious character, no term of communion." But with regard to his position on baptism, Rice came as near pinning him to the wall as he ever experienced in his long polemic career:

After all the gentleman's declamation against creeds, his churches actually have a creed. They have not adopted the constitution he offered them, but still they have a creed. It is

---

[71]*Millennial Harbinger,* 1849, p. 611.

short—containing *two articles*, the substance of which is—1st.
That immersion only is baptism; 2nd.   That infant baptism
is not to be tolerated.   They will receive no one into the church
who has not been immersed, and they will not permit their
members to have their children baptized. . . . .

. . . .

They do not profess to take the New Testament, as Mr. Campbell interprets it; nor as each little church interprets it; but as
each individual understands it.   Now, suppose I should take
the gentleman upon his own principles, and apply for membership in his church.   He would ask me, "Do you believe that
Jesus Christ is the Son of God?"   I answer in the affirmative.
He would ask again, "Are you willing to be baptized?"   I answer, I have been baptized.   Will he receive me?   He will not.
He demands that I be *immersed*.[72]

Campbell never directly came to grips with the charge
of making an oral creed at this point, and attempts to
defend him against the charge have been difficult.   It
is true that on three occasions he preached a sermon on
baptism in which he said: "As I am sure it is unscriptural to make this matter a term of communion, I let
it slip.   I wish to think and let think on these matters."
The catch in this is in the fact that those three occasions
were on February 3, 1810; May 19, 1811; and June 5,
1811, prior to his own immersion in the year 1812.   However, as late as the year 1837, he was castigated by some
of his more conservative brethren for his liberal attitude on baptism.   He responded to that criticism:

. . . We gave it as our *opinion* that there were Christians
among the Protestant sects; an opinion, indeed, which we have
always expressed when called upon.   If I mistake not, it is
distinctly avowed in our Extra on Remission. . . . In the article
alluded to, we have said that we "cannot make any one duty the
standard of Christian state or character, not even Christian
immersion." &c.   Again, we have said that "there is no occasion
for making immersion on a profession of faith absolutely essen-

---

[72]*Campbell-Rice Debate*, p. 883.

tial to a Christian, though it may be greatly essential to his sanctification and comfort."[73]

In the light of the above article in which the unimmersed are recognized as Christian, there are submitted below two other quotations which reveal once more the basic conflict between Campbell, the legalist, and Campbell, the ecumenical Christian. It must be noted that both these quotations are taken from the *Christian Baptist,* and were published within two and one-half years of one another, the one in November, 1825, the other in May, 1828. The first is:

As to the "purblind Pharisee who strains out a gnat and swallows a camel," because he will not have full communion with all the evangelical sects in the mass, I have to remark, that it is not optional with me or you whether we would have christian communion with them. They have something to say on that subject.

. . . .

Dear sir, this plan of making our own nest, and fluttering over our own brood; of building our own tent, and of confining all goodness and grace to our noble selves and the "elect few" who are like us, is the quintessence of sublimated pharisaism . . . the longer I live . . . the more I am assured, that all sectarianism is the offspring of hell; and that all differences about words, and names, and opinions, hatched in Egypt, or Rome, or Edinburgh, are like the frolics of drunken men; and that where there is a *new creature,* or a society of them, with all their imperfections, and frailties, and errors in sentiments, in views, and opinions, they ought to receive one another, and the strong to support the infirmities of the weak, and not to please themselves. To lock ourselves up in the bandbox of our own little circle; to associate with a few units, tens, or hundreds, as the pure church, as the elect, is real Protestant monkery, it is evangelical pharisaism.[74]

[73]*Millennial Harbinger,* 1837, p. 506.
[74]*Christian Baptist,* III, 238-239.

The second quotation is selected from a reply made to a request for Campbell to discuss a certain constitution drawn up for one of the infant Disciple congregations. Besides objecting to the form of the constitution, Campbell objects to the content:

. . . This Constitution or Covenant . . . is objectionable because it admits an *unimmersed* person to all the ordinances of the christian community or congregation, as an *occasional* member; and yet refuses to receive such as regular and constant members. I know of no scriptural authority for such a discrimination. It is arbitrary and unreasonable. If I can admit an unimmersed person once a-month for a year to all social ordinances, I can for life or good behaviour. When I say, *I can do so,* I mean that all precepts, precedents, and scriptural reasons, authorize such a course.

But I object to making it a rule, *in any case,* to receive unimmersed persons to church ordinances:

1st. Because it is nowhere commanded.

2nd. Because it is nowhere precedented in the New Testament.

3rd. Because it necessarily corrupts the simplicity and uniformity of the whole genius of the New Institution.

4th. Because it not only deranges the order of the kingdom, but makes *void* one of the most important institutions ever given to man. . . .

5th. Because, in making a canon to dispense with a divine institution of momentous import, they who do so assume the very same *dispensing power* which issued in that tremendous apostacy which we and all christians are praying and laboring to destroy.[75]

Here was the conflict within Campbell at its keenest! "Welcome all Christians in all the world whom Christ would welcome," the liberalist shouted. "Except the unimmersed," the legalist appended. The Young Campbell has sometimes been called the literalist, and the Elder Campbell the liberalist. It would be truer to history to say that the elder Campbell was an unconscious

---

[75]*Ibid.,* VI, 527-528.

attempt to resolve the conflict between the literalism and the liberalism of the younger Campbell.

C. *Church Courts*

That "monster horrific, shapeless, huge, whose light is extinct," called an esslesiastical court. . . . Whether such an alliance of the priests and the nobles of the kirk be called a session, a presbytery, a synod, a general assembly, a convention, a conference, an association, or annual meeting, its tendency and result are the same. Whenever and wherever such a meeting either legislates, decrees, rules, directs, or controls, or assumes the character of a representative body in religious concerns, it essentially becomes "the man of sin and the son of perdition."[76]

If the Antichrist of ecclesiasticism used the clergy as its high priests, and creeds as its shibboleths, it used its ecclesiastical courts as its sanhedrins in its tyranny over the free spirit of man. In fact, it would not misrepresent the spirit of Campbell to use the modern analogy that the clergy was the ecclesiastical Nazi party, creeds its *Mein Kampf,* and ecclesiastical courts the Gestapo by which it sought to purge itself of those who dared hold a minority opinion. However, Campbell was careful to include in his indictment of church courts not only their lack of right to conduct church trials, but their absence of right even to legislate the laws by which the trials were held: "By an ecclesiastical court, we mean those meetings of clergy, either stated or occasional, for the purpose of either enacting new ecclesiastical canons or of executing old ones." In other words, an ecclesiastical court was any supralocal body which arrogated to itself the right, under whatsoever name or claim, to speak authoritatively for the local congregation, on any question whatsoever. "An individual church or congregation of Christ's disciples is the only ecclesiastical body recognized in the New Testament." "The amalgamation

---

[76]*Ibid.,* I, 72-73.

of christian communities into one solid, compact, and
united body, by representation in ecclesiastical councils,
was not then heard of." The fact that, in some cases, the
"laity" was granted representation, altered the evil of
such a church court not a particle: "Whether the assembly is composed of none but priests and levites, or
of one half, one third, or one tenth laymen, it is alike
antiscriptural, anti-christian, and dangerous to the community, civil and religious."

Against such a court, Campbell inveighed with all the
anathemas which he hurled at other forms of ecclesiasticism: (1) not only were they antiscriptural, their very
existence implied the claim of infallibility; (2) they were
proscriptive, "whomsoever they will, they kill, and
whomsoever they will, they save alive"; (3) not one ever
contributed to the progress of religion, being always opposed to reform; (4) they forever sought to build up the
power of the priesthood against the people. But Campbell had a few choice charges to bring against church
courts, in addition to his general indictments against
other ecclesiasticisms. Their decisions were notoriously
in error:

. . . I never had much faith in Sanhedrims, because they have,
to say the least, been oftener wrong than right. In this San-
hedrim which condemned the Messiah to death, the votes stood
for crucifying, 70; for releasing, 2, (Nicodemus and Joseph of
Arimathea.) Jesus had two votes out of seventy-two. This
event has incurably prejudiced me against ecclesiastical councils.[77]

Perhaps his most telling blow was the charge that
their character was antirepublican in combining the
various branches of government in one assembly:

. . . What, at the best, makes but a bungling job of the whole
of such systems, is that the same assembly is this moment leg-

_____

[77] *Millennial Harbinger*, 1830, p. 245.

islative, and anon judicative; not only is it the maker, but the executor of its own laws; thus opening a door for the most tyrannical exercise of power.[78]

In this connection, his most powerful invectives were reserved for his former love, the Baptists, as a result of the "Dover decrees." Issued by the Dover Association of Virginia, these decrees announced that it could not in future act in concert with any church which should countenance the ministrations of six prominent ministers known to be sympathetic to the teachings of Campbell. After charging the Association with having violated both its own charter and those of the churches, Campbell continued:

. . . I ask the Virginia Baptists, the sons of the fathers of American liberty, the advocates of the trial by jury, of the *habeas corpus*, of an independent judiciary, of placing legislative, judiciary, and executive powers in different hands; is it republican, is it American, is it safe (to say nothing of the Bible) that such a power should be placed in the hands of any single representative body—of any court, or tribunal of judgment, unguarded by any court of appeal, any superior or controlling, independent tribunal, to which the aggrieved may appeal?[79]

His final thrust in the direction of the un-American nature of the decrees was one of his most bitter:

. . . Ought [the accused not] be permitted to be present, in person or by their attorney, and have a hearing on the indictment, before sentence was pronounced against them? . . . The accused were not invited, most of them absent, no testimony heard; and even the forms of justice were dispensed with. In all other courts, the allegata must be proved, testimony adduced, the law must be applied, and that before an independent tribunal; but these unfortunate brethren were before-written to condemnation.[80]

---

[78]*Christian Baptist*, IV, 314.
[79]*Millennial Harbinger*, 1833, p. 113.
[80]*Ibid.*, p. 113.

Campbell's response to church courts was that any supralocal meeting whatever was unauthorized, save occasional "conventional" meetings, and these could serve only for "social worship and praise," and the "hearing of the reports of the brethren." It was a stand which led his group to the brink of ecclesiastical anarchy, and its specter was to rise up and haunt him in future years. Sometimes its ghost still attends the conventions of Disciples of Christ.

D. *Theology and Orthodoxy*

. . . Who that has his eyes open has not seen that men of the lowest intellect and of the lowest moral endowments are the most zealous in the cause of orthodoxy? and that the reason is, they are conscious that unless they can raise a clamor about orthodoxy they are likely to pass off the stage as they ought? I have always found those of the most orthodox scent the slowest in the race, and the loudest in the sound. The foremost hound makes the least noise about the course, but those hindmost are always sounding lo here! or lo there![81]

Orthodoxy was the myth, the mystical concept, by which ecclesiasticism maintained the fear and support of the masses. Theology was the propaganda by means of which orthodoxy's converts were made. Here again Campbell's intrepid spirit of inquiry led the way, and he challenged all orthodoxies not only because they tyrannized the minds of men, nor because they insisted on uniformity of thought, but because in so doing they thereby sought to abort the spirit of investigation, defying "common sense, reason, and revelation." We have seen how Campbell, in his debate with Rice, maintained that there was variety of teaching and belief in the New Testament church. His opening gun in his attempt to rid Christianity of persecuting orthodoxies was a *crusade for variety of opinion.* "When men make communion in religious worship dependent on uniformity of opinion,

[81]*Christian Baptist,* IV, 275.

they make self-love, instead of the love of God, the bond of union.''[82] But variety of opinion was more than a desirability, it was an *actual necessity*. To hold opinions contrary to the majority or the national creed to be an injury was to ''establish a principle of calamitous consequences.''[83] Opinions were encouraged. But they were not to be imposed on others, they were to be held as private property.

If Campbell's first thrust at orthodoxy was to espouse variety of opinion, his second was to actually champion heterodoxy. A true picture of him cannot be painted until he is portrayed as the avowed heretic of his day. His method of expressing himself often caused him to be misunderstood, and there is reason to believe that at times he was deliberately misrepresented, and as a result he was accused of many heresies which he consistently denied. Still, from the standpoint of orthodox Christianity as constituted in his time, he was heretical. He not only ever stood for the spirit of inquiry, he praised the spirit of scepticism:

To what was it owing, my fellow citizens, that we have a constitution so favorable to the utmost liberty of conscience, so congenial to that spirit of enquiry which is essential to our knowing and enjoying the true substantial bliss; a constitution the wonder and the admiration of the virtuous—the fear and the dread of the tyrant, and the oppressor in all nations; a constitution . . . the most illustrious feature, of which, is . . . that generous philanthropy which it expresses in these golden words —''*All men are born free*''? . . . I am persuaded that it was owing more to the scepticism that prevailed in that most illustrious of all national conventions, that which framed this Magna Charta of American liberty, than to any other cause. Had sectarian priests framed our Constitution, do you think, that I, my friends, dare have stood here, as I do this day, in opposition to the very principle which is the basis of all religious establish-

[82]Robinson, *op. cit.*, II, 224.
[83]*Ibid.*, p. 133.

ments? No, my friends, there would then have been a more summary way of settling such controversies.[84]

His final blow at orthodoxy was simply an attempt to eliminate the foundation on which it rested. That foundation was philosophical and theological speculation. He almost reminds one of the refrain of Islam that "Allah is Allah" in the simplicity with which he would dispose of theology: "Call Bible things by Bible names." There was a sort of linguistic asceticism in the way in which he insisted on a "pure speech." "Let us give to divine institutions divine names, and to human institutions human names." "There must be, and there shall be, an abandonment of the new and corrupt nomenclature, and a restoration of the inspired one." He insisted on having nothing to do with the "abstract and metaphysical dogmas" of theology. They only served to create churches of "religious speculators . . . empanneled to sit in judgment on the preacher's orthodoxy."

One cause of Campbell's being misrepresented in his theology was this refusal to discuss the more abstract theological speculations of his day. Once, when asked the question "Did humanity die and divinity leave the Son of God?" he refused to discuss the question, saying:

. . . It has arisen from the dissecting knife of theological anatomists. It is the northern extreme of frigid Calvinism. The immense ice mountains of those regions have prevented their most expert captains from finding a passage to those latitudes which would confirm their theory of sphere within sphere. They are as skilful to separate and treat of humanity and divinity in the Son of God as is Colonel Symmes in forming this globe into so many hollow spheres, each having its own proprieties and inhabitants.[85]

"Allah is Allah." "The Son of God," said Campbell, "is the Son of God." He insisted that he was neither

---

[84]*Campbell-Maccalla Debate*, pp. 216-217.
[85]*Christian Baptist*, II, 169.

Unitarian nor Trinitarian, although charged by either side as being the other. In speaking of the doctrine of the Trinity, he said:

... I object not to this doctrine because it is contrary to reason, or revelation, but because of the metaphysical technicalities, the unintelligible jargon, the unmeaning language of the orthodox creeds on this subject, and the interminable war of words without ideas to which this word *Trinity* has given birth.[86]

Such dogmas, he held, were "farther from the comprehension of nine-tenths of mankind than the words employed by the Holy Spirit." He would free the human spirit from the tyranny of such abstractions by making the Bible its own interpreter and every believer his own exegete. In order to do this he gave much attention to the principles of biblical interpretation.[87]

An interesting commentary on Campbell's opposition to theology is the bias which most Disciples of Christ have to this day even to the term "theology."[88] Their schools for the ministry are consistently called "Bible Colleges," in which they, as a rule, have no departments of theology, but have instead, departments of "Church Doctrine." They seem not to have discovered such passages from his pen as the following, in which he indicts the term "doctrine" as fully as he ever did the term "theology":

---

[86]*Millennial Harbinger,* 1833, p. 155.

[87]In this connection, T. W. Grafton says: "I was a student at Bethany in 1874-78. The memories and traditions of Mr. Campbell were hanging over the college as the autumn haze hangs over the lovely Ozark hills of Missouri. I copied this key which he gave to his classes: 'I suggest gentlemen, as a key to open to you the scriptures, that you use the "W" key. Who writes or speaks? To whom is he writing or speaking? Where did he write? When did he write? What did he really say? What purpose did he have in writing? What lesson for our age? What principles involved? What lessons for me?' All this is the A B C of higher criticism. Alexander Campbell was on the track of modern biblical scholarship, was actually an incipient higher critic. ... It must be remembered though, that Campbell —even if he did initiate methods of study which higher critics use today— never doubted the Bible or anything in it." *Alexander Campbell, Leader of the Great Reformation of the Nineteenth Century,* pp. 216-219.

[88]In this connection, Fred West has properly shown that even though Disciples of Christ have historically followed Campbell in his aversion to theology, Campbell himself became a theologian in opposing theologies. See West, Fred. *Alexander Campbell and Natural Religion,* p. 475ff.

We read in the Christian Scriptures of *"doctrines"* or *"the doctrines and commandments of men."* We also read of *"the doctrines of demons"* and of *"strange doctrines;"* but never once of *"sound doctrines,"* nor of *christian doctrines,* never once of *orthodox doctrines.* These all were generated, and born, and nursed, and cherished in the bosom of the mother of harlots, and in the bosom of her meretricious daughters.

No Christian man of a *pure* speech, well educated in the Christian Scriptures, ever represents the inspired teachings of the Holy Spirit by the terms "Christian doctrines."[89]

E. *The Agencies of Ecclesiastical Propaganda —Sunday Schools and Missionary Organizations*

. . . Nothing can be done worthy of admiration by the christians of this age, with any reference to the conversion of the pagan nations, until the christians separate themselves from all the worldly combinations in which they are swallowed up, until they come out from amongst them that have a form of godliness, but deny the power of it . . . until they form themselves into societies independent of hireling priests . . . until they cast to the moles and to the bats the Plutonic speculations, the Pythagorean dreams and Jewish fables they have written in their creeds; until they return to the ancient model delineated in the New Testament.[90]

If theology constituted the propaganda by which ecclesiasticism perverted the minds of men, Sunday schools, missionary organizations, and all "human agencies" of the like were the vehicles through which it was propagated. As such, they fell under the iconoclastic ban.

Campbell's attitude toward these agencies constituted one of the points at which unquestionably he reversed his position later on. How he could have continued throughout his life to insist that he "hadn't changed his position" always promises to remain a puzzle in the face

---

[89]*Millennial Harbinger,* 1864, p. 201.
[90]*Christian Baptist,* I, 16.

of such contradictory statements as the following. The first two selections, it will be noted, were written during his writings prior to the year 1840, while the latter two are selected from his writings subsequent to that date:

. . . The New Testament . . . churches were not fractured into missionary societies, bible societies, education societies; nor did they dream of organizing such in the world. . . . They dare not transfer to a missionary society, or bible society, or education society, a cent or a prayer, lest in so doing they should rob the church of its glory, and exalt the inventions of men above the wisdom of God.[91]

We have always and uniformly borne our testimony in favor of temperance, righteousness, benevolence, and the co-operation of all christians and christian churches in the grand enterprize of converting the world; but at the same time we have borne our testimony against. . . . Missionary Societies, and every other human institution opposed to the honor, dignity, and usefulness of the Christian Institution.[92]

. . . The cause of missions is a cause that first of all, and most of all, commends itself to the affections of the whole Christian community.

We are, therefore, peculiarly gratified, to see with what unanimity, zeal, and liberality, the whole brotherhood assembled at the late Cincinnati Convention, have entered into this great work of evangelizing.[93]

. . . I doubt not that our brethren in all places will see it a duty they owe to themselves, to the church, and to the world, either to have in every church a Sunday School of their own, or to unite with the Sunday School Union in their truly benevolent and catholic institution.[94]

But Campbell's contradictory position with regard to missionary endeavor was not confined to a difference in his earlier and his later thought. There was confusion and contradiction even in his earlier antagonisms. During this period his opposition largely was based on two

[91]*Ibid.*, pp. 6-7.
[92]*Millennial Harbinger,* 1835, p. 388.
[93]*Ibid.*, 1850, p. 76.
[94]*Ibid.*, 1847, p. 201.

grounds: first, that all auxiliaries of the church were simply agencies by which the clergy propagated the ecclesiastical theologies; second, that the multiplicity of such agencies lessened the power and glory of the church by fracturing it into little groups.[95] He insisted that he was irrevocably in favor of both a specific program of religious education, and also of a grand program of missions for the evangelization of the world. With regard to the latter plan, it was an atomistic one, with individual disciples taking it on themselves to go to foreign lands as ambassadors of Christ. When individual disciples accepted their true office as such ambassadors, there would be no need of missionaries. But a single month prior to this suggestion he had questioned the very validity of missions, and had suggested that the missionary work was completed with the cessation of the power to work miracles.

Here again was a conflict between the literalist and the liberalist! And here again is data which suggests that, instead of antipodes between the earlier and the later Campbell, the later Campbell was the result of an effort to resolve a basic contradiction in the thought of the earlier Campbell, of the nature of which he never seemed to be aware.

Thus we have seen that until the third decade of the 19th century Campbell's career was marked by a violent antiecclesiasticism. That antiecclesiasticism rooted back both in Campbell's historical experience and his psychological make-up. It was absolutistic in its sweep, and sought to brush aside all existing Christian sects with their media of propagation. It was supported by both a literalism and a liberalism within Campbell which led

---

[95]*Christian Baptist*, I, 6-8. This was one of the keenest educational insights Campbell ever showed, one in which he anticipated many modern advocates of a unified church program. It is regrettable that he did not pursue that insight more faithfully in his later years.

him to the brink of religious atomism, and made him "exclusively-inclusive" while striving for ecumenicity.

Beginning in the middle of the third decade, and reaching its peak in the fourth and fifth decades of the 19th century, Campbell applied himself to the constructive period of his career, and struggled to create the type of Christian community which would meet the dictates of what he considered to be both reason and revelation. This was his period of growth, maturity, and Christian statesmanship. The remainder of this study will be devoted to a consideration of the results of these constructive efforts.

CHAPTER TWO

THE CHURCH UNDER A CHRISTOCRACY

It is not the object of our efforts to make men think alike on a thousand themes. Let them think as they like on any matters of human opinion and upon "doctrines of religion," provided only they hold THE HEAD CHRIST and keep his commandments.[1]

Nowhere was the dichotomy between Campbell's literalism and his liberalism more sharply drawn than in his conception of the nature of revelation. On the one hand revelation was final, complete, and arbitrary. It had its alpha and its omega in the fiat of God:

There are no new discoveries in Christianity. It is as old as the sacred writings of the apostles and evangelists of Jesus Christ. *Our whole religion, objectively and doctrinally considered, is found in a book.* Nothing discovered by any man, that has lived since John wrote the Apocalypse, is of any virtue in religion; nay, indeed, is no part or parcel of Christianity. All that can now be pretended or aimed at, by any sane mind, is *the proper interpretation of what is written in Hebrew and Greek* and translated into all the modern languages in the civilized world. Whatever in Christianity is new is not true.[2]

On the other hand, the discovery of truth was progressive, cumulative, and unfolding. It had its genesis is a scientific spirit of inquiry. The following is typical of

---

[1]*Campbell-Rice Debate,* p. 797.
[2]*Millennial Harbinger,* 1848, p. 280.

any number of statements of like effect: "Weak minds are the slaves of old times, and of old customs. They need the crutches of antiquity, and human authority. But men of vigorous minds ask, *what is truth?* not *who* says it."[3]

Within the confines of the scriptural canon Campbell built his whole system of thought on the basis of progressive revelation. In a day when there was a tendency to blot out the lines between the Old and the New Testaments he first aroused the opposition of some of the leaders of the Redstone Baptist Association because of his "Sermon on the Law," in which he divided the epochs of the kingdom of God into three progressive dispensations called the Patriarchal, the Jewish, and the Christian.[4] But with him the progress of revelation went not one word beyond the last spoken by the apostles.

With Campbell, all was either black or white. When it came to Christianity, white consisted in what he called the "gospel facts," black in what he called "human speculations." Any satisfactory understanding of Campbell must take into account the distinction which he drew between the two. He spent his life trying to call the religious world away from "speculation" to "fact." What was fact? He does not leave us in doubt:

The gospel is not a *theory,* a *speculation,* a *philosophy,* a *doctrine;* but a *matter of fact message;* an official communication of stupendous facts and documents, sent by specially commissioned heralds, to Jews, Samaritans, and gentiles, without exception. These facts and events, these precepts, promises and

---

[3]*Campbell-Rice Debate,* p. 608.

[4]It will be noted that both references above are taken from what was distinctly the later period in Campbell's career. The first was contained in the *Millennial Harbinger* in the year 1848, the second from the debate with N. L. Rice in 1844. This is mentioned because of the insistence of most biographers that Campbell's literalism marked his earlier career while his liberalism marked his later career. "There was something of literalism, of going to extremes, a certain note of finality, which I must depict as an integral part of Mr. Campbell's teachings in this magazine. . . . It must be constantly kept in mind that Mr. Campbell, while dogmatic and narrow during this period, was brave enough to reverse himself later on. He abandoned his literalistic teachings almost entirely, and preserved only the constructive part." Smith, Benjamin L. *Alexander Campbell,* p. 137.

threatenings, communicated by special heralds—sometimes called "apostles, prophets, evangelists," or proclaimers of good or bad news—are the contents or materials of inspired embassadors of the Lord Messiah. Persons, their sayings and doings, promises and threatenings, events and issues, are the staple, or materials, of the so called Four Gospels, and the Acts of Apostles.[5]

. . . In his letter to the Ephesians, (chap. 4, 7) [Paul] presents the strongest arguments for union, Christian union, ever expressed by mortal man. These are, We have but *"one body, one Spirit, one hope, one Lord, one faith, one baptism, one God and Father of all,* who is above all, and through all, and in you all."

These seven superlative *facts*—not theories, not speculations, not opinions, not doctrines, not philosophies, not ordinances, not human institutions;—these seven facts, we say, are the bases or pedestal, the die and the cornice of the house of God, which Jesus *the Christ* founded, which Peter opened to Jews and Gentiles, and Paul preached, taught, and developed to the whole Gentile world in his fourteen elaborate epistles.[6]

On the other hand, human speculation consisted not only in any philosophy or theology or church polity developed since the close of the New Testament canon, it also included any interpretation given to any part of that canon which Campbell felt to be in error. Reflecting the Lockian influence, he believed that truth was truth and that the human mind was so constituted that it could not refrain from assent to the plain truths of the New Testament if it would but rid itself of its prejudices. Firmly believing that he had so rid himself, he then believed that the only things which prevented all others from seeing simple facts of the gospel as he saw them were the prejudices and traditions from which they had been unable to free themselves. A direct result of this position was the charge on the part of his opponents

---

[5]*Millennial Harbinger*, 1862, pp. 16-17.
[6]*Ibid.*, pp. 49-50.

that his real distinction between fact and opinion was that "fact" meant his own interpretation of the Bible while "opinion" meant any interpretation which differed from his, and that his interpretation thus became his unwritten creed.

When Campbell thus pleaded for human freedom and responsibility, it must be understood that the freedom for which he pleaded was never the freedom to disregard nor to question the "gospel facts." Again there were two areas as distinct as black and white. One represented the area of the absolute sovereignty of Christ, the other the area of the complete freedom of man.

I. *The Lordship of Christ*

The *Christening,* or anointing, of Jesus as autocrat of the universe was . . . the most grand, august and sublime event ever that transpired; and the proclamation of it the most thrilling and soul-subduing annunciation ever uttered on earth.[7]

The widespread impression that Alexander Campbell was the apostle of democracy in regard to church polity is somewhat at variance with the facts. In the first place, he scorned the whole idea of church polity, and attributed the divisions of Christianity to its church polities rather than to difference in faith:

. . . May we not safely affirm, on the premises of the seven isms, that their great central idea is, that church *politics,* rather than piety, humanity, or faith, are the great magnetic centres of all sects and schisms in alienated Christendom?

Why inscribe on their banners their ecclesiastic *politics,* rather than their Christian *doctrine, faith,* or *worship,* if they do not give a paramount value to church polity?[8]

In the second place he particularly discounted the worth of all existing forms of church polity:

[7]Selina Huntington Campbell, *Home Life and Reminiscences of Alexander Campbell,* p. 160.
[8]*Millennial Harbinger,* 1855, p. 362.

Democracies belong to earth, merely to manacle and fetter human ambition. But there is no democracy nor aristocracy in Christ's true earthly kingdom, nor is there any democracy in heaven. Patriarchies, Papacies, Prelacies, and Presbyteries are the four capital PS. of ecclesiastical Politics, and ecclesiastic ambitions.[9]

As if this were not enough he scoffed at the very idea of a "church government":

... After all that has been said upon the subject of church government, lodged in human hands; after all the angry contests, whether an episcopacy similar to a monarchy; whether a presbytery similar to an aristocracy, or an independency similar to a democracy, be the government instituted by God, or authorized in the New Testament—it might perhaps appear, upon an impartial examination of the scriptures, that the whole controversy is a mere *"vox et preterea nihil"*—a sound and nothing else; that there is no such a thing as "church government," in the popular sense of the terms.[10]

Instead of seeking democracy in church affairs, Campbell, therefore, sought to free the church from all existing church governments. Every local church was to be free of all outside dominion, every believer was to be free of all proscriptive creeds, but only in order that they might come under the absolute authority of Christ. From the dawn of his plea for restoration until the twilight of his career at Bethany, there was one theme which threaded his thought, and that was that God had made Christ the absolute monarch of the universe. There were many terms which Campbell used to express this idea, including the application of the terms "king" "monarch," and "autocrat" to Christ. But there was one word which he used over and over again, a term which, according to his statement, he seems to have coined himself. That term was "Christocracy":

[9]*Ibid.*, 1858, pp. 517-518.
[10]*Christian Baptist*, I, 25.

It is to us surpassing strange, that we, as a people, are the only people, now within the precincts of modern christendom, so called, whether under the name of a presbytery, a prelacy, a papacy, or a patriarchy, that have given, or now give, in any of their books, or in any of their pulpits, known to us, any special or particular prominence to this most important fact, oracle, or annunciation ever uttered or heard by mortal ear upon earth. There is no end, no terminus, to church and State *democracies, aristocracies, monarchies, oligarchies, theocracies,* but not one word, not even in Webster's Dictionary—of a *christocracy,* and yet, in very deed, this is *the only liege designation title, or name, of the present government of the universe; and especially of that of the Christian church.*[11]

This "Christocracy," or absolute sovereignty of Jesus Christ, was the only government of the church which Campbell recognized. "There is no other authority recognized, allowed, or regarded, by a society of christians, meeting in one place as a church of Jesus Christ, than the authority of its king or head."[12] He further called this the "subbasis" on which he had built for forty-six years, and declared that such complete adherence to the sovereignty of Christ was all that could do a helpless sinner any good. Although he vigorously objected to the combining of the legislative, executive, and judicial powers in any man or set of men, he insisted that all these branches of government were completely combined in the Lordship of Christ.

The basis of the Christocracy was Christology, which embraced the person, the office, and the work of Christ, the "Son of God and the Son of Man" and redeemer of the world. Here again we run across one of those amazing contradictions in Campbell. One moment he embraced and advocated the study of "Christology" as essentially indispensable because it has to do with the person, mission, character, and work of Christ. In al-

[11]*Millennial Harbinger,* 1857, p. 490.
[12]*Christian Baptist,* I, 26.

most the next breath he completely repudiated the whole idea of "Christology." And on what grounds? Because the literal word is not found in the Bible! Those apologists for Campbell who would confine his literalism to his earlier days and would place his liberalism in his later days will note that the two following (and thoroughly contradictory) statements are taken not only from his later writings, but from the same volume of the *Millennial Harbinger,* and from successive issues, published in June and July, 1861:

Of all the governments that ever existed under any name, that of the *Christocracy* is the superlative. But to appreciate it, the study of Christology is essentially indispensable. Christology is the whole—the perfect and complete development and appreciation of the *person,* the *mission,* the *character and the work* of the Lord Jesus.[13]

Christianity is an abstract term—a speculative idea, never once named by an inspired apostle, evangelist, pastor, or teacher. . . . We have a real, positive and actual *Christ* and *Christian* in the evangelical terminology of inspiration. They are positive and real existences. But Christianity, theology, Christology, orthodoxy, heterodoxy, are pure speculative abstractions of human reason or imagination. Hence they are wholly contraband, unscriptural, and unauthorized by any divinely commissioned apostle, prophet or evangelist found in the volumes of Divine inspiration. We, therefore, reprobate and repudiate them *in toto.*[14]

On the basis of the latter quotation, those Disciples who hold a bias against theology, a bias which reflects the lingering influence of Campbell, would do well to explain why they do not abolish the term "Christianity" on the same grounds. It is also regrettable that Campbell did not explain why he did not repudiate his favorite term of "Christocracy" on the same basis that he insisted on rejecting the terms mentioned.

---

[13]*Millennial Harbinger,* 1861, p. 364.
[14]*Ibid.,* 1861, pp. 561-562.

On any basis but one this contradiction is inexplicable. That basis is the one which has been suggested, that the contradictions in Campbell were rooted in two presuppositions which he never succeeded in reconciling. At one time, Campbell the discoverer, the irrepressible seeker after truth, was writing. At another time, Campbell the literalist, the authoritarian, was expressing himself. Difficult as it is to confess, the attempt to restrict Campbell's literalism to his younger days smacks as much of an attempt at wishful thinking as the attempt to squeeze his liberalism into his later writings. Both strains ran concurrently in all his thought.

A. *The Scope of Christ's Reign*

Campbell attached much importance to a correct understanding of the exact beginning of the reign of Christ. Here again we find elements in his thought which are both conformative and creative. At one moment he speaks prophetically:

> Family religion was the only social form of religion from Adam to Moses. The national succeeded it; but the ecumenical is destined to permeate the world. . . .
>
> The Lord Jesus Christ is reigning monarch. . . . He has worn the crown of thorns, and he must wear the crown of glory, of enduring righteousness, holiness, and peace.[15]

On the other hand, Campbell had a categorical mind, one which not only thought in terms of only two shades —black and white—but one which was burdened with types, allegories, dates, and numbers. To him the history of religion signified not only a growth of accumulated values, as suggested in the preceding quotation; it also represented a fiat of God who had arbitrarily divided the history of the world into the patriarchal, the Jewish, and the Christian dispensations in such a

---

[15]*Ibid.,* 1861, p. 464.

way that a correct understanding of the latter depended
on recognizing its types in the former two. Campbell
attributed much of what he considered the error in
existing sects to a mistake in dating the beginning of
Christ's reign with his birth rather than with the first
Pentecost following his death:

> . . . Much of the confusion on the subject of Christianity has
> grown out of a failure clearly and fully to recognize this great
> fact, that the Christian Dispensation commenced on the day of
> the first Pentecost after the coronation of the Lord Jesus Christ.
> When our great constitutional lawyers would settle any great
> elementary principle of the government, they go back to the
> history of its first constitutional organization. A mistake here
> is fatal—fruitful of the wildest licentiousness in the interpreta-
> tion of our *Magna Charta;* and it is precisely so in reference to
> the Kingdom of Christ. I attach great importance to this prop-
> osition, because of the comprehensive bearings that it has upon
> many points of departure from the ancient order of things in
> the Christian Church.[16]

Campbell prided himself on making this discovery for
the Christian world:

> The era of a son's birth was never, since the world began,
> the era of his reign, or of the commencement of it. It is a
> strange fact, to me a wonderful fact, . . . that we, as a commu-
> nity, are the only people on the chequered map of all Christen-
> dom—Greek, Roman, Anglican, or American, that preach and
> teach that the commonly called Christian era is not the era of
> the commencement of the Christian church or kingdom of the
> Lord Jesus—*the Christ.*
>
> The kingdom of the Christ could not antedate his coronation.[17]

But if Christ's monarchy had a beginning in time, it has
no end. The latter terminus of his reign is conjoined
to eternity: "He will and must reign without a successor, until the last scene of the last act of the grand
drama of ransomed humanity."

---

[16]*Ibid.,* 1859, p. 150.
[17]*Ibid.,* 1860, p. 607.

The area of his Lordship includes not only the church but the whole of humanity. "He is crowned Lord of all glorified humanity—and Lord of all the estates in creation's entire area."

All the expense and machinery of all the political governments of the world are a result only of the failure or refusal of humanity to acknowledge the Lordship of Christ.

The media by which Christ's sovereignty was to be maintained were three. The first was the delegation of the apostles as his representatives:

. . . He placed the twelve apostles upon twelve thrones, and commanded the nations to obey them. I find, therefore, that the Lord Jesus is the governor, and the twelve apostles under him, sitting upon twelve thrones, constitute the government of the church of Jesus Christ.[18]

But the lives of the apostles were not commensurate with the length of Christ's reign. Did they delegate a succession of representatives? By no means, said Campbell. After their death, the inspired word of the Bible was supreme, final, and complete:

The Bible alone must always decide every question involving the nature, the character, or the designs of the Christian institution. Outside of the apostolic canon, there is not, as it appears to me, one foot of terra firma on which to raise the superstructure ecclesiastic.[19]

. . . His will, published in the New Testament, is the sole law of the church; and . . . every society or assembly, meeting once every week in one place, according to this law, or the commandments of this king, requires no other head, king, lawgiver, ruler, or lord, than this Mighty One; no other law, rule, formula, canon or decrees, than his written word.[20]

Not that the entire Bible was to be the law of the church. Campbell sounded almost Barthian in his contention

---

[18]*Christian Baptist*, V, 441.
[19]*Richardson, op. cit.*, II, 495.
[20]*Ibid.*, I, 26-27.

that the Bible "contained" the word of God, while granting that it also contained other materials. Here again we find evidences of a critical approach:

> I have just now found on my desk a few questions. . . .
> The first is, *Are the books composing the Old and the New Testaments the only books of divine authority in the world?* I answer positively, Yes. I have already said, that the books composing the two Testaments contain more than what is properly called a *Divine Revelation*. They contain much history which can with no propriety be called a Divine Revelation; for example, the history of the deluge—the confusion of human language—the dispersion of the human family—the biography of the patriarchal judges—and kings of Israel—the chronicles of Judea and Israel. All the things recorded in these sections were known before written, and therefore could not be REVELA-TIONS.[21]

But here, again, Campbell's critical spirit was held in leash by his authoritarianism. Another question which was put to him at the same time as the former had to do with the authorship of the Book of Job, parts of Deuteronomy containing accounts such as the death and burial of Moses, and the authorship of the Epistle to the Hebrews. Campbell replied:

> . . . My belief in the authenticity and authority of [the] book [of Job], and all anonymous parts of the Old Testament, is founded upon the following basis. The Jewish scribes received them; the whole Jewish nation received them; their own internal evidence attests their pretensions; and, above all, they were quoted as genuine, and approbated as parts of the sacred records and revelation, by Jesus Christ, or his Apostles, concerning whose inspiration and certain knowledge of the character of these works we cannot entertain a rational doubt.[22]

The third means by which the sovereignty of Christ was to be maintained, said Campbell, was by the Holy Spirit. Attacks on his belief about the Holy Spirit never

---

[21]*Campbell-Owen Debate,* p. 352.
[22]*Ibid.,* p. 354.

ceased to plague him. His opposition to emotional revivalism, his insistence on the prominence of volition in conversion, his definition of the nature of faith, and his emphasis on the authority of the written Word, drew down upon his head the charge that he did not believe in the Holy Spirit. He conducted a number of extended discussions with some of his contemporaries, particularly with Barton Warren Stone with whose "Christian" group his "Disciples" had united, and with Andrew Broadus of the Baptists, on the general subject of the work of the Holy Spirit in conversion. Campbell consistently denied that he had negated the work of the Holy Spirit, but sought to define that work in terms which he felt would not do violence to man's free will. He insisted that the Holy Spirit operated "through the Word of God, and not separate and apart from it." That he did assign a place to the Holy Spirit in the government of Christ may be seen in the following:

"The government of Christ in his church, is by the established record of Faith and Practice, in the Scriptures, and by the immediate work and guidance of the Holy Spirit, in accordance with that record."[23]

. . . The Christian institution in a Christocracy, or a Christ government.

Jehovah, in the person of the *Father*, and as the God of Abraham, was the head of the Jewish Institution. And Jehovah, in the person of the *Son*, is the head of the Christian Institution. And Jehovah, in the person of the Holy Spirit, is the guest—not the *Ghost* of it.[24]

B. *The Nature of His Reign*

If Campbell looked for identifying resemblances between the Christian and Jewish dispensations, he also stressed what he believed to be distinct differences. Here we find him expressing some of his finest thought,

---

[23]*Millennial Harbinger*, 1837, p. 87.
[24]*Ibid.*, 1861, p. 462.

much, indeed, having been written during that period which some would indict as his period of literalism.

With the coronation of Christ, said Campbell, there was a new era "evangelical and not legal, pursuant upon the descension of the Holy Spirit, to remain always in the church, as its quickening, sanctifying, soul-inspiring life." It was not a formal, visible kingdom, but a spiritual and invisible one, "not a kingdom of this world, but a kingdom in this world." It was to be marked by "an inhabitation of God through the Holy Spirit, now the holy guest in the members of that spiritual community called the body of Christ, or the house of God, the pillar and support of the truth in the world." It was intimately personal as well as spiritual, owing its existence to "an infinitely sublime, official person—Jesus the Messiah, the Christ, or the 'Anointed of God.'" Not only did it make "subject, object, intercourse and communion" all personal, it placed personality supreme on the list of values:

Society was not made—neither political nor religious society —was constituted—for the sake of law-givers, Law-expounders, Law-executors, but these were created and constituted for man. Just as the Great Teacher once said—to the too ceremonious *Pharisees*—"The Sabbath was made for man, not man for the Sabbath." Mark ii :27. So we say—Law-givers, Law-interpreters, Law-executors were created and are sustained, not for themselves . . . but for the State. They are *public* servants of the *sovereign* people confederated. So precisely are Christian *Ministers*, Christian *Teachers*, Christian *Evangelists*.[25]

Since Christ's reign was held to be personal, the only test of Christian character which could be required must also be personal.[26] The personal relationship of believer to Christ was not so much that of subject to master as that of those who have been emancipated to

---

[25]*Ibid.*, 1857, p. 587.
[26]*Ibid.*, 1855, p. 365.

their emancipator. The believer was governed by principles rather than by laws:

As young men arrive at the full age of mankind they are emancipated from the government of more precepts, and put under the government of principles. Here is the secret. The Jews were under a government of precepts—we are under a government of principles. Hence all was laid down to them in broad and plain commandments; and the book which contained their worship was a ritual, a manual of religious and moral duties, accurately defined to the utmost conceivable minutia; insomuch that nothing was left to discretion—nothing to principle.

There is nothing like this in the New Institution. We have no ritual, liturgy, or manual.[27]

While holding that immersion and the Lord's Supper are positive institutions under the Christian dispensation, Campbell insisted that they are still in harmony with the principle of freedom:

. . . There were more directions about the celebration of the Passover and the observance of the Sabbath, than is to be found in the whole New Institution. Nay, indeed, there is nothing of that sort in the christian economy. No mode of eating the supper, no mode of observing the Lord's day is suggested in the apostolic writings. In this christians are left to the discretion of full grown men to the government of principle.[28]

While the reign of Christ was held by Campbell to be based on principle in preference to any code of laws, forms, or ceremonies, there is one principle which he held to be the basis of the whole system:

. . . All the principles of obedience, all the principles of action, how numerous soever we may suppose them, are reducible to one great principle, sometimes called the new commandment. Now, says Paul, "the end or object of the commandment is love out of a pure heart, out of a good conscience, and from faith unfeigned."[29]

[27]*Christian Baptist*, VII, 655.
[28]*Ibid.*
[29]*Ibid.*

The "Christian Institution" he held to be not only personal and based on the principle of love, it is distinctive in its creative power. It "creates in the heart of man this love. It gives it birth and being. It is a love of a higher order, or a sublimer genius, than any former age or economy could produce."

The reign of Christ, being a reign of love, opened the only door to perfect freedom and liberty, a freedom won by perfect slavery to the King. It would be difficult to produce anything from Campbell's so-called "liberal" period which transcended the following conception, selected from the last volume of the *Christian Baptiot*:

> The dominion of love is the dominion of favor, and its service the easiest conceivable. . . . All who serve any favorite principle feel themselves free. The man who toils harder than any menial bondman ever did, provided he toil in the service of some grateful principle, . . . feels perfect liberty. Liberty is all in the mind. Hence the slaves of Jesus, or the slaves of love, are the veriest freemen in the world.

> .   .   .   .

> The christian scheme is the wisdom and power of God in producing this principle. When created its aliment is the will of God. On the sincere milk of the word it feeds. This nourishes and strengthens it. To its government the new man is subjected. Hence, the obedience of faith is also the obedience of love.

> .   .   .   .

> But that which calls for our notice here, is that God now deals with us as sons, and not as servants—not as sons who are minors, but as sons who are full of age.[30]

II. *The Priesthood of the Believer*

. . . [Jesus] begins with the Jews, proceeds to the Samaritans, and thence to all the nations of the earth. He founds a new kingdom under a large commission. . . . He establishes the doc-

---

[30]*Ibid.*

trine of personal liberty, of freedom of choice, and of personal responsibility, by commanding every man to judge, reason, and act for himself.[31]

Campbell proceeded from the doctrine of liberty in Christ to the doctrine of the priesthood of believers. He insisted that Protestantism had done violence to this great concept in that its clergy had continued to arrogate to itself as exclusive privileges rights which properly belonged to all believers.

A. *Freedom the Basis of the Priesthood of the Believer*

Campbell rested his case for the priesthood of the believer on a much broader foundation than simply that of the nature of the Christian institution. He appealed to the nature of personality itself as being not only free but of supreme worth as well. He held that Christ not only frees the person, he recognizes a freedom which already inheres in personality. His views in this connection are best found in his voluminous writings in favor of universal suffrage and of universal education, and against war and human slavery. As a member of the general convention of the state of Virginia in the year 1829, he said:

While I am on the subject of such a state of nature, or viewing man as coming into society, may I not take occasion to observe that man exhibits himself as possessing the right of suffrage anterior to his coming into the social compact. It is not a right derived from or conferred by society, for it is a right which belongs to him as a man. Society may divest him of it, but it cannot confer it. But what is the right? It is that of thinking, willing, and expressing his will. A vote is nothing more nor less than the expression of a man's will. God has given to man the power of thinking, willing and expressing his will, and no man ever did, as a free agent, enter into any society

---

[31]*Christian Baptism: With Its Antecedents and Consequences*, pp. 109-110.

without willing it. And, we may add, no man could enter into
a social compact without first exercising what we may call the
right of suffrage. It is a right *natural* and *underived,* to the
exercise of which every man has by nature as good a reason as
another.[32]

Campbell held not only that the right of suffrage is
natural and underived, but that the very nature of man
is such that he cannot be restrained. In his debate with
Robert Owen, feeling that Owen's twelve "laws of human nature" did violence to man's volitional nature,
he asserted that said laws would apply to a goat or any
other animal as well as to a man. He, therefore, presumed to add other laws to Owen's in which he more
adequately sought to describe man's nature as being
insatiable for knowledge, for fellowship, for happiness,
and for personal growth:

. . . As these are the beginning of a new series for Mr. Owen,
I will call my first the thirteenth "law of human nature."

13. That man has aspirations after knowledge, which would
not cease, did he know and perfectly comprehend every particle
of matter in the globe, in the solar system, in the universe with
all its laws, properties, and modifications; and never can he
feel so well pleased with his acquisitions of knowledge as to fix
a period to his inquiries.

14. That man has a taste for society which the largest and
most accomplished society which could exist contemporaneously
with himself cannot gratify.

15. That he has desires for happiness which no circumstances
on earth can satisfy; and that these desires are commensurate
with infinite objects which the present state of existence cannot
present to him.

16. That when he has formed the best conceptions of himself
which all earth-born opportunities present, he feels himself *pain-
fully* ignorant of every grand fact connected with the origin of
his existence and of every grand result involving his own ultimate destiny.[33]

---

[32]Richardson, *op. cit.,* II, 311.
[33]*Campbell-Owen Debate,* pp. 447-448.

Campbell further insisted that the human spirit could not be restrained permanently because of the very nature of will. He thought of God as essentially a "willing" spirit, and man's will as the essence of his affinity with the divine.

While Campbell was, therefore, a "Christocrat" as regards man's relationship with God, he was a thoroughgoing republican as regards man's relationship with men. Shortly after his immigration to America he wrote his uncle Archibald in Scotland expressing an appreciation of the republicanism in America, a gratitude which he ever maintained:

"I cannot speak too highly of the advantages that the people in this country enjoy in being delivered from a proud and lordly aristocracy. . . . I have had my horse shod by a legislator, my horse saddled, my boots cleaned, my stirrup held by a senator. Here is no nobility but virtue, and knowledge. . . . I would not exchange the honor . . . of being an American citizen for the position of your king."[34]

It would be a mistake, however, to picture Campbell as an unconditional democrat. With him freedom always involved responsibility, and was conditioned on the fulfillment of certain requirements. Much as he campaigned for universal suffrage, he campaigned even more for universal education as a prelude and a prerequisite to that universal suffrage:

. . . If it should yet require the appropriation of a hundred millions of dollars to bring a good education to the door of every American citizen, to compel the education of all, when it cannot otherwise be accomplished, we would be wanting in the grand elements of Christian community, nay, of a wise and prudent and moral people, if we should not, situated as we are, make vigorous efforts to raise that sum, and devote it to that use.[35]

---

[34]Richardson, *op. cit.*, I, 465-466.
[35]*Millennial Harbinger*, 1837, p. 64.

The purpose of such education was to develop the free powers with which Campbell believed man to be endowed, in a way which would make possible his more effective functioning in the personal, social, and cosmic order:

> Education . . . is teaching a person to think, to reason, to act for himself, and from himself, in harmony with the constitution of the universe; or in unison with himself and with all the relations in which he stands to God and man—to things past, present, and future. Such is a rational and moral education.[36]

In the year 1836 Campbell issued an "Extra" of the *Millennial Harbinger* on the subject of education, parts of which might well become a primer of the modern progressive education movement. In this essay he held that the human soul can operate only through its organs, an organ being a natural instrument such as the brain or the eye. A faculty is the power of the organ, an eye being the organ, and seeing its faculty. An operation is the act of the organ in using its faculty. A faculty is improved and an organ enlarged by repeated operations, by exercise directed by reason. At this point Campbell anticipated E. L. Thorndike's studies in the transfer of training:

> It must be laid down with all the formality of a positive precept that *the exercise of any one organ only improves itself.*

> . . . .

> "Under whose care soever a child is put to be taught, during the tender and flexible years of life, this is certain, it should be one who thinks *Latin and language the least part of education.*"

> . . . .

> A reason for the neglect of moral culture is found in a very common error, viz., in the supposition *that in cultivating the*

---

[36]*Ibid.*, p. 256.

intellect we are cultivating the moral sentiments and feelings— that in enlightening the head we are improving the heart.[37]

On another occasion Campbell used a telling illustration in advocacy of what today would be called "life-centered" education:

> . . . What reply would you make to a teacher of instrumental music who would thus accost you? "Sir, I have clearly, emphatically, and repeatedly pronounced in the ears of your daughters the whole science of instrumental music; I have explained all its principles, and the peculiar powers, and laws, and susceptibilities of the Piano. Besides, sir, I have exemplified these principles and laws to your family by playing before them in every instructive manner I could imagine . . . and yet, sir, I am sorry to inform you that not one of your family can play a single tune."
>
> Would you not immediately rejoin, "Why, sir, did you practice them? Did you make them apply their fingers and their ears to the instrument? In one word, sir, did you train them to the principles and examples which you delivered?"
>
> .   .   .   .
>
> Training sons is much more laborious than teaching sons.
>
> .   .   .   .
>
> Does any one desire that his son shall be of a generous and benevolent spirit and character? Let him accustom him to perform acts of this kind from his earliest capability of action. Let him be often sent on errands of mercy and employed in acts of beneficence. Take him with you while visiting and relieving the miseries and misfortunes of the sick and the afflicted.[38]

When Horace Bushnell was still fresh out of Yale Divinity School, Alexander Campbell was pleading for Christian nurture and stressing the importance of the formative period prior to the age of speech in the child:

> Some principles of religion and morality, or of irreligion and immorality, must be imbibed . . . by every child before it can

---

[37]*Ibid.*, 1836, pp. 587, 590, 594.
[38]*Ibid.*, 1842, pp. 16-17.

reason or judge for itself; and the only alternative left is to decide whether parents and teachers shall leave it to accident what these principles shall be; or whether they shall attempt, in obedience to philosophy, to Solomon, and to Paul (for in this, these three are one), to "train up the infant in the way he should go," in the persuasion that "when he is grown he will not depart from it."

The soil of the human understanding . . . must receive some seed before we arrive at boyhood, much more before we arrive at manhood.

. . . .

Another reason why the moral feelings ought to be first cultivated is found in the fact, that if not cultivated soon, they can never be so fully and successfully cultivated afterwards. This Nature points out by giving them the greatest susceptibilities at first. Indeed, the excellency of the human constitution requires this: for if at more advanced developments of the mind . . . the moral nature of man could easily take on a new color, or immediately assume another hue, then stability, the very basis of character, without which everything in morals is modish and freakish, would be unattainable.[39]

As to the nature of the Christian nurture, Campbell again bore striking resemblance to Bushnell's thought, not only by vigorously opposing the Calvinistic conception of conversion current in his day, but by affirming that it was mediated by conduct in the matrix of the family life, and made explicit in language:

. . . We want, and must have, a radical and thorough reformation in family religion and family education. In respect to both personal and family religion and education, we need more reading of God's Book, more meditating upon it, more conversation about it, more praying, more singing, . . . more rejoicing, more zeal, more morality, more truth, more honesty, and infinitely less dissimulation, duplicity, bargain and promise-breaking, selfishness, and carnality among professors, than we now find amongst large masses of the evangelicals of our day.[40]

[39]*Ibid.*, 1836, pp. 597ff.
[40]*Ibid.*, 1837, p. 538.

But Campbell sought to develop an over-all system of education which would provide for the total span of life. In the year 1840 he proposed a plan for a literary, moral, and educational system which would unite four institutions in one—a combination of the family, the primary school, the college, and the church in one great system of education. Bethany College was a direct result of this plan, and Campbell attempted to anticipate the noble project of Dr. Arnold Gesell of Yale by advocating a system of nursery schools for the preschool child:

. . . It is then true in philosophy, because true in fact, that moral culture must be attended to in perfect infancy and childhood, if we would have our pupils to attain to high degree of moral excellency.[41]

To the domestic and infant school system of moral training, which gives a bias to virtue and sows the seeds of moral excellence in the human constitution, must be added the influence of every school and every seminary through which the pupil advances in his literary career.[42]

Campbell actually founded an infant school and a primary school in connection with Bethany College. Both closed—for lack of pupils.

As has been pointed out previously, Campbell constantly urged the incorporation of religion and the Bible in all systems of education. Shortly after his debate with Bishop Purcell on the Roman Catholic religion, he rejoiced:

I had the pleasure to see even the Catholic Bishop of Cincinnati, with all the Clergy of all denominations—Episcopal, Presbyterian, Baptist, and Methodist—then present at a meeting of the College of Teachers in that city, voting in favor of my amendment of a resolution of give the Bible to every school in the country, without one sectarian or denominational note or comment; and that, too, in one year after the debate on Roman-

[41]*Ibid.*, 1836, p. 599.
[42]*Ibid.*, p. 602.

ism, growing out of that cardinal tenet of Protestism, viz.—the
Bible, the whole Bible, and nothing but the Bible, as the rule
of Christian faith and manners.[43]

While Campbell bemoaned the sectarian divisions
which barred the uninhibited teaching of religion in the
public schools, he not only affirmed that in America we
have a by-law-established religion, he further asserted
that we have a common core of religious faith which
could be taught:

It is also becoming more and more evident that, notwithstand-
ing all our sectarian differences, we yet have something called
a *common* Christianity—that there are certain great fundamental matters—indeed, every thing elementary, in which is properly called piety and morality—in which all good men of all
denominations are agreed; and that these great common principles and views form a common ground on which all Christian
people can unite, harmonize, . . . and co-operate in one great
system of moral and Christian education.[44]

Thus, while Campbell advocated universal suffrage,
it can be seen how he would have conditioned that suffrage. He would have withheld the right of suffrage until
the individual had qualified himself with some such educational training. He demanded not only an educational democracy, but educated democrats. To him it
was unthinkable that the vote of an ignorant mind
should be allowed to nullify the vote of an educated
mind. The implications of such a sentiment as the following had an important bearing on Campbell's whole
idea of the organization of the church:

. . . Tell it not at Mecca, publish it not among the wild men
of the forest, that in the civilized and Christianized State of
Virginia, there are in a single county 2100 persons of mature
age and reason that can neither read nor write! Yet they must
vote; and their illiterate vote must, in our government, out-

[43]*Ibid.*, 1841, pp. 445ff.
[44]*Ibid.*

weigh the vote of two thousand and ninety-nine Solomons, could they be found. Is this rational? Is this right? Is this an oracle of wisdom or of folly? If we must have universal suffrage, let us have universal education. I would limit the one by the other. Till I have got another . . . sort of world than this, I cannot consent to swear that it is good, or reasonable, or fair, or honorable that the vote of a Franklin, a Jefferson, a Madison, or a Washington, should be neutralized by that of one who never knew the letters that compose his own name. . . . That ignorance should neutralize intelligence, and that two thousand uneducated persons should decide the election of a state or the fate of a nation, is, to my mind, no less preposterous than our system of naturalizing certain foreigners who swear to support a constitution, one word of which they have never heard, and can never read.[45]

If Campbell's conception of the free nature of man was reflected in his advocacy of universal education and universal suffrage, it was evidenced no less in his condemnation of the institution of war and the institution of human slavery. His unflinching opposition to war was one of the subjects on which he was ever consistent, even through the critical days of the War between the States. Going further, and holding that wars of any sort, political, theological, or Christological, "never had a warrant from the present reigning Monarch of the Universe," he called upon Christian nations to devise a strategy for peace. He even doubted that a Christian could engage in war, suggesting that the contrast between the gospel of Christ and the genius of war easily could be seen by imagining a Chaplain, on the eve of battle, addressing the soldiers on the text "love your enemies, bless them that curse you, etc."

But Campbell was not content simply to condemn war. He was ready with practical and constructive suggestions for its abolishment. The first was a program of education for a Christian internationalism to replace

[45]*Ibid.*, pp. 455-456.

what he felt to be a narrow patriotism. The second was to advocate the settling of international disputes not only by an impartial umpire, but by the establishment of an international court to adjudicate such controversies:[46]

But how are all national disputes to be settled? Philosophy, history, the Bible teach—that all disputes, misunderstandings, alienations, are to be settled, heard, tried, adjudicated by impartial, that is by disinterested umpires. No man is admitted to be a proper judge in his own case. Wars never make amicable settlements, and seldom, if ever, just decisions of points at issue. We are obliged to offer preliminaries of peace at last. Nations must meet by their representatives, stipulate and restipulate, hear and answer, compare and decide.

In modern times we terminate hostilities by a treaty of peace. We do not make peace with powder and lead. It is done by reason, reflection, and negotiation. Why not employ these first! . . .

Why not have a *by-law established Umpire?* Could not a United National Court be made a feasible and as practicable as a United States Court? Why not . . . a Congress of Nations and a High Court of Nations for adjudicating and terminating all international misunderstandings and complaints, redressing and remedying all wrongs and grievances?[47]

On the problem of slavery Campbell demonstrated at once some of the finest Christian statesmanship and some of the most literalistic restraint of his entire career. His statemanship was clearly manifest in that he was successful in guiding his 600,000 followers through the perilous years of 1860-1864 without a split over the slavery question when such churches as the Methodists, the Baptists, and the Presbyterians were broken asunder on that jagged rock. Campbell's feat

---

[46]This is an amazing anticipation of the United Nations today. Campbell's attitude toward war is considered briefly here only as it bears on his conception of the freedom inherent in man. A fuller treatment of his contribution at this point may be found in Harold Lunger's book, *The Political Ethics of Alexander Campbell.*

[47]*Millennial Harbinger,* 1848, pp. 382-383.

was all the more remarkable when it is noted that the great bulk of his following at that time was in such states as Virginia, West Virginia, Kentucky, Tennessee, Pennsylvania, Ohio, Illinois, and Missouri. These were largely border states on both sides of the Mason-Dixon Line. To make matters more precarious, Campbell himself lived in a slave state, and had at one time been a slaveholder. In addition, as on most critical issues of the day, he intrepidly advanced to express his own views and position. That position was in favor of neither abolition nor slavery:

> I am just as fully convinced that my views on the whole premises, when fully comprehended, will be found to be more truly philanthropic and Christian, than any other scheme before the American people, touching the entire subject of American slavery—that they are more practically beneficial to master and servant—to the true interests of both ends of the Union, than Abolitionism or anti-Abolitionism as now understood and developed.[48]

In a word, Campbell stood for emancipation but not for abolition. As early as 1830 he had pled for the education of the Negro, at the same time asserting that "knowledge and slavery are incompatible—the priests made this discovery before Alfred the Great mounted the throne."

At this point Campbell's literalism and his liberalism again clashed. His literalism said to him that there had been slaves, with apparent divine sanction, in Old Testament times, and that Jesus had not only not condemned slavery, but had apparently sanctioned the relationship between "master and servant." On the other hand, his liberalism said to him that slavery was an inhuman institution, that it violated everything in which he believed about the human spirit, and that in addition it was a distinct social and economic liability. Here

---

[48]*Ibid.,* 1845, p. 314.

was truly a poser for him, and for once it would be expected that he would be compelled to examine more critically his basic presuppositions. But not for a mind as agile as that of Campbell! He had an amazing solution! The Bible sanctioned slavery, but not American slavery, nor any other existing slave institution, "whether in Algiers, West Indies, Africa, Italy, or America!" Asserting that he greatly preferred the condition and prospects of the free states to those of the slave states, he said:

When I affirm that the New Testament recognizes *without censure* the *relation* of master and slave, I do not say that it sanctions the *legalized treatment* of either masters or slaves according to the American or any other code. . . . While, then, I affirm the conviction that the relation of master and slave, by the providence and law of God, is, in certain cases and conditions, morally right, I also affirm the conviction that in this age and in this country it is not expedient.[49]

Once he had made peace with his literalistic requirements, he loosed all his persuasive powers not only to warn of the threat to the nation economically, socially, and morally, but to plead in the name of liberty for the slave. When Harriet Beecher was still in pigtails, Alexander Campbell was pleading in the state assembly that Virginia lead the way for the slave states toward such emancipation.

On the other hand, Campbell feared that the abolition movement would issue only at the point of the bayonet:

. . . *Anti-slavery* is a generic, while *abolitionist* is a specific term. Anti-slavery men are many, while abolitionists are comparatively few. All at the North, and some at the South, are anti-slavery. I have always been anti-slavery, but never an abolitionist. . . . All men of good sense and of humanity contemplate an end of slavery in all its obnoxious attributes; but

---

[49]*Ibid.,* p. 237.

no one expects a sudden, an immediate termination of it, except at the point of the bayonet.[50]

Having inherited slaves f r o m his father-in-law, Campbell set them free, and later purchased two slaves from a Methodist minister, not only setting them free in violation of the laws of Virginia, but going their bond for good behavior.

As a contemporary of Henry Clay in the Virginia Assembly of 1832, Campbell suggested a measure looking toward the gradual emancipation of the slaves. The debt on the Revolutionary War had just been paid through a tax which amounted to about $10,000,000 per year. Mr. Campbell opposed Mr. Clay in his stand that the tax should continue to be collected by the Federal Government and then paid back to the states:

. . . We regret to see Mr. Clay urging this project. Rather, infinitely rather, would I have heard him introduce the following resolution:

. . . .

"Be it enacted, That from and after the first day of January, one thousand eight hundred and thirty-four, the sum of *ten millions of dollars* shall be annually appropriated to the colonization of all people of color, either slaves or free persons, in ——, until the soil of our free and happy country shall not be trod by the foot of a slave, nor enriched by a drop of his sweat or blood, that the whole world may believe that we are not a nation of *hypocrites,* asserting all men to have certain natural and inherent rights, which in our practice we deny; and shedding crocodile tears over the fall of Warsaw, and illuminating for the revolution of the Parisians, while we have millions of miserable human beings at home, held in involuntary bondage, in ignorance, in degradation, and vice, by a *republican system of free slave-holding;"*

. . . .

But Virginia can, and she will, rid herself of the curse; and

[50]*Ibid.,* p. 358.

we say, the sooner she does it, the better for herself. . . . But should the nation take it up, how gloriously would the cause triumph! And as sure as the Ohio winds its way to the Gulph of Mexico, will slavery desolate and blast our political existence, unless effectual measures be adopted to bring it to a close while it is in the power of the nation.[51]

This was twenty-nine years before the outbreak of war. But the bill was defeated, and soon problems more directly related to church order began to arise. The Methodist church divided over the slave issue, and the problem of retaining fellowship with owners of slaves began to arise in some of the Disciple churches. Here was truly a grievous problem, and here was where the theme song which Campbell had been singing for a quarter of a century paid dividends:

. . . Amongst the peculiarities of our profession there is a prominent one—that *we are not allowed to make our own private judgment, interpretation, or opinion, a ground of admission into, or of exclusion from the Christian church.* . . . Opinions as to the policy or impolicy, the prudence or the imprudence of any set of measures, or of what other persons ought to do in certain circumstances, whether similar or dis-similar to our own, not being matters of revelation, or of express precept, are not to be causes of alienation and schism among the members of the household of faith.

. . . .

. . . I affirm the deep and solemn conviction, that any Christian man who exacts more from master or slave than the duties enjoined upon each towards the other, as these duties are developed and defined in the Holy Scriptures, as a term of communion in the Christian church, does that which neither Jesus Christ nor any of his Apostles has authorized him to do, and makes himself a transgressor of the law of Christ.[52]

Campbell stood undeviatingly on this proposition like a rock, and it weathered the storm! The same princi-

---

[51]*Ibid.*, 1832, pp. 87-88.
[52]*Ibid.*, 1845, pp. 233-234.

ple of freedom which prompted him to oppose slavery
demanded that he grant to those who differed with him
the right to hold their opinions without making them a
test of fellowship.

For once Campbell's spirit of inquiry and his devotion to the literal "facts" of the gospel seemed to go
hand in hand. The conception which he evidenced of
the nature of personality as revealed in his attitude
toward education, suffrage, war, and slavery, dove-
tailed very easily into what he conceived to be the
apostolic doctrine of the priesthood of all believers.

B. *The Scope of the Priesthood of All Believers*

While admitting that in all organized communities there
should be official persons to attend to all public duties, it does
not follow that these public duties cannot, or should not be performed in special cases and occasions by unofficial persons.[53]

Campbell believed that Protestantism had never followed out the implications of its doctrine of the priesthood of believers. He felt that too largely it had been
restricted to the right to read and interpret the Bible
for oneself, and that even here, church creeds and the
clergy greatly limited the real freedom of the individual. But in addition to the right of access to the scriptures, Campbell contended that the priesthood of believers secured two other great types of privilege. First,
the right of volitional acceptance of the Lordship of
Christ, or entrance into his kingdom; second, the right
of functioning in any capacity in the service of that
kingdom. The first of these implications led Campbell
to reject infant baptism on grounds other than his belief
in immersion, to relentlessly combat current doctrines
of the influence of the Holy Spirit in conversion, and
to offer what he considered to be both a rational and
a scriptural definition of faith. The second led him to

[53]*Ibid.*, 1858, p. 445.

advocate the use of a "lay" ministry in the church, to deny the clergy the exclusive right of performing the ordinances of the church, and, in fact, to think through anew the whole problem of the structure of the church.

1. *The Right of a Volitional Entrance into the Kingdom*

Newton entered life without a single idea; so have all the men of all the ages of time. Man has capacity or susceptibility from the hand of his Creator; no more. He is, therefore, passive before he can be active. He receives impressions before he makes them. That something we call *mind,* acts not till acted upon through the medium of the machinery of sense. The animal frame, the five senses, like the five mechanical powers, are but the machinery through which and by which the mind acts, and is acted upon. The material universe enters the soul, or acts upon the mind only by the medium of sense; and no other universe can enter the soul but through the material universe. So that the Great Spirit operates upon the human mind through the material universe.[54]

If the believer is free, said Campbell, he is free to believe or not to believe. In any case, no other person is authorized to commit him to the dominion of Christ either against his will or without his consent. This conviction led him to oppose the practice of infant baptism on even more vigorous grounds than on the grounds of his adoption of immersion as the mode of baptism. It was at this point that Campbell radically diverged from the position of Bushnell. Whereas Bushnell held that the child should grow up a Christian and "never know himself to be anything else," Campbell held that he could not become a Christian until he had arrived at the age where he could make that choice for himself. Here again was one of those tenuous lines which Campbell had the knack of drawing. Few men have written as much or as vigorously as did he in behalf of Christian nurture, or on the importance

---

[54]*Ibid.,* 1836, p. 152.

of the first tender years. For years he conducted as a feature of the *Millennial Harbinger* a series of articles entitled "Conversations at the Carlton House" which was a model for conversations about religion in the home. He urged again and again that the child be "trained up in the way he should go." And yet the child could not be a Christian!

Parents and children are now alike to act for themselves. It is he, and only he, "who believes and is baptized, that shall be saved." In the Lord's kingdom there is neither Jew nor Gentile, Barbarian nor Scythian, bond nor free. Indeed there is neither male nor female, parent nor child, under his administration. Intelligence and candour, faith and obedience, are supposed to be possessed by every member of Christ's kingdom. There are not two classes of church members in Christ's church, any more than there are two sorts of citizens in the United States.[55]

Because the Pedobaptist churches invoked their creeds on the "helpless infant," invoking their traditions on him, and committing him to those traditions, Campbell held that they had not fully abjured popery. The following was written, not during the so-called "anti-ecclesiastical" days, but in the year 1846:

No religion preached on earth is so favorable to human liberty as the Christian. Indeed, it prescribes the only rational foundation of liberty ever submitted to the human understanding. This it does by making every man's destiny forever depend upon his own choice. If he must be judged for himself, he must think and choose for himself is as sound logic, as sound theology, as ever preached. His father cannot act for him unless he be judged for him. No Pedobaptist has, therefore, fully abjured popery. He carries a pope in his bosom so long as he will vow for his child, and then by the force of that vow teach his son that he is obliged to join his father's church, because in that church he was sealed, signed, and delivered by the divine warrant of infant baptism.

---

[55]*Christian Baptism: With Its Antecedents and Consequences*, pp. 109f.

. . . .

This new species of ecclesiastic fatalism is not confined to Cal-
vinists, but extends into the bosom of the Arminian churches.
They all, more or less, and sometimes, while disavowing it, impose their solemn rites upon their infant offspring by dedicat-
ing them to God; and that in connexion with certain ecclesiastic
formulas of faith and manners.[56]

Here again the irreconcilable elements in Campbell
seemed to be waging an undeclared war without even
being conscious of it. The only hint as to how he could
draw such a fine line as to condemn a formal act of
dedication while advocating the permanent shaping of
the mind through a constant program of Christian nurture is found in statements such as the following:

The Christian church is the only perfect cradle of human
liberty, as it is the only proper school of equal rights and immunities on earth. It commands every man to think, speak, and
act for himself. . . . It guaranties freedom of thought, of speech,
and of action, to every citizen under the Messiah's reign—provided only, he speaks and acts as the oracles of God require.[57]

"Provided only, he speaks and acts as the oracles of
God require." This sounds suspiciously like the old
refrain "error has not the same rights as truth." Campbell did not stop at condemning infant "sprinkling,"
but infant "dedication" also, and affirmed that the
Christian religion knew "no sponsorship, no godfather,
nor godmother." Campbell, in so many words, expressed a concern that infants so baptized would be
bound to grow up in the religion of their parents:

. . . Infants cannot choose whom they should serve, and whose
name shall be stamped upon them, because they cannot consider
and compare rival candidates.

. . . .

If Jesus commands infants to be baptized, it morally or politi-

[56]*Millennial Harbinger,* 1846, p. 310.
[57]*Christian Baptism: With Its Antecedents and Consequences,* p. 110.

cally obliges them all to the same course of action. If it binds one to the religion of his parents, it binds all; and then it is in every case a barrier interposed between God and human liberty of choice. Every baptized infant is bound to follow the religious belief and profession of his parent or godfather without consideration, comparison, or choice.[58]

On just what grounds Campbell felt justified in charging that children of Pedobaptist parents were more likely to grow up in the faith of their fathers than children in homes practicing the kind of Christian nurture which he, himself, diligently advocated is not clear. While it is true that he urged the use of the deliberative principle in such Christian nurture, he adduced no evidence as to why the deliberative principle might not just as well be used in Pedobaptist family circles.

Attention should be called to the fact that in condemning infant baptism Campbell also rejected the type of theology which necessitated the "regeneration" of the infant for the sake of original sin. His very doctrine of personal accountability was a denial of all such theology. Further, he denied all doctrines which portrayed the Holy Spirit "operating" on a person without that person's volition:

The New School avers its belief that not even an infant can be saved without *the special operations of the Holy Spirit* upon its constitution, anterior to its hearing, knowing, or believing the truth; thus making regeneration to consist in a special physical operation, without argument, motive, or persuasion: for, of these, infants of a few months old are insusceptible; yet, according to the doctrine of the New School, such infants, without a single idea, are proper subjects of such special operations, and cannot be saved without them! These operations, too, cannot be superinduced by the infant—they are as sovereign as absolute will; and they are not the fortune or lot of all, but of some infants; for while only some *experience,* all infants *need* this regeneration. . . . Unless, then, there are two sorts of regenera-

---

[58] *Ibid.,* p. 110f.

tion, . . . —one for infants and another for adults—the destiny of every individual cannot in the least depend upon himself any more than his parents, his country, or surrounding circumstances. This is Owenism with a witness.[59]

Campbell was no less rigorous in his opposition to any doctrine which taught that the Holy Spirit operated on an adult with any kind of regenerating influence which hinted of the "miraculous." Any conception of the work of the Holy Spirit which impinged on the free decision of the believer was repugnant to him:

No theory of spiritual influence in conversion is the influence of the Spirit. Therefore, to deny any theory is not to deny the influence of the Spirit.
The theory which has frequently led to enthusiasm and fanaticism, and which necessarily tends that way, and which directly makes the testimony of God of no value, is the only theory which our views of propriety would permit us to oppose. That theory of regeneration which imparts a holy principle, regenerates a person, or works faith in his heart physically, or without the instrumentality of the word, independent of the word and without any knowledge of it, is, in our judgment, of ruinous tendency.[60]

In accordance with his position that the Holy Spirit operated only through the spoken or written Word of God, Campbell proposed his definition of faith as "the belief of testimony," as contradistinct from any type of magical or miraculous gift of the Holy Spirit operating independent of the Word. He sought to make a careful distinction between faith, knowledge, and opinion:

. . . Faith is the simple belief of testimony, or confidence in the word of another. Knowledge is the experience we have of things within us; or the information we acquire by the exercise of our senses and judgment on the things without us. Opinion is no more than probable evidence, the view or conclusion which

---

[59]Millennial Harbinger, 1837, pp. 437-438.
[60]Ibid., pp. 536-537.

the mind forms by its reasonings and reflections on those things
of which there is no certain evidence within one's reach.

. . . .

In conclusion, be it observed, that testimony, without being
or fact, is as impossible as testimony without a testifier; that
faith, without testimony—knowledge, without experience or the
evidence of sense—and opinion, without speculation, are as impossible as an effect without an adequate cause.[61]

In keeping with this view of faith, Campbell defined
Christian faith as the belief of the testimony of the
inspired scriptures about the person of Jesus. He
distinguished between "faith" and "the Faith."
"Faith" he held to be a belief of testimony about facts,
but "the Faith" involved not only a belief in the
testimony about Jesus, but such a trust in his person as
to act in accordance with that testimony. The glory of
the priesthood of the believer was his freedom, by a
volitional act, to act in accordance with that testimony,
and thus to receive of the pardon of Christ. Entrance
into Christ's kingdom he thus considered to be consequent upon a rational procedure as follows:

That a person must believe, and believe before he can repent,
and repent before he can be scripturally baptized; and that
all these must precede his admission into the Christian church
and the enjoyment of the privileges of the new covenant, is
most scripturally true; but yet this is not the gospel . . . the
gospel is the proclamation in the name of God of remission of
sins and eternal life through the sacrifice and mediation of
Jesus Christ, to every one that obeys him in the instituted way.

It is not the preaching of faith, but of *the faith;* it is not a
display of the significance, value, and importance of faith, repentance, baptism, regeneration, justification, sanctification, or
any other word or phrase, or thing in the Bible; but it is clear,
full, and authoritative statement of pardon and eternal life

---

[61]*Ibid.,* 1836, pp. 166f.

from the philanthropy of God through the interposition of Jesus in a positive institution. It is pardon and eternal life by putting ourselves under the guidance of Jesus Christ.[62]

Much as he attached importance to the act of baptism, Campbell was emphatic in denying that he attributed to it any mysterious or magical power. Rather, it was a means by which the volitional act of faith was to be expressed in placing one's self under Christ's sovereignty:

. . . How do men receive the gospel? Not simply by believing it true, but by actually receiving or appropriating it to themselves. This, it may be assumed, is a mental, and not a bodily act. But we do not admit that any act is merely a bodily act that proceeds from the understanding, the conscience and the heart. It is, indeed, an act of the whole man. . . . Now, our voluntary reception of Christ and his gospel, is an act of the whole man. His understanding, and conscience, and affections are all employed in it. Baptism is, therefore, the form and expression of a voluntary reception of Christ in his death, his burial and his resurrection. In this act the mind and heart are active and the body passive. It is the divine formula of putting on, or receiving, Christ in his personal glory and official fulness. Hence God is pleased to make it and regard it as the actual reception of the gospel, on which he formally and actually remits all our past sins.

. . . .

The efficacy still is in the faith confessed, and not in the water. . . . It is a sign and pledge of his pardon, and not the pardon itself. We are justified by faith, and neither by water nor immersion in it.

. . . .

There is no one that will ever read these lines who has more faith in faith, or in the blood of Christ, than myself as the ground of pardon.[63]

[62]*Ibid.*, 1837, pp. 535-536.
[63]*Ibid.*, 1849, p. 611.

2. *The Right to Function in the Service of the Kingdom*

. . . How little depends upon high official dispensations of ordinances may be learned from the fact that the person sent to baptize the great Apostle to the Gentiles has no other honor, office, or designation, than that of "a certain disciple named Ananias." What a rebuke to those who assume that either baptism or "confirmation" must be administered by ecclesiastically administered hands, in order to their validity and salutary efficacy! Ananias was, like many other disciples . . . of that age, possessed of spiritual gifts. But that he held any official rank, cannot be shown by any proper evidence. Indeed, his designation as a mere disciple precludes any such assumption.[64]

The priesthood of the believer, Campbell affirmed, involved not only the freedom of a volitional entrance into the kingdom, but the right to perform the functions of the Christian ministry as well, including the administration of the ordinances of the church.

On no subject was Campbell more pragmatic than on this one, and at no point did he present greater transitions of thought. Various years of his writings represent three changing attitudes. But none of these attitudes represented any departure from his basic presuppositions. In each of the three attitudes referred to he supported his position by: an appeal to free inquiry, and an insistence on conforming to the authority of a fixed scriptural canon. Remarkably enough, both criteria came to his aid in meeting three practical situations with which he was confronted. In his earlier period of iconoclasm, when he had little following and depended for his following on winning supporters away from the existing clergy, he advocated a program of a pretty thoroughgoing lay ministry for the church:

. . . To be more explicit in expressing my views of the means which the church is to use for the salvation of the world, I would

[64]*Ibid.*, 1846, p. 667.

remark, that having the record, or testimony of God in it, and
every member professing it, it becomes the duty and high privilege of every member of it to be a preacher of the gospel, in the
only sense in which any person can now be called a preacher.

. . . .

The young women are to declare to their coevals . . . the young
men and elder men to theirs, the glad tidings, and to shew the
evidence on which their faith rests.   This, followed up by a
virtuous and godly life, is the most powerful mean left to
illuminate and reform the world.[65]

In this first volume of the *Christian Baptist*, Campbell continued to outline a program whereby the local
bishops, or elders, who were selected from the membership of the local congregation, would instruct the congregation.   To complete the pure atomism of his program at this time, he concluded:

. . . The church of the living God is thus independent of theological schools and colleges for its existence, enlargement, comfort, and perfection; for it is itself put in possession of all the
means of education and accomplishments, if these be widely
used.[66]

This was distinctly not the program of the man who
later founded Bethany College, and pled for a trained
and educated ministry!

The second stage of Campbell's thought on this subject is reflected in his writings during the third and
fourth decades of the nineteenth century.   This was the
period in which he had developed a following—but in
which that following was suffering for the lack of leadership.   His agile mind again met the exigencies of the
situation by calling both reason and scripture to his aid
in support of a pragmatic view that specially designated
ministers, officers, and leaders were needed, but that in
their absence, or even in conjunction with them, the lay

---

[65]*Christian Baptist*, I, 70.
[66]*Ibid.*, p. 71.

members were authorized to perform the functions of
the ministry. His viewpoint at this period is well illustrated in his debate with Rice in the year 1844:

> . . . When, then, any one desires baptism, any one to whom he
> applies may administer it. When a few brethren in one family,
> or neighborhood, organize themselves to meet once a week to
> shew forth the Lord's death, to read the scriptures, sing and
> pray together, having no ordained officer among them, they ap-
> point one of themselves, to break "the loaf of blessing" and
> distribute "the cup of salvation." All this, the New Testament,
> reason, common sense approve.[67]

The third stage of Campbell's thought regarding the
individual believer performing the functions of the ministry is found in the later years when, with a firmly
established following, he was no longer an advocate of
heresy but of orthodoxy, no longer an opponent of sem-
inaries but the president of Bethany College, and the
ghost of his former "independency" was stalking
through the brotherhood. At this stage he is the opponent, not of an organized clergy, not of ecclesiastical
"popes," but of "individual popes" who dared to in-
flict their individual opinions on the churches without
constituted authority. It would be misleading to leave
the impression that Campbell had departed from his
conviction of former years that unofficial persons were
permitted to perform the ordinances of the church. He
was consistent in that belief throughout. The efficacy
of these ordinances he held to reside not in the administrator. "Grace in . . . Christian institutions consists
not in, nor depends on, the grace, or office, or power, of
him that dispenses or administers them." But those
unofficial persons were not to be independent of the
Christian community. They owed their authority to
that community. In the year 1858 Campbell wrote:

---

[67]*Campbell-Rice Debate*, p. 580.

. . . While good order and general satisfaction demand that everything in the Christian church should be done decently and in order, persons qualified for every work and duty should be selected and appointed by the common consent of the whole community, or by those already selected or ordained for this purpose.[68]

Thus the three stages of Campbell's thought regarding the priesthood of believers performing the functions of the ministry were: in the beginning he believed they were under a scriptural injunction to perform them, since they were all "preachers of the word"; later he held that they were permitted to perform them in the absence of regularly ordained officers; finally he insisted they were unauthorized to perform them without the consent of the Christian community.

---

[68]*Millennial Harbinger*, 1858, p. 449.

CHAPTER THREE

THE CHURCH AND ITS MINISTRY

That institution which separates from the world, and consociates the people of God into a peculiar community; having laws, ordinances, manners, and customs of its own, immediately derived from the Saviour of the world, is called the *congregation* or *church* of the Lord.[1]

In seeking to arrive at Alexander Campbell's conception of the church some things stand out with unmistakable clarity, others present considerable difficulty in interpretation. It is clear that in Campbell's thinking certain features of the church were divinely ordained to be immutable and unchanging. It is just as clear that he considered it his mission to help restore the church to what he considered to be its apostolic and primitive state.

On the other hand, care needs to be exercised in examining Campbell's prolific writings on the church, not only because of the evolution of his thought on the subject, but because, like so many writers, he used the term "church" in so many varied senses. In his case, the problem created by the latter fact is accentuated by his tendency toward the use of superlatives. He frequently used the term in a particular sense, while his extreme method of expressing himself conveyed the impression that in his mind that was the only sense in which it could be used.

---

[1]Alexander Campbell, *Christian System*, p. 72.

I. *The Church*

The *true* Christian church, or house of God, is composed of all those in every place that do publicly acknowledge Jesus of Nazareth as the true Messiah, and the only Saviour of man; and, building themselves upon the foundation of the Apostles and Prophets, associate under the constitution which he himself has granted and authorized in the New Testament, and are walking in his ordinances and commandments—and of none else.[2]

Campbell gave his definition of the church on innumerable occasions. The investigator is sometimes uncertain as to how comprehensively his definitions are supposed to be taken. Frequently, as in the above definition, the church is composed of "all those in every place," and so forth. On other occasions, especially during the *Christian Baptist* days of emphasis on the autonomy of the local congregation, the emphasis is on the church as all those meeting in "one" place:

. . . I am taught from the record itself to describe a church of Christ in the following words:—It is a society of disciples professing to believe the one grand fact, voluntarily submitting to his authority and guidance, having all of them in their baptism expressed their faith in him and their allegiance to him, and statedly meeting together in one place, to walk in all his commandments and ordinances.[3]

On yet other occasions Campbell left no doubt whatever that he conceived the term "church" to be taken in a universal as well as a particular sense. He appealed to the use of the term in both senses in the scriptures to support his position:

As though we had never before thought on the subject, let us, then, in the true inductive style, institute an examination of the sacred history of the word *ekkleesia,* as found in the Christian scriptures.

---

[2]*Ibid.,* pp. 73-74.
[3]*Christian Baptist,* I, 70.

. . . .

It is found in the singular number, seventy-eight times, and in the plural number thirty-seven times. But the most important fact is; *that it is used in the singular number, in two distinct senses*—one indicating a single community, meeting in a single place—the other indicating the congregated multitude of all these communities, as existing in all ages and nations. We have, then, the church universal, and a church particular.[4]

Another point of difficulty is that of determining to what extent Campbell equated the church of Christ with the kingdom of Christ, or the kingdom of heaven. There were times when he seemed to distinguish between the two. On these occasions he would speak of the kingdom of Christ, the kingdom of God, or the kingdom of heaven in more comprehensive terms than the church. Richardson lists as one of Campbell's "important additions to the truths developed during the progress of the Reformation" the fact that he had pointed out that the term "kingdom" was a compound one, embracing at least three distinct conceptions. Whatever the historical facts about this, it does seem safe to conclude that Campbell for the most part equated the church with the present reign of the kingdom of Christ upon the earth. This conclusion seems justified because in discussing the so-called "visible" and "invisible" kingdoms, he denied knowing anything about any "invisible" kingdom[5]; because he used identical descriptive terms when speaking of the church that he did when speaking of the kingdom; and finally, because he specifically used the terms interchangeably. The following is typical:

As the church, or congregation, or assembly, (as it is expressed by all these names,) is repeatedly called a kingdom—

---

[4]*Millennial Harbinger*, 1849, p. 221.

[5]This position was in entire harmony with Campbell's conception of psycho-physical unity as seen in his insistence that mind could gain no knowledge except through the organs of the body, that the Spirit could operate only through the Word in appealing to the mind of man, and that the visible act of baptism was one with the spiritual decision of acknowledging the Lordship of Christ.

the kingdom of God, and the kingdom of heaven, it is fairly to be presumed, from the terms themselves, that the government under which the church is placed, is an absolute monarchy. There cannot be a kingdom, unless there be a king. They are correlative terms, and the one necessarily supposes the existence of the other. . . . On this, as a first principle, I found all my views of what is commonly called church government. All the churches on earth that Christ has ever acknowledged as his, are so many communities constituting one kingdom, of which he is the head and sovereign.[6]

Unless, then, there are qualifying expressions or other evidence suggesting a limited or different use of the word, the investigator may be safe in assuming that when Campbell used the term "church" he meant by it the visible kingdom of Christ on earth. Further, the term may refer either to a particular local congregation or to the universal aggregate of those congregations.

A. *The Scope of the Church*

We must understand the type, or we cannot understand the antitype. We must understand that which is natural before we can understand that which is spiritual. What, then, are the essential elements of a kingdom as existing among men? They are five, viz: King, Constitution, Subjects, Laws, and Territory. Such are the essential parts of every political kingdom, perfect in its kind, now existing on earth.[7]

With his love of types and antitypes, Campbell used five terms to describe either the kingdom of Christ or the church of Christ. These terms were: king, constitution, subjects, laws, and territory.

The church not only derived its nature from the fact that it had Christ as its King, said Campbell. The grand fact of Christ as the Son of God was the very foundation on which the church was built. "The church is founded on the thing confessed. Christ himself is,

[6]*Christian Baptist*, V, 428-429.
[7]Alexander Campbell, *Christianity Restored*, p. 150.

indeed, the rock; but figuratively, the truth which represents him.''

The church first assumed a name and a local habitation in the capital of Judea, ''separate from the world, in the world, but not of the world.'' But whereas the territory of Christ's church, or kingdom, began there, it did not stop there: ''He begins with the Jews, proceeds to the Samaritans, and thence to all the nations of the earth. He found a new kingdom under the large commission. He sends them into the whole world, and commands them to convert all nations.'' In all his cries to ''come out from among them,'' Campbell was proceeding in accordance with his conception of the evangelical and proselyting nature of the church. This conception also had much to do with the emphasis which he placed on the function of the individual members of the church as preachers: ''When the Apostles had set in order the Christian temple they died. . . . The church, the whole church, was thus constituted one great converting institution.'' Because of its evangelical nature, it was also missionary in character: ''The spirit of Christianity is essentially a missionary spirit. Christianity began with a mission, and is the fruit of a mission from heaven to earth.'' But it was qualitative as well as quantitative in its territorial designs. For that reason, it sought to make inroads into all the areas of man's experience: ''We have long since expressed a conviction that the church of Jesus Christ is a Missionary, Temperance, Bible, Education, and Philanthropic Society; that, in the church capacity, Christians move in all spiritual and moral good.''

The means for accomplishing the evangelical work of the church were two: the Holy Spirit operating through the oracles of God, and the conduct of the disciples.

The church was thus evangelical in its nature. But it was never designed to be fractured either into competing sects or into rival ''auxiliary'' organizations. It was the dream of its founder that it be "essentially, intentionally, and constitutionally one." For that reason, the bond of union was simple:

The societies called churches, constituted and set in order by those ministers of the New Testament, were of such as received and acknowledged Jesus as the Lord Messiah, the Saviour of the World, and had put themselves under his guidance. The ONLY BOND OF UNION among them was faith in him and submission to his will.[8]

Reviving therefore the cry "in essentials unity, in nonessentials liberty, in all things charity," Campbell pointed to what seemed to him to be two more areas which were as distinct as black and white:

. . . To ask for a *positive* precept for everything in the details of duties growing out of the various and numerous exigencies of the Christian church and the world, would be quite as irrational and unscriptural as to ask for an immutable wardrobe or a uniform standard of apparel for all persons and ages in the Christian church.

. . . .

We must make a broad, a clear, and an indelible distinction between elements of *faith, piety,* and *morality,* and matters of temporal expediency.[9]

Campbell therefore drew a strict line between what he called the essentials of faith and the nonessentials of expediency. In the essentials, man was not to reason why, but to accept without question the edict of the church's constitution. In all nonessentials he was to be given absolute liberty.

As to the constitution of the church, Campbell left no doubt where he stood. The foundation of his platform had been:

[8]*Christian Baptist,* I, 6.
[9]*Millennial Harbinger,* 1849, pp. 269-270.

Note

. . . We have proposed . . . a return to the faith and manners anciently delivered to the saints—A RESTORATION *of original Christianity in both theory and practice.* The three capital points of which are:

I. The Christian Scriptures, the only rule and measure of Christian faith and learning.

II. The Christian confession, the foundation of Christian union and communion.

III. The Christian ordinances—baptism, the Lord's day, and the Lord's supper, as taught and observed by the Apostles.[10]

With the slogan "no creed but Christ, no book but the Bible," Campbell held the Bible aloft as the constitution of the church, denying the validity of any laws or edicts passed or issued by any council, synod, or association. At first this denial seemed to be categorical, but later was limited to those matters which had to do with "faith and morals." So far as these were concerned, the Bible continued to be his one and only constitution for the church:

Faith, piety, and *morality* . . . are wholly and exclusively of Divine authority. No church, synod, council, or general assembly, can of right, add to, change, or modify any one of these. They are all forever fixed by the Messiah in person, and by his inspired and Divinely comissioned law-givers, apostles and prophets.[11]

In referring to the Bible as the "constitution" of the church, Campbell was very careful to demarcate between a "constitution" and a "charter." Insisting that a "charter" was not enough for the government of a church, the Bible was therefore infinitely more than a "charter"; the latter could regulate only public bodies, while the Bible regulated individuals as well:

I object to considering the bible merely as a charter granted by a legislature or civil government, because the bible does

[10] *Ibid.*, 1847, p. 487.
[11] *Ibid.*, 1849, p. 270.

more than erect congregations, or constitute religious bodies invested with peculiar privileges. It gives them many laws for their general and particular behavior. It authorizes the existence of congregations, or, as you call them, "corporate bodies," but it does more than any charter ever granted by any legislature ever did. It prescribes to the members in particular every requisite rule of behavior, for their thoughts, words, and actions. . . . The apostles taught christians a thousand times more than any charter teaches; and while the constitution of the christian church is laid down most fully in these writings, every important item of christian duty requiring, the attention of christians, either in public or private capacity is also laid down. In representing the bible, then, only as the charter of the church, injustice is done to it as great as I can conceive of. And the book is divested of all its utility in regulating the conduct of individuals. . . . Charters regulate public bodies, and not individual persons; whereas almost the whole New Testament is engrossed with the regulations and rules and precepts which are to govern individuals.[12]

But while Campbell would at one time speak of the Bible as containing laws, precepts, rules, and regulations for the Christian community, there is a question as to whether or not on these occasions he was giving play to his love of drawing analogies between his "types and antitypes." For he would at other times affirm that the Christian community was under principles rather than precepts, and under liberty rather than law. The difficulty attended in determining exactly what he meant to convey when speaking again and again of the "laws" of the church may be seen in comparing such a statement as the following with the previous quotation:

They greatly mistake who expect to find a liturgy, or a code of laws in the New Institution, designed to govern christians either in their private or public relations and character. . . . The nation of the Jews affords both demonstration and proof

---

[12]*Christian Baptist,* V, 444.

that man cannot be governed or controlled either in piety or morality by any extrinsic law, however excellent or spiritual.[13]

Two or three considerations, when combined, may be of help at this point. The first is the flair, already mentioned, which Campbell seemed to have for "types and antitypes," and the attendant drawing of terms from his "types." A correlate of that was a tendency toward a rather loose use of terms. In one article, written in 1829, he asserted that the Christian church was under principles, that it had no code of laws; and in the same article praised the Christian "law" of love. But even when these factors have been taken into account, they do not seem to be the whole story. After allowance has been made for an inexact use of terms, the fact still seems to be undeniable that Campbell made room in his thinking for both "law" and "principle," for both "legalism" and "liberty," especially in regard to the ordinances of the church.

B. *The Ordinances of the Church*

In Campbell's thinking, the constitution of the church provided for three ordinances. The observance of these ordinances was held to be indispensable. At this point he distinguished between the "fact" of an ordinance and the "method" of its observance. That the observance of an ordinance was indispensable to the Christian was a fact. But the method of the observance of the ordinance was not a fact. In that, each particular congregation, or believer, exercised liberty.

The three Christian ordinances, said Campbell, are (1) the Lord's day, (2) the Lord's Supper, and (3) baptism. Since the Bible, as the constitution of the church, instituted them, their observance, he held, was indispensable to the very fact of being a Christian:

[13]*Ibid.,* VI, 500.

It is not alleged by me that there are no divinely instituted acts of christian worship nor ordinances in the christian church; nay, the contrary I have undeviatingly affirmed. These are a part, an essential part, of the Institution of Favor. It is not discretionary with disciples whether they shall or shall not enter the kingdom without obtaining the remission of their sins by immersion; whether christian societies shall regard the first day of the week to the Lord; whether they shall show forth the Lord's death at the Lord's table till he come to raise the dead; whether they shall continue in the fellowship for the saints and the Lord's poor; whether they shall sing psalms, hymns, and spiritual songs; unite in social prayers, and in reading the sacred writings in their regular meetings. These are the traditions of the Holy Apostles who were commanded to teach the disciples to observe all things which the King in his own person commanded them.[14]

But the new institution, being only under the law of love, made no specifications as to how these ordinances were to be observed. All it did was to institute them:

. . . The New Constitution and Law of Love does no more than institute the converting act, the Lord's supper, and the Lord's day. Immersion, or the converting act, by which persons are brought into the kingdom of principles and introduced into the rank of sons, is not so much an ordinance in the kingdom as that which brings us into it. The Lord's supper, a weekly commemoration of the great sacrifice, and the day of the resurrection of Jesus, though positive institutions, are not presented to christians accompanied with directions for the mode of celebration, as were any of the former institutions under the Jewish age.[15]

In the manner of observance, the individual congregation and the individual believer were left at liberty:

. . . No mode of eating the supper, no mode of observing the Lord's day is suggested in the apostolic writing. In this christians are left to the discretion of full grown men to the govern-

[14]*Ibid.*, VII, 656.
[15]*Ibid.*, p. 655.

ment of principle. All things are to be done decently and in order; but the modes of decency and order in the celebration of these christian institutions are no where pointed out.[16]

The last three quotations form the basis of a truly interesting study. Cumulatively, they stress freedom and liberty in the method of observance of the so-called three indispensable ordinances of the church. But let us examine that freedom. Campbell had a habit of adding a great deal of content to his initial selection of terms. A close examination will reveal some surprising restrictions on the "liberty" announced in the observance of these ordinances.

Indeed!

1. *The Lord's Day*

The freedom granted in the observance of the Lord's day was conditioned on the fact that Campbell insisted they had no choice about receiving an offering. That was not a matter of "discretion." Neither had they any choice about uniting in social worship. That was an essential condition to a proper observance of the Lord's day. And having met in social worship, it was not a matter of freedom with them whether they would "sing psalms, hymns, and spiritual songs; unite in social prayers, and in reading the sacred writings in their regular meetings." These were the traditions of the apostles, and therefore binding.

But there were other ways in which the observance of the Lord's day should be limited, according to Campbell. It was a desecration of Christian worship to erect ornate and gaudy edifices of worship. Worship should be marked by simplicity, and the use of instrumental music in the worship service was anathema. In the *Christian Baptist* he complained: "The original and scriptural simplicity of the Baptists is fast departing in the introduction of these associations, instrumental

---

[16]*Ibid.*, VII, 655.

music in their worship, and such matters.'' The personal presence of Campbell in holding his followers together was no sooner missed than the group began to be rent asunder over this, and similar limitations placed on ''complete freedom in the method of observing the Lord's day.'' The pages of the *Millennial Harbinger* began to be filled with controversial articles on these subjects in the very year of Campbell's death. Jesse Kellems, in discussing Campbell's ''law of expedience,'' says:

Nothing has more frequently caused dissension, in one case even to the point of division among the Disciples, than a failure to understand this Campbellian principle. The schism which arose over the position of instrumental music in the worship of the church, resulted from a failure to realize that the whole question belonged to the realm of expediency, and not to that of divine revelation.[17]

If that be true, then the same charge will have to be brought against Campbell himself, for whether we like it or not, there is not one line in his writings to suggest that he ever, at any time, retracted his censure of the use of instrumental music in worship.

2. *The Lord's Supper*

The first limitation which Campbell placed on freedom in the manner of observing the Lord's Supper is found in the phrase ''the Lord's supper, a weekly commemoration of the great sacrifice.'' Obviously this at once became a limitation not only on the manner of observing the Lord's Supper, but on the Lord's day as well. The Lord's day was to be observed by observing the Lord's Supper, and the Lord's Supper was to be observed every Lord's day.

A further limitation placed on the observance of the Lord's Supper had to do with inviting unbaptized per-

---

[17]Jesse R. Kellems, *Alexander Campbell and the Disciples* (New York, Harper & Brothers, 1930), p. 391. Used by permission.

sons to participate. In response to an interrogation sent to him by the Churches of Christ in England in the year 1859, he replied:

> . . . That unbaptized persons may have sat down to the Lord's table amongst our brotherhood, without invitation, is not wholly improbable but I know of no church that has formally invited them to participate with it on such occasions.
>
> We do not, indeed, on any such occasions, known to me, *"invite"* or *"debar,"* in the usual currency of these words, any one unbaptized to participate with us in any act of social worship.[18]

This limitation, seemingly, was a double-barrelled one: local congregations, while free in their observance of the Lord's Supper, were permitted neither to invite nor to debar unbaptized persons. They were simply to ignore them.[19]

In other respects, however, Campbell consistently stood for freedom. In answer to the same group of Disciples in England which inquired about admitting unbaptized persons to the Lord's table, he answered a question asked twenty-five years earlier regarding the admitting of colored brethren to the table, whether they were admitted, and if so, if they sat at the same table. Campbell drew no color line:

> A number, a goodly number, of these bondmen are members of our churches. In these churches they assemble around the same table, and are recognized and treated as brethren in Christ. I never knew an instance in which they had a separate table in a church where there were any white members. I do not say, however, that they fully enjoy in all places that

---

[18]*Millennial Harbinger,* 1860, pp. 407-408.

[19]This position of Campbell's occasions surprise on two counts. The first is the fact that the very act which occasioned the heresy trial of his father, Thomas Campbell, was his invitation to members of other Christian sects to participate in the communion service at which he officiated. The second is the fact that Disciples of Christ, historically, have been characterized by the practice of what is called "open communion," without any discrimination.

share of respect, and attention, and education in Christ, which is due them as joint heirs of the blessings of his salvation.[20]

Still another point at which Campbell advocated freedom was in the administration of the Lord's Supper. Stating that "we regard the loaf or cup as receiving no virtue from official hands" he affirmed that anyone who had a right to partake of the supper had a right to officiate at it. This was in harmony with his position regarding the priesthood of believers:

> May not, then, *holy* and *royal* priests thank God for the Lord's table, its loaf, and cup of wine? May they not, without a *human* priest to consecrate the way for them, approach the Lord's table, and handle the loaf and cup? . . . [If not,] then they know not how to appreciate the consecration of Jesus, nor how to value their high calling and exalted designation as kings and priests unto God.[21]

Finally, Campbell expressly asserted freedom as to time and posture, saying that there was no prescription concerning the time of meeting, "or whether they shall eat the Lord's supper standing, sitting, kneeling, or reclining."

3. *Christian Baptism*

We have seen how Campbell would have limited the freedom of the church in regard to baptism to its administration only to those who had made a volitional decision to accept the Lordship of Christ and be baptized. On this ground he would necessarily prohibit the baptism of infants. While holding that there was no code of laws directing the method of its administration, he would have limited it further by defining it so as to be equated only with immersion. His writings on this point were prolific, and the evidence which he called forth in support of his position was drawn from varied sources. In short, conceiving baptism to be the divine formula

[20]*Millennial Harbinger*, 1835, p. 18.
[21]*Christianity Restored*, p. 316.

for putting on Christ, a dramatic representation of the death, burial, and resurrection of Christ, and the only mode of baptism known to the New Testament church, he charged the translators of the King James version of the scriptures with transcribing the term *baptizo* from the Greek rather than translating it, and in his new translation of the New Testament, inserted the words "immerse" and "immersion" in all instances in which the Authorized version contained the words "baptize" and "baptism."

On the other hand, any volitional candidate for baptism was to be received on his simple confession of faith in Christ, and baptism administered, without any restraint on the part of the congregation: "During the ancient order of things there was no church meeting for the purpose of receiving candidates for immersion. There were no monthly meetings to decide who should be baptized." Also, along with the administration of the Lord's Supper, he held not only that the local congregation had the right to authorize any member of the church to baptize, but that the validity of the ordinance was not contingent on the hands which administered it. Neither was there any restraint on the place where, the time when, nor the manner in which the candidate was immersed, so long as it was done "decently and in order."

C. *Membership in the Church*

The church was held by Campbell to be constituted not only of King, territory, constitution, and laws, but, obviously, of members. This necessary element has been reserved to the last in our discussion because in the mind of Campbell, the nature of the membership was so directly related to the nature of the ministry of the church.

It is difficult to decide whether his conception of the membership of the church should be characterized as being marked by an inclusive exclusiveness or an exclusive inclusiveness. There were times when he would oppose all church councils and church creeds on the ground that they might shut out one heretic whom Christ would receive. He pleaded for freedom and toleration, and opposed "tests of fellowship" which excluded. He referred to those who would not have fellowship with all the evangelical sects as "purblind Pharisees who strained out the gnat and swallowed the camel."

A common charge brought against him was that his group made room for all sorts of heretics. He called down the rebukes of some of his brethren because he specifically stated that he believed there were Christians among the Pedobaptist sects. In later years he urged the Disciples to co-operate heartily in interdenominational movements such as the proposed Protestant Federation, the Sunday school, and the American Bible Society. And be it said to his credit that there is no record of his ever, at any time, having refused to have fellowship with any religious group in worship.

On the other hand, there was the notable occasion when he journeyed from Bethany to Nashville, Tennessee, in order to carry the day against a pastor of Disciples of Christ who was reputed to be heretical. He entered the minister's pulpit, denounced him from his own pulpit for three successive nights, and having successfully unseated him, returned to Bethany and published an article in the *Millennial Harbinger* entitled "The Fall of Mr. J. B. Ferguson."

In addition, while he affirmed an ecumenicity of fellowship, he so defined the way in which a person could become a Christian, that the *koinonia* seemed to become greatly reduced:

Of all the Christian ordinances, baptism is by all Christendom acknowledged to be the act of naturalization—the eccle-

siastic new birth—the door into the church. A birth of water
and of spirit is essential to entrance into Christ's kingdom.

. . . .

He, therefore, that has not received Christian baptism cannot be a constitutional citizen, and certainly not an officer of
Christ's church.[22]

The unbaptized was not only not qualified to be a constitutional citizen or an officer, he was not qualified to
participate in the fellowship of the church:

I object to making it a rule, *in any case,* to receive unimmersed persons to church ordinances:

1st. Because it is no where commanded.

2d. Because it is no where precedented in the New Testament.

3d. Because it necessarily corrupts the simplicity and uniformity of the whole genius of the New Institution.[23]

When it is recollected that Campbell equated baptism
with immersion only and that the two quotations above
were written twenty-eight years apart, we may safely
conclude that in his judgment the unimmersed could not
be "constitutional" members of the church. But when
we further recollect that he repeatedly affirmed that
there were not two kinds of church members but one,
we must conclude that his system provided for none but
"constitutional" members. This kind of exclusive inclusiveness reminds one of the story which Campbell
himself once used in pleading with the Christian sects
of his day that they grant greater freedom of opinion,
greater personal liberty. He related how a military
chieftain, desiring to appear republican on the eve of a
hazardous undertaking, addressed his troops thus:

. . ."Soldiers, your country has important duties for you to
perform. It has placed you under my command. This author-

[22]*Millennial Harbinger,* 1843, p. 223.
[23]*Christian Baptist,* VI, 527-528.

ity I wish to exercise with all republican virtue. I wish you, therefore, fellow-soldiers, to have the most perfect freedom in every act of your obedience to my orders. Now as this is an arduous service which I require of you, I wish you to act like volunteers; and I, therefore, hazard all that the crisis requires. ... [You have] the most perfect liberty of choice. ... Say what you will do; only remember that he who refuses to accompany me and to do his duty, shall be brought up and shot without benefit of court martial or clergy!''[24]

When, then, Campbell defined the membership of the church as consisting of those who exhibited ''faith in Christ and submission to his will,'' we are to remember the content which he put into the phrase ''submission to his will.'' Remembering this, it would seem fair to say that in his conception the church was composed of those men, women, and children of the age of ''decision,'' who had by a volitional act expressed their faith in Jesus as the Christ, the Son of the living God. This faith, involving repentance for all past sin, was expressed in the divinely ordained act of immersion: ''Baptism is an ordinance by which we formally profess Christianity. It is the first constitutional act in the profession of Christianity.'' This act was at once a visible expression of a voluntary reception of Christ in his death, burial, and resurrection, and a visible act of putting on Christ, the efficacy of the act being in the faith thus confessed, and ✓ not in the water.

Those who had thus received Christ, Campbell said, were to disavow all human appellations as to their religious faith, and were to be known simply as disciples, disciples of Christ, or individually as Christians. They knew no hierarchy of classes or groups, but were all on an equal footing in the sense that all were priests unto God. No one was called of God any more than they were all called of God. The church knew nothing of anything but one class of members: ''There are no patricians nor

[24]*Millennial Harbinger*, 1834, p. 142.

plebeians, no feudal barons nor feudal serfs, amongst all the faithful in Christ Jesus. All are one in rank and privilege in Christ's kingdom. It is not flesh, but spirit, that characterizes Christ's membership.''

Whatever might be said one way or another about Campbell's conception of the method of becoming a church member, his conception of their status, once they were members, became the foundation on which he understood not only the nature of the Christian ministry to rest, but also the foundation on which his whole theory of church organization and church government stood.

II. *The Church's Ministry*

Bishop Purcell: I really do not know what Mr. Campbell's tenets are, or what he believes . . . what qualifications, what marks of a divine call to the ministry he considers necessary, if indeed he believes in any peculiar separation of any man or set of men, for priestly functions.[25]

We have noted Campbell's opposition to the doctrine of apostolic succession. We have considered his crusade against what he was wont to call the "kingdom of the clergy." We have studied his insistence on extending the doctrine of the priesthood of believers to include the right of any believer to perform the functions of the ministry in the administration of the ordinances of the church. These teachings of his, when combined, caused many, like Bishop Purcell, to question whether he believed in the setting apart of any man or set of men for priestly functions. The earlier part of his career left some ground for question as to where he stood regarding the ministry of the church, and undoubtedly there was an evolution of his thought on this subject. On the other hand, there was no time in his career that he did not believe in the setting apart of designated leaders for designated functions in the church. Since a detailed study of those functions would involve us in his concep-

---

[25]*Campbell-Purcell Debate*, p. 44.

tion of the structure of the church, we may best understand his teachings on the ministry at this point by
studying: A. The types of ministry; B. The credentials
of the ministry.

A. *The Types of Ministry*

. . . The scheme of a learned priesthood chiefly composed of
beneficiaries, has long since proved itself to be a grand device
to keep men in ignorance and bondage; a scheme, by means of
which the people have been shrewdly taught to put out their
own eyes, to fetter their own feet, and to bind the yoke upon
their own necks. From this iniquitous scheme, a knowledge
of the New Testament is the only means that can set the people
free.[26]

Denying that the New Testament knew anything about
such officers as priests, deans, archbishops, archdeacons,
local preachers, circuit preachers, presiding elders,
friars, priors, abbots, cardinals and popes, Campbell affirmed that the only ministry which was authorized for
the church was of two classes. These were officers
"plenipotentiary," and officers "ordinary."

1. *Officers Plenipotentiary*

The officers plenipotentiary were those who had received their commission directly from Jesus Christ.
There was some variation in the types of ministers which
Campbell placed in this category. His usual classifica-
tion included three types—apostles, prophets, and evangelists. On other occasions the list included two others
—pastors and teachers. When the latter were included,
however, Campbell made a careful distinction between
the nature of their commission and the offices of "pastor" and "teacher" as currently known in the 19th-
century church.

---
[26]*Christian Baptist*, I, 18.

His officers plenipotentiary not only owed their commission directly to Jesus Christ, they were miraculously equipped with the qualifications of their offices:

. . ."He hath poured out that which you now see and hear." These "distributions of the Holy Spirit," as Macknight renders *Heb*. ii.4, issued in the perfect qualification of apostles with the "word of wisdom;" prophets with the "word of knowledge;" evangelists with "tongues and miracles;" pastors with an immediate possession of all the requisites to feeding the flock.[27]

They were not only supplied with special qualifications, they were granted special powers. They were the representatives of Christ, and as such, the authority that was his as King inhered in them. In speaking of the great commission as found in Matthew, Chapter 28, Campbell, insisting that it was given only to those disciples present, said:

This commission created plenipotentiaries: it reared up ambassadors, and gave to the apostles the same power of erecting the church, which God gave to Moses for raising the tabernacle in the wilderness. They had all the authority of Christ to set up what orders they pleased.[28]

In addition to being characterized by having received their commission, special qualifications, and special powers from Christ, the officers plenipotentiary owed their existence to a specific need of the kingdom. That need was the establishment of the church. That work of "initiation" included not simply the baptizing of converts, and the organization of congregations, but the bringing of those congregations to a position of self-sustenance as well.

Since the work of these plenipotentiaries was for a specific task, said Campbell, it was obvious that it was of a limited duration. For the same reason, there was

[27]*Ibid*., II, 95.
[28]*Campbell-Purcell Debate*, p. 52.

no need of their having any successors. It was just as obvious that this limited time had expired, and that, therefore, such officers and offices no longer existed in the Christian church.

But, divine wisdom having foreseen that since neither these special officers nor their converts would be able to be present at the setting up of new congregations throughout the history of the church, adequate provision for the church in its subsequent history had been made by these special officers before their death. "This object was answered by their discourses and their writings."

2. Officers Ordinary

"All . . . that we learn . . . on the subject of the Christian ministry, is, the general design of that ministry immediately bestowed on the primitive church; but that very design clearly intimates that when that crisis which called for those gifts should be accomplished, all those supernatural offices or gifts should cease. This order was therefore temporary and introductory to an ordinary ministry."[29]

The "ordinary" officers of the church, according to Campbell, were those who owed their offices to the authority of the officers plenipotentiary. "As the Apostles were commanded to preach the gospel to every creature, so they commanded these things to be done by others." Since the apostles were possessed of divine authority, this conferred a divine right upon those whom they had appointed:

. . . They had all the authority of Christ to set up what orders they pleased. They created both bishops and deacons; and as they had a divine right to do so, so those created by them have a divine right to officiate in the duties of those offices.[30]

[29]*Millennial Harbinger*, 1842, p. 445.
[30]*Campbell-Purcell Debate*, p. 52.

As in the case of special officers, Campbell's list of ordinary officers varied in its categories on different occasions. His earlier classifications almost always included only two types of "ordinary" officers. These were bishops and deacons. In later years he more frequently classified deacons, pastors, and evangelists in this group. There were other variations so far as terms were concerned. For instance, he equated missionaries with evangelists in regard to function, and frequently he would use the terms "elder," "presbyter," and "bishop" interchangeably. It was his argument that they were but three terms denoting one office. On other occasions his republican sentiments led him to use the term "senate" when applied to a group of these officers: "The Apostles, at the command of the King, ordained a senate, a presbytery, an eldership—three names for the same thing—'in every church' which they set in order."

There was not as much difference in Campbell's earlier and later classifications of these "ordinary" officers as might appear on the surface. The fact is that his conception of the office of "bishop" was broad, and included that of "pastor." In other words, a "pastor" was a bishop with a particular assignment. The chief point to be noted is the difference between his use of the term "pastor" in his earlier and his later writings. In his *Christian Baptist* days he applied the term to one of the special offices of the early church which had been abolished; later he came to recognize the continuing need of the "pastor" in the ongoing work of the church.

The office of evangelist also represented a change in Campbell's thinking. He came to recognize the need of a type of ministry especially sent out to establish new churches, and accordingly made this addition to his "ordinary" officers.

As Campbell's term implied, "officers ordinary" referred to those officers whose functions were needed in the ordinary work of the ministry, in each local congregation. "Bishops and deacons" could not exist separate and apart from a local congregation, and therefore could come into being only after the congregation existed:

> . . . The apostolic writings . . . teach us that the office of bishops was the last thing instituted, or, in other words, that the apostles and evangelists, had fulfilled their commission, i.e. had proclaimed the gospel, made disciples, baptized them, convened them, and taught them the christian doctrine, before they suggested to them the necessity, utility, and importance of the office of a bishop.

. . . .

> From these premises it must follow that, as the enlisting of soldiers is previous to their training; the making of disciples, to teaching them; the gathering of congregations, to setting them in order; necessarily the bishop's work is different from that of a missionary, a preacher, an evangelist, in the New Testament import of these terms.[31]

The ministry of the church since the days of the New Testament, then, according to Campbell, included: for the work of establishing churches, missionaries, and evangelists; for ministering to the needs of churches having been established, bishops (including pastors), and deacons.

B. *The Credentials of the Ministry*

> . . . While we contend that every citizen has a right to be heard, as well as to hear, in the christian community; and that every one who, in his intercourse with society, finds an unbeliever, has a right and command to *preach* to him the gospel, and to baptize him if he ask it of him; yet we have no idea that every disciple is to become a public preacher, baptizer, teacher, critic, at his own volition, option, or solicitation, by virtue of his discipleship.[32]

---

[31]*Christian Baptist*, III, 231-232.
[32]*Millennial Harbinger*, 1832, p. 501.

While Campbell denied any right of apostolic succession, and while he further repudiated any doctrine of a special and miraculous operation of the Holy Spirit in calling men to preach, he was just as definite in opposing the type of "independency" which led some to insist on preaching without the proper credentials.

Campbell insisted that all who were to officiate or function in any capacity in the church's ministry do so only when armed with the proper credentials. Only those who were called were to serve. And in what did that call consist? Campbell was clearer and more consistent on no subject than this. The call to the ministry consisted neither in a personal ambition on the part of the one called nor in a mandate from the Holy Spirit, but in a social contract with the church. Whatever the changes which Campbell made in the types of officers of the ministry, there is no hint of his having changed in his conception of the nature of the call to the ministry. The office of the ministry was in the nature of a social relationship, and call, appointment, and ordination were all integral to a social contract with the congregation:

. . . Every thing essential to appointment, call, or ordination was vested in the minds of the brethren. Their desires, however expressed, gave the office to the candidate, however he was announced.

. . . .

No instance can be found in the inspired writings, where the circumstances are detailed, of the call and appointment of any brother to any office, where the call and appointment is not distinctly represented as the act of the brethren, and in no case is an ordination or appointment made without them. But their call is what, in all cases, gives the right to officiate.[33]

On the part of the church, the calling of a man to an office represented a delegation of power and responsibility which was resident in the congregation to the officer

---

[33]*Christian Baptist*, I, 261.

chosen. It did not therefore conflict, Campbell said, with his insistence that all believers were eligible to perform the functions of the ministry, and responsible for those functions:

But we shall be asked, "Is not preaching, and baptizing, and even teaching, the common privilege of all disciples, as they have opportunity?" And we also ask in answer, "Is it not the privilege of all fathers to teach their own children, and to preside over their own families?" But who will thence infer, that all fathers are teachers and presidents, does not more shock common sense, than he who infers that all disciples, as such, are evangelists, pastors, and teachers, because we concede that in certain cases it is the privilege of all the citizens of Christ's kingdom to preach, baptize, and teach. Every citizen of Christ's kingdom has, in virtue of his citizenship, equal rights, privileges, and immunities. So has every citizen of the United States. Yet all citizens are not legislators, magistrates, governors, &c. Before any community, civil or religious, is organized, every man has equal rights to do what seemeth good in his own eyes. But when organized, and persons appointed to office, then whatever rights, duties or privileges are conferred on particular persons, cannot of right belong to those who have transferred them.[34]

Even when an individual member of the church exercised his right of priesthood to function as an officer for a single occasion, it was still, said Campbell, to be a social contract, and by authority of the "brethren": "Hence, no one acts either pro tempore an elder or overseer for a single day, but by the choice or appointment of the brethren."

The call to the ministry as a social contract Campbell held to be functional in nature. It was not the office but the work to be done which was to be considered:

Little men in office are great officers. They have much to say about official duty and official power. Great men in office lay much less stress upon the office than upon the qualifications

[34]*Christian System*, pp. 80-81.

necessary to the discharge of its duties. They regard the duties
above the office, and the office for qualifying them for discharg-
ing its duties, rather than as imparting any virtue to their
acts.[35]

These functions to be served became, then, the only occasion of the social contract, and apart from such functions, no "call to the ministry" existed:

> The only call which any man could urge with either scrip-
> ture or reason on his side, was his competency to instruct, and
> the need for it. The same call which the rich man has to re-
> lieve the poor when he discovers them, is that which an intelli-
> gent christian has to instruct those ignorant of God.[36]

On the part of the congregation, the selection of those
who were to be "called" was to be guided by (1) the
nature of the functions to be performed, and (2) the
qualifications of those called to perform them:

> . . . Some were better qualified to preside, to rule, and to
> teach, than others; and the constitution of man as an individ-
> ual, and of men in society, is such as to require, for the sake
> of intelligence, order, peace, harmony, and general good, that
> there be persons set apart or appointed to certain functions,
> which are necessary to the good of the whole associate body.[37]

These qualifications were to be specific as well as general,
and directly related to the milieu in which the "minister" was to serve:

> . . . The call is based upon the qualifications; without these
> he is not eligible; with them he is eligible. Consequently a due
> estimate of his endowments must be formed by somebody; and
> most certainly not by himself, nor by those who belong not to
> the flock to be instructed. . . . By whom then? Assuredly by
> those amongst whom he is to labor. . . . His qualifications in the
> intellectual department must then be viewed in relation to the
> capacity and attainments of the flock; for a man may be fit to

---

[35] *Millennial Harbinger,* 1840, p. 507.
[36] *Ibid.,* 1831, p. 114.
[37] *Christian Baptist,* III, 232.

teach, and to preside over one flock, who would not be qualified
to teach or preside over another. The flock then in calling or
electing a person to this office will turn their attention to
themselves as well as to the candidate . . . and will conclude
whether his aptitude to teach and his capacity to preside is of
such a degree as will correspond to their circumstances.[38]

1. *Obligations of the Contract on the Minister*

On the part of the individual called, Campbell held
that his eligibility involved three things: (1) that he
possess the intellectual and spiritual endowments requisite to the functions of the office; (2) that he under-
gird those endowments with a specific program of education and training; (3) that he be willing to devote his
time and talents to executing the functions of the office.

In the first class of requisites, Campbell included such
traits as "a good character, a good spirit, and a good
talent for business—these are the three indispensables."
To these he added "intelligence, discretion, and gravity."

In regard to special training for the ministry, Campbell's later views represented quite a departure from
his earlier position. In the year 1825 he wrote: "The
christian bishop pleads no inward call to the work, and
never sets himself to learn it. . . . The christian bishop
is called by the brethren, because he has the qualifications already." In that period, Campbell seemed to
think a knowledge of the Bible, coupled with an evidence
of faith in its teachings, sufficient to a minister's educational talents:

. . . If, then, we would appear credible, or worthy of the
audience of the people, we must appear before them, not under the assumption or pretension of ambassadors from heaven,
or as God's special ministers; but as the pious, and humble and
devout students of the Bible; as persons who have believed the
gospel ourselves, and upon such grounds and reasons as will not

---

[38]*Ibid.*, IV, 260.

make us ashamed to give a reason of the hope which we entertain.[39]

But by the year 1835 Campbell had developed a considerable following, much augmented in that year by
the union with Barton W. Stone and the "Christians" of
Kentucky. As the movement swelled in the center, it
began to fall apart at the seams, and the leaks were
around the rivets of an uneducated leadership. Moore
says of this period:

. . . It is an undeniable fact that many of the churches suf-
fered on account of the incompetency of the eldership.

· ·

In the days of the *Christian Baptist* Mr. Campbell had severely
chastised the clergy. . . . His reformatory movement was now
reaping some of the results of his own teaching.[40]

Without admitting either that he had been in error
or that he had changed his views, Campbell, in harmony
with his principle that the important thing was "the
work to be done," began to reverse his former stand,
and to complain of those "expounders" who were ignorant of all the laws of language, the force of words,
the logical point in an argument, and their inaptitude to
expound and apply the word of truth. He concluded:

. . . The cause of reformation would ere now have overrun
the whole community but for . . . a class of unsent, unaccom-
plished, uneducated advocates who plead it.

· ·

Many and various instances could be given of the inadequacy
of all accidental checks and restraints to perfect a Christian
ministry; yet all agree that the perfection of the mass very
much depends on the perfection of this class of citizens in the
Christian kingdom.[41]

[39]*Ibid.*, VI, 632.
[40]W. T. Moore, *A Comprehensive History of the Disciples of Christ*, pp.
311-312.
[41]*Millennial Harbinger*, 1842, pp. 244-246.

He accordingly began to appeal to the Christian scriptures for the authority of an educated ministry. Speaking of Timothy, he said:

. . . That he might travel with Paul acceptably, he accommodated his education and training to the times and people amongst whom he had to labor. So ought churches still to commend persons worthy of the ministry to those who may make them more useful and circumcise them of their ignorance, prejudice, and vulgar notions.[42]

College!

The third requirement which Campbell listed as a condition of a "brother's" eligibility for a call to the ministry was that he be willing to commit his time and his talents to the work, "that he give himself wholly to the work, that his improvement may keep pace with the growth of the body, and be apparent to all." Needless to say, this view also represented some departure from his earlier stand, and from his own earlier practice, since, after his own ordination, he had practiced the vocation of a husbandman rather than receive remuneration for his services as a minister.

2. *Obligations of the Contract on the Church*

The contract which involved the three conditions of native equipment, training, and commitment on the part of the one called to the ministry bound the congregation likewise with three basic requirements: (1) the setting apart of the one called by a special service of ordination; (2) recognition of and a respect for the authority and responsibilities thus delegated to him; and (3) the meeting of his material needs with monetary support for his services.

Campbell had been ordained to the ministry on January 1, 1812, and throughout his ministry he affirmed the service of ordination as one having New Testament

---

[42]*Ibid.*, 1842, p. 242.

Stepping away from
the sacrament of
ordination.

146   APOSTLE OF FREEDOM

authority. However, he held that the only way the grace
of God attached to the service was in the fact that God
had granted the church the right to "call" its ministry.
In fact, he continued, the service itself was simply an
"inauguration" which attested the "call" which had already been given. The validity was in the call rather
than in the inauguration:

> Every thing essential to appointment, call, or ordination was
> vested in the minds of the brethren. Their desires, however
> expressed, gave the office to the candidate, however he was an-
> nounced. The apostles so taught them. They, in the first in-
> stance, took a part, not in the call or appointment; but in the
> introduction and inauguration of the bishops elect. This was
> done in conformity to the Jewish custom of imposing their
> hands upon the head of the person or animal devoted. . . . The
> brethren called or elected, and the eldership expressed their
> concurrence, and the brethren's desire, by a formal sign ex-
> pressive of the devotion of the person to the work. I say this
> is all that can be legitimately gathered from the volume, as
> to the forms of investiture; but as to the right of the brethren
> so to choose, and of the bishop, on this choice to officiate, there
> is the most ample evidence.
>
> Here I would take liberty to remark that in process of time,
> as corruption and defection progressed, it came to pass that
> what was, with the apostles, but the mere sign or mark, ex-
> pressive of their concurrence with the brethren's election and
> appointment, came by degrees to be considered as the ordina-
> tion itself, independent of the brethren's voice.[43]

While Campbell's views regarding the ministry
changed with the changing years and his changing circumstances, his views on the nature of the service of
ordination as a formal appointment to office in fulfillment of a social contract was substantially the same
thirty years after he wrote the article previously quoted.
The setting apart of a man to the ministry was, according to Campbell, in all cases to be done by a local

---

[43]*Christian Baptist*, IV, 260-261.

is the College does not ordain, but the church itself.

congregation, or by local congregations acting in unison, never by any supralocal ecclesiastics. In some cases, he held that inferiors in office or station could officiate in ordaining superiors in station, but the more proper procedure was by the laying on of the hands of the bishops, who were in all cases officers in one local congregation, never having jurisdiction over more than one. Whatever the procedure, whether by one congregation or several, or whether the laying on of hands was by laymen or bishops the authority resided in the whole church. Here Campbell expressed his faith in the common mind of the church. "The voice of the whole people is the voice of God—because it is the voice of reason and of truth. It is his providential call."

At first Campbell held that the ordination qualified the one called to serve only the group ordaining him. The procedure he preferred was that of the congregation first electing and ordaining a plurality of bishops and deacons, then from among the bishops elected, the selection of one as the "shepherd of the flock." Later, however, an ordination to the work of a shepherd, or pastor, was held by Campbell to qualify a man to serve in any congregation which chose to engage his services, but he served said congregation in the capacity of a representative of the one which had first ordained him. Each congregation ordaining a man to the ministry was thus under a solemn responsibility:

. . . Impose hands suddenly on no man; or, Invest no man with sacred office until he is first approved; for should you ordain to office an incompetent person, you must, to a certain extent, participate in his sins of mal-administration.[44]

Inherent in the social contract which the congregation made with its ministry, whether those called as deacons and bishops or those called from among the bishops as

[44] *Millennial Harbinger*, 1840, pp. 71-72.

shepherds,[45] was the responsibility on the part of the church to recognize the authority which it had thereby delegated to its officers: "Whatever rights, duties, or privileges are conferred on particular persons, cannot of right belong to those who have transferred them." This transfer, however, could never relieve the individual members of the congregation of responsibility, as it could never be absolute:

> . . . Parents cannot wholly transfer the education of their children to others; neither can a master transfer all his duties to a steward or overseer. No more can the citizens of Christ's kingdom wholly transfer their duties to preach and teach Christ.[46]

The third obligation devolving on the congregation by virtue of its social contract with the minister, Campbell held, was the responsibility of providing for his financial support. This, again, represented a change from his earlier views. Not that he had ever completely advocated an unpaid ministry. But two factors served to create a very general impression that he was so opposed. The first was his very definite attack on the "hirelings" of the clergy in his earlier days. The second was the fact that he boasted that he had never accepted a dollar in remuneration for his services as a minister.

While it is true that his attitude toward a paid ministry was misinterpreted, it is also true that his views did change. In the year 1825 he wrote:

---

[45]Certain obscurities are to be noted in Campbell's teachings so far as methodology of ordination is concerned. These obscurities have so burdened Disciples of Christ that as late as 1935, at San Antonio International Convention, a "Commission on Ordination" was set up to study the whole problem. These obscurities center around the fact that by insisting that the "shepherd," or "pastor" had only the rank of a "bishop" in the local congregation, no distinction was made in the procedure of ordaining them. This has continued to posit the right of ordination of ministers in the local congregation. On the other hand, Campbell, inconsistently enough, by insisting that the "bishop" was an "elder" by virtue of age, placed a barrier against a young ministry. Further, by leaving the ordination of ministers purely to the local congregation, and at the same time urging each congregation to consider its own intellectual level in making its choices, he went a long way toward defeating his own campaign for an educated ministry. Both these problems still, to some extent, plague Disciples.

[46]*Christian System*, p. 82.

A hireling is one who prepares himself for the office of a "preacher" or "minister," as a mechanic learns a trade . . . and agrees by the day or the sermon, month or year, for a stipulated reward.

. . . .

[The christian bishop] accepts of the office for the congregation of which he is a member, and takes the oversight of them, and receives from them such remuneration as his circumstances require.[47]

The distinct implications here were against a stipulated salary for the ministry, and for a diversified ministry from "within" the local congregation. This position led to the growth of "part-time" ministers among Disciples, often paid with sacks of flour and bags of potatoes.

Coincidental with his recognition of the need of a full-time educated ministry, Campbell began to try to undo his teachings regarding the support of the ministry. He wrote many times pleading for the churches to become conscious of their "scriptural" duty to support the ministry. The following is typical:

. . . Would it not . . . be a very imprudent policy on the part of a Christian community, to have its evangelists plowing, teaching school, making shoes or tents, when they ought to be, every day, working in Christ's vineyard, and winning souls to God, or preparing themselves for this great work?

. . . .

I allude to the ordinance: "That they who preach the gospel should live," not *on* the gospel, but *of* (or by) the gospel. The philosophy of this is, that every man, as a general rule or law, must faithfully and industriously pursue that calling on which he depends for support.[48]

The call to the ministry then, according to Campbell, was a social contract, based on a social relationship, and involving reciprocal relations and responsibilities.

---

[47]*Christian Baptist*, III, 233.
[48]*Millennial Harbinger*, 1850, pp. 486-487.

CHAPTER FOUR

THE STRUCTURE OF THE LOCAL CHURCH

. . . Organs are, indeed, essential to the growth and action of every body—vegetable, animal, political, ecclesiastic or religious. Hence, in all conventions of the people, literary, moral, political or religious, the first act is organization. Then the body is created, lives, moves, acts, and enters upon its mission.[1]
. . . Has the King of the kingdom of heaven himself laid down no system of organization!? Then he has no kingdom of heaven —no church on earth! He may have a people, but without organization, he can have neither church nor kingdom, for those terms indicate organized bodies.[2]

With the rapid growth of Campbell's following in the fourth decade of the 19th century, he began to apply himself to the problem of a valid type of church organization. His categorical denunciation of the existing forms of church government had helped to throw the spotlight upon him. His constructive abilities were now to be put to the test.

While always affirming that he believed in order, his writings in the *Christian Baptist* had revealed a skepticism of "church governments," holding that the "constitution" of the church provided for all the government which the church needed, under Christ as absolute monarch. By the year 1834 his writings began to reflect a different tone. By the year 1838 he was definitely strug-

---

[1]*Millennial Harbinger*, 1855, p. 373.
[2]*Ibid.*, 1855, p. 380.

gling to avert a threatened anarchy in the ranks of his
followers:

There are the extremes of Congregationalism and monarchical
despotism. There is popery and a fierce democracy. Neither
of these is the Christian Institution. Mobocracy may become as
tyrannical as unlimited monarchy. Both are to be eschewed for
the same reasons.[3]

But to leap at this change in the tone of Campbell's
writings as an evidence of his abandonment of his earlier
"literalism" would be to do violence to the facts. It was
an evidence of growth away from his earlier extreme
"independency," but his dependence on the letter of the
Bible was just as great at this time, and continued to be
as great, as it had been previously. The chief difference
was that he had learned to look for a different kind of
letter. He was just as quick to seek a "book, chapter,
and verse" as authority for his views in 1835, 1845, and
1855, as he was in 1823. In 1842 he wrote: "Outside of
the apostolic canon there is not, as it appears to me one
solid foot of terra firma on which to raise the superstructure ecclesiastic." In the year 1847 he wrote:
"God is the author of one book. Everything spoken by
him in that book, or by his authority, is infallible. The
human race cannot add to it one new idea worth an
hour's discussion."

But, interestingly enough, during this same period he
was appealing to the Bible itself as evidence that it was
not sufficient to govern the church:

A book is not sufficient to govern the church. No book ever
governed any community—not even the Book of the Law, or the
Book of the Gospel, else Moses would have resigned when he
wrote the Law, and would never have laid his hand upon
Joshua; else Jesus would never have sent out Apostles, Prophets, Evangelists, Pastors, and Teachers of the New Testament.[4]

---

[3]*Ibid.*, 1838, p. 128.
[4]*Ibid.*, 1841, pp. 533-534.

The Bible, further, became the *jus divinum* by which, in numerous articles, Campbell sought to marshall his followers to the adoption and support of the principles of church organization which he advocated.

But he at the same time was calling his spirit of inquiry into play in his attempt to conceive an effective system. His understanding of the term "church" as designating either a local congregation of believers, or the aggregate of all those congregations, became the basis upon which he constructed the framework of the church as a social organization. He continued to affirm the autonomy of the local congregation over all matters concerned with its internal affairs, but insisted that its independence was not an independence of all other congregations in matters which concerned the kingdom. He likened this independent-interdependence to the family as a social organism in the state:

. . . Every family in Pennsylvania is independent of every other family in the State, in all that enters into the idea of a private family; but in whatever appertains to the State, it is not independent of any other family, nor any other family in the State independent of it. It belongs to the State, and the State to it. So of the church of Christ; it belongs to every particular church, and every particular church to it.

If the Christian Church or community be a church of Christians, or a community of communities, then, indeed, not one church can be absolutely independent of every other church belonging to the community or church of Christ.[5]

Since Campbell assiduously sought to maintain this distinction between the "private life" of a local congregation and the mutuality of each congregation's "public life" with all other congregations, this chapter will deal with a study of his conception of the structure of the local congregation. Chapter Five will then devote itself to his conception of the structural relationships of

Ibid., 1850, p. 286.

the local congregation to the aggregate of all the local
congregations.

I. *The Organic Framework of the Local Church*

There is now heard from the East and from the West, from
the North and from the South, one general, if not universal,
call for a more efficient organization of our churches.

. . . .

I have always been a pleader for organization; still organization
is not faith, nor humility, nor liberality. We have very compact and efficient organizations in our country without intelligence, faith, or true religion. . . .
But we want organization—the setting in order of the things
wanting to perfect the church and convert the world.[6]

The first step which Campbell took in the attempt to
construct an effective organization in the local church
was to recognize that it had its existence in a social context. This he conceived to be at once its opportunity
and its danger. The initial problem became that of relating the organization of the church to the social and
civic milieu in a way which would safeguard it against
any disrupting influences in its environment, and at the
same time in a way which would give effectiveness to its
work. For this reason he was suspicious of all political
and legal entanglements. While the genius of the Christian organization had to adapt itself to the "peculiar
exigencies and mutations of society," Campbell insisted
on the necessity of distinguishing between "the family
of God and its circumstances, between the Christian institution and its accidents." The church was therefore
to make use of natural groupings and boundaries in defining the territorial limits of each congregation, and for
the relating of individual congregations into groups. At
first Campbell inclined to the view of only one church in
a locality:

---

[6]*Ibid.,* 1849, pp. 90, 92.

. . ."When they refer to any circumscribed or limited situation, as a town or city, they, in all such cases, use the singular number, as the church at Ephesus, at Corinth, at Cenchrea, which was about two miles from Corinth; evidently because there was no christian society in any of these places, but one, to which the designation *church* justly belonged.

But when they come to speak of a certain district of country, in which there was a number of such assemblies, they as invariably use the plural number, as "the churches of Galatia."[7]

But since Campbell also believed in the greater effectiveness of small congregations of believers fellowshiping together in face-to-face relationships, he necessarily had to abandon the idea of one church to a city as his movement continued to grow. Strangely enough he used the same scriptural terms to support his "more than one church" that he had used twenty-three years earlier in supporting his "only one church" to a city:

There may, indeed, be "churches of God," "churches of Christ," "churches of the Saints," in a city, as well as in a province, or an empire. And there may also be but one church of Christ in a city or in a province. In both cases, however, a church of Christ is a single society of believing men and women, statedly meeting in one place, to worship God through the one Mediator.[8]

But while Campbell advocated that the church make use of natural groupings and boundaries in defining its own limits, he was insistent that its members recognize these boundaries as the "circumstances" rather than the reality of the church. The churches of Christ in America must assiduously avoid the political implications of such terms as "the American church" or "the church of America":

It is worthy of remark, that we never read of a church *in* or *of* any province or district, such as the church of England; the

[7] *Christian Baptist*, IV, 315.
[8] *Millennial Harbinger*, 1849, p. 223.

church of Scotland, or the church of Geneva. We might as rationally look for the church of America, or the church of Africa, as for any national or provincial church.

. . . .

A church of churches, or a church collective of all the churches in a state or a nation, is an institution of man, and not an ordinance of God.[9]

While making use of political boundaries in its organization, the church was not only to avoid any identity with political groups, its members were to guard as well against confusing their loyalties. Campbell, while holding that both the church and the state are divine institutions, insisted that the church is paramount to the state, and that therefore the Christian's relations to the church are paramount to his relations to the state, as well as to every other temporal institution. As a safeguard against any such confusion of loyalties, Campbell preferred that the church administer its affairs without resort to such legal devices as charters and articles of incorporation. Dependence on such legal instruments for the administration of its affairs, he held, might lead to a lessening of dependence on Christ, and to the danger of being blinded to the grand principles of Christianity. Likewise he feared the reactionary influence of endowments and legacies for ecclesiastical purposes on the future thought and program of the church.[10]

The local congregation, then, while an organism within a social and political framework, was to sedulously guard and maintain both its structural and functional autonomy. It was to accept its obligations both to the church at large and to society at large, but it was not to permit either ecclesiastical or mundane matters to usurp the

---

[9] *Ibid.*, p. 222.

[10] *Christian Baptist*, VII, 571. While we later find Campbell both securing a charter for and leaving a bequest to Bethany College, we find no record of his renunciation of his original stand on these items regarding the church, per se.

divine prerogative of the society of believers to direct
its own destiny.

The care with which Campbell sought to draw a distinction between external factors which he felt might
thwart the autonomy of the local congregation, and internal factors which he believed that autonomy could
control, is illustrated in the fact that while he was suspicious of any written instrument which might bind the
program of the congregation either to its own past, to an
overhead ecclesiasticism, or to the state, he at the same
time encouraged the use of such written instruments as
had to do with the internal life of the congregation, and
over which the congregation had control. In such a class
he considered church histories, minutes of church meetings, constitutions and by-laws for church boards, and
personal case histories of members.

In regard to church records and other written instruments intended to facilitate the functioning of the organization, he typically appealed to the Bible for authority,
and observed:

> . . . The Bible is all the proof we need. Reference is frequently
> had to other church and family records, . . . such as those of
> Iddo and Jasher. These public documents were authentic, and
> used by the inspired writers.
>
> . . . .
>
> But it is objected, that these records may become church
> articles, and bonds of union; and thus we may degenerate into
> church covenants, creeds, and all other sectarianisms. I pre-
> sume there is no hypothesis more unwarrantable from all his-
> toric record, and from our own experience. I have never read
> nor heard of any society, confounding its *own history* with its
> faith.
>
> . . . .
>
> I should not think that such a subject deserved a grave argu-
> ment, were it not, that some christians within my knowledge,
> have been so alarmed on the subject of articles, and rules of

faith and manners, as to think it unsafe to have pen, ink, and paper within the walls of a meeting house; or to have their names enrolled, lest, by some strange vicissitude, it might be converted into a creed for posterity.[11]

The local congregation, then, was held by Campbell to be free to use any techniques which it might find suitable to its needs and purposes, so long as in using them it did not sacrifice any portion of its autonomy.

But if the congregation was to be structurally insulated against any outside encroachment on its freedom, what was the internal framework by which it was to exercise that freedom? Campbell was ready with book, chapter, and verse scriptural references with which he sought to support his claim that while all matters of faith, piety, and morality were immutable, and subject only to the inviolable sovereignty of Christ, the exercise of judgment in all matters of "expediency" was lodged in the "brethren."

But the biblical precedent for the exercise of this authority in matters of expediency, as well as for regulating matters in the realm of faith, was by the selection by the "brethren" from among themselves of officers to whom were delegated specific powers which inhered in the congregation. These powers were never to be absolute, and the "brethren" always retained the right of referendum and the right of veto. In the event of the congregation overriding the action or decision of its officers, the officers were either to abide by the action of the congregation, or, if they could not conscientiously do so, they were to resign their offices. In the absence of a majority action vetoing the decisions of the officers, all members were to abide by them:

... The election to rule is, on the part of the electors, an engagement to submit to the elected. On any other hypothesis an election or ordination is a farce. . . . All that promote to any

---

[11]*Millennial Harbinger*, 1834, pp. 503-504.

office a brother, are obliged by every principle of piety and congruity to submit to the administration of that person so long as he exhibits himself faithful to the Lord and the brethren.[12]

Both officers and members were bound to abide just as religiously by any rules of order by which they had agreed to operate: "So soon as people agree to act by any rules, they oblige themselves to act according to them; because they have, on conviction of their truth or expediency, adopted them."

The officers to whom these delegated powers were to be committed, Campbell affirmed, were of two classes, and two only. These were bishops and deacons, of whom there was to be a plurality of each class in every congregation: "Each community has its own bishops and deacons, its own presbytery and diaconate." Of these functionaries, so long as each congregation had a plurality, the exact number and, in some respects, their character and attainments, were to depend on "the number and attainments of the church's members, and surrounding circumstances."

From among the "bishops" there was to be selected one who would serve as "president" of the congregation. At first, Campbell also held that from among the bishops a diversified ministry was to be selected, including both those who "taught" and those who "shepherded" the "flock." He warned the churches against depending on the services of "itinerant" pastors, meaning by "itinerant" all who were not permanently members of one congregation. Later, appalled at the inefficiency of local bishops who were "untrained and untaught," he abandoned his earlier position and embraced the idea of a "one-man" ministry. He did not, however, abandon his position that the rank of the pastor was simply that of one of the bishops.

---

[12]*Ibid.*, 1840, p. 217.

Elections were evidently to be for the term of good behavior, and Campbell specifically went on record in opposition to "annual" elections. This was in harmony with his idea that duties were derived from relationships, and officers from duties. He looked upon the election to office of any man for any duration other than that of good behavior as simply an expedient.

On the other hand, while officers elected by a congregation were for "life" or good behavior, any officer either visiting or removing to another congregation appeared in his new relationship as purely an unofficial disciple. The election to office by one congregation gave him no prerogative in another congregation. To suppose the contrary, Campbell asserted, would be to constitute different orders of men, and to create supralocal officials.

Those who were members of the congregation were to be enrolled as such upon their having satisfied the requirements for membership. Both officers and members were to be functionally related to the total organization according to their diversified gifts and the needs of the congregation. In all matters, with a single and singular exception which we shall later note, the majority rule was to prevail in all decisions requiring the congregational voice.

II. *The Authority and Functions of Officers*

There never was a community that got along peaceably and profitably for any length of time that presumed to settle all matters . . . by a public vote in a public assembly. Such societies as have advocated this wild democracy have either broken themselves to pieces, or greatly dishonored and injured the profession.[13]

Campbell sought to make a clear distinction between the authority, responsibilities, and functions of the two classes of officers which he advocated. His combined

---

[13]*Ibid.*, 1840, p. 217.

writings on the subject of the bishops of the church
would fill many volumes. On the occasions when he
mentioned the deacons, he greatly stressed the importance of the office, but singularly enough, his references
to them are both rare and meager.

A. *Bishops, Elders, Presbyters, Shepherds, Rulers*

All the above titles were applied by Campbell at one
time or another to refer to the same office in the church.
When referring to a group of such officers, he added both
the terms "senate" and "episcopacy," maintaining that
the latter term referred to the same type of office in the
New Testament as the terms "elder," "bishop," and
"presbyter." Thus, he affirmed that in the New Testament sense of the terms he was both Presbyterian and
Episcopalian as well as Congregationalist.

To be qualified to occupy the office of a bishop, Campbell held that a man must be an "elder" not only in
years, but in Christian maturity. He must further be
the head of a family:[14]

. . . A strippling, married or unmarried, is not eligible. A
person of middle age, if recently converted, is not eligible. And
a man who has had no experience in domestic management is
illy qualified to manage the family of God.[15]

In addition, Campbell believed that the bishop should be
possessed of all the native endowments previously listed
as qualifications of the ministry of the church. But,
while he literally insisted on what he conceived to be
Paul's specifications regarding the qualifications of a
bishop, he did not hesitate to add a few of his own, holding that bishops must be characterized by "justice, energy, and discretion." "No man," he said, "destitute

---

[14]Here is another point of obscurity in Campbell. Since he insisted that
the "minister," or "pastor," is a "bishop" or "elder," the implication would
be that the minister must also be the head of a family. As in the case
of the age of the minister, Campbell nowhere clears up this point.
[15]*Christian Baptist*, VII, 581.

of decision, of character, of self-government, and energy, ever can well manage any concern, domestic, ecclesiastic, political.''

Campbell was anxious that the church refrain from using the term ''bishop'' in any honorary sense which might favor the idea of the bishop as a ''supra-local'' functionary. He asserted that such a practice was what had caused the Presbyterians and Baptists to permit the Methodists and Episcopalians to appropriate the term to an office the Lord never intended, and as a result would not consent to the application of the term to himself—he was not ''the overseer'' of a single congregation. ''A bishop without a charge or cure,'' he said, ''is like a husband without a wife.''

Campbell held that the duties of the bishops related to three functions, namely: shepherding the flock, ruling the congregation, and instructing the members. Some of these functions were to be met by the appointment of specific bishops to the execution of these responsibilities, while others were to be the corporate responsibility of the entire eldership.

The work of shepherding included three classes of duties, which Campbell designated as watching, feeding, and healing. This work was the special responsibility of the pastor, who, as shepherd, was ''more than a bishop'' in regard to function, but not more in regard to rank. As shepherd, the pastor was an administrator, looking after ''the common interests of the kingdom in those places and districts'' in which he was located. He was to watch over the welfare of the members as a shepherd watches over a flock.

But the fact that the pastor was an overseer, a shepherd, an administrator, did not mean that he was a ruler, any more than all the bishops were rulers over the congregation. Neither was the president of the congregation a ruler in any special sense. He was simply to preside, and if in special instances he made appointments, it was to be understood that it was the congregation making the appointments through him.

In fact, while the work of shepherding and the work of teaching, as well as particular administrative duties such as that of presiding, were to be assigned to specific bishops who evidenced qualifications for those responsibilities, Campbell would not grant that the work of "ruling" belonged to any one person. That duty was a function of the bishops as a corporate body. Campbell never ceased to be too suspicious of the insidious will to power within man to sanction the delegation of the authority to rule in one pair of hands.

As time progressed Campbell began to stress more and more the importance of the function of bishops as rulers. He seemed to be more conscious of the necessity of securing more orderliness in the ranks of the congregations which were afflicted with "individualism." Several instances arose in which open church trials were held for the purposes of disciplining some recalcitrant member. Disturbed by the ill effects of these "open trials," Campbell time and again stressed that in such matters the "senate," or eldership, should properly dispose of such cases without airing them before the public. The following is typical of his writings in this regard:

> . . . We ask, Whence originated the idea that the whole congregation must try all offences; that it must be a sort of Court of Common Pleas, a tribunal of Oyer and Terminer, to hear and decide all controversies? Certainly not from the Jewish or Christian constitution or laws. . . . There is no statute nor law known to us, requiring all offences, whether public or private, to be tried in a public assembly. It would, indeed, make the Christian community an anomaly among all human institutions —in a point, too, where much would be always endangered and nothing gained.
>
> . . . .
>
> There is . . . neither wisdom nor propriety in calling a whole

community together to prove a fact, or to examine an evil report against a brother. This is the duty of the elders of the
church. The whole church are not *bishops*. Their official duties
reach to these cases. They examine the report and collect the
evidence. They ascertain the fact. . . . [They] state the fact
to the community . . . and so the matter ends. . . . If . . . not,
the bishops resign either the case or their office, and the community appoint other persons to judge the case, or succeed
them in office.[16]

But while Campbell insisted on the ruling nature of the
bishop's office, he made it clear that the bishop's power
did not extend to that of determining the beliefs or opinions of the members of the congregation. The eldership,
in other words, was to rule, but it was to be no heretic
detector, no court of inquisition:

As government has respect to *actions,* not to opinions nor
sentiments, the Christian senate or eldership can never, legiti-
mately, become guardians or censors of men's notions, of their
opinions, or of articles of belief. When, therefore, we speak of
the duties of ruling and teaching, as connected with the elder's
office . . . we do not contemplate them as censors of opinions or a
tribunal of critics on matters speculative or doctrinal, but as
vigilant superintendents of the education and behavior of the
Christian communities.[17]

Even in cases of public immorality requiring the disciplinary action of the elders, that action was ever to be dispensed according to the Christian principle of love, and
the human issue, more than all else, was to be the basis
upon which their decision was reached. Any disciplinary
action was to be characterized by an aim at the conversion of the transgressor. Final exclusion was not to
be attempted until admonition, reproof, and persuasion
had failed to effect a change in his behavior, and even
though both public and private good might require the

---

[16]*Millennial Harbinger*, 1839, pp. 339-340.
[17]*Ibid.,* 1842, p. 328.

exclusion, he was not to be treated as an enemy, but admonished as a brother.

The functions of the bishops, then, Campbell held to be primarily concerned with the spiritual welfare of the congregation. While they were to use what means they found or believed to be effective, they were to be supremely motivated by a desire for the spiritual good, and were to guard against any purely legal demands which might fetter the spiritual good. The same principle was to apply to any instrumental device used in administration. For this reason, he feared resort to any kind of inflexible rules, or the adoption of inflexible programs. He guarded against the requests which came to him to suggest set routines of administration, and on one occasion observed:

It is always more or less detrimental to the ascertainment of truth to allow our previous conclusions to assume the position of fixed and fundamental truths, to which nothing is to be at any time added, either in the way of correction or enlargement. On the contrary, we ought rather to act under the conviction that we may be wiser to-day than yesterday, and that whatever is true can suffer no hazard from a careful and candid reconsideration.[18]

Campbell felt that the bishops could function best as spiritual overseers by keeping themselves free from detailed tasks. He even denied that the New Testament required them to preside at the Lord's table. He therefore deemed it wise for the bishops to assign most of the specific details of operation to other members of the congregation, particularly to the second class of officers, the deacons.

B. Deacons, Stewards, Deaconesses

Considering the importance which Campbell attached to the office of deacon, the investigator is surprised to

---

[18]*Ibid.*, 1842, p. 327.

find him writing so little about it.[19] As in the case of
bishops, he held that there was to be a plurality of
deacons in each church, and that the exercise of their
office applied only to one church. Affirming that "the
deacon's office is more important than many imagine,"
he used the term alternately in two different senses. On
the one hand, he held that any member who rendered a
service to the church was a deacon:

> . . . They are all *deacons* in the unappropriated sense of that
> word. *Diakonos,* or *deacon* is found *30 times* in the Christian
> Scriptures. It is in the Common Version, represented by *min-*
> *ister* and *servant,* and only three times retained or transferred
> —*deacon.* . . . Apostles—civil magistrates and houschold *servants*
> (not slaves) are in the Christian Scriptures called *deacons.*
> They are never called *douloi* or *slaves;* but only *servants, volun-*
> *tary servants; ministers* sometimes of high, and sometimes of
> low commission.[20]

On the other hand, Campbell specifically designated
the deacon as one of the two kinds of officers in the
church. Between these two kinds of officers was a clear
distinction of function. The bishops were to "superin-
tend the spiritual concerns of the people," while the
deacons "were only to attend to secular things." They
were more than mere church ushers or servers of the
Lord's table, although the latter called them into being.
They were business managers and, as such, were due the
respect owed to ministers of the church. They administered both the "domestic and foreign" interests of the
local congregation. As in the case of bishops, the church
was cautioned by Campbell against calling any man a
deacon who did not function as one.

Since Campbell held that the deacon's office had respect to the temporalities of the church, and as these

---

[19]This surprise is all the greater, considering that in the average church
of the brotherhood so greatly influenced by Campbell, the deacons on the
"church board" usually outnumber the bishops or "elders" about three to
one.

[20]*Ibid.,* 1857, pp. 586-587.

are generally connected with pecuniary matters, he identified the steward, the almoner, the treasurer, and the deacon with the same office. They were to take care of all pecuniary matters, and out of the same fund "three sets of tables" were to be furnished. These were the Lord's table, the bishop's table, and the poor's table. That was to say that the deacons were to provide the physical mechanics and services of worship, to be responsible for providing the minister's salary, and to look after the needy in the community, "according to the exigencies of each and the ability to contribute."

Campbell attributed the admission of women to the office of deaconess, or to use his term, "female deacon," to the eleemosynary function of the office. "Amongst the Greeks who paid so much regard to differences of sex, female deacons were appointed to visit and wait upon the sisters." Campbell nowhere suggested the admission of women to any other office or ministry of the church than that of deaconess. Neither does he suggest the use of women even in that capacity in any of the public functions belonging to the deacon's office.

Thus, in the offices or ministry of the church, Campbell sought to establish a distinct dichotomy between spiritual and temporal affairs, even to the point of distinguishing between those officers responsible for them. It may be noted, in passing, that this was the only instance in which he made such a distinction. The visible act of baptism he had held to be essentially conjoined to the spiritual quality of faith, the visible church he had identified with the present invisible reign of Christ on earth, and the spoken or written Word he had held to be the only avenue through which the Holy Spirit operates on the heart and mind of man, and man in turn can learn only through the instrumentality of his physical organs. But it never occurred to him that what he called the "temporal" affairs of the church might have a spiritual reference, that the Christian stewardship expressed through the investment of funds in the program of the church could be made a significant spiritual experience. His liberal spirit suggested to him that the church should avoid "different orders of men" which might give rise to supralocal ecclesiastics. But the literal scriptural references to deacons serving tables and to bishops shepherding the flock led him to create two orders of officers within the local congregation, the one dealing with sacred spiritual things, the other with mere temporal things, a distinction which has caused many a Disciple congregation to be strife ridden, and many a church officer to be offended when elected only to the office of a deacon when he felt that he merited the office of an elder. As much as Campbell had to say about psycho-physical unity on the one hand, and about the distinction between the legislative and executive branches of government on the other, it is an occasion of surprise that, since he insisted on two classes of local church officers, he did not achieve the concept of one class as legislators of the program and another as executors, but both of equal importance, and both dealing with the total life of the church as a unit.

III. *The Privileges and Functions of Members*

. . . A society without a social compact to me is unintelligible. Society is not a number of persons covering a certain piece of ground like the trees in our forests. They must congregate upon some stipulations, expressed or implied.[21]

In his discussion of the place of the membership in the organization of the church, Campbell maintained all that he had said about the priesthood of believers. The individual, as a holy priest unto God, enjoyed the right of the private study and interpretation of the Bible, including the right to his own opinions. He further enjoyed the right of a volitional decision in accepting

---

[21]*Campbell-Owen Debate*, pp. 392-393.

Christ as his Lord, and entering into the church, and was privileged, should the occasion demand it, to perform the services of the ministry, including the administration of the sacraments.

In addition, the believer, said Campbell, enjoyed the rights inhering in the social contract which the church had entered into with its officers and ministry. These included the right of receiving instruction, pastoral care, and discipline from the elders, and the right of being waited upon by the deacons. They included also the right of a voice in electing the officers, and the right of referendum and veto of any undesirable decision which the officers might make.

As to the functions of the members, they were in turn to fulfill their part of the social contract with the officers. This included the function of setting the officers apart with a service of ordination, of respecting the authority which had thus been delegated to them, and of supporting them morally and, when proper, financially, in their work.

A. *The Deliberative Group*

But in dealing with the actual relationships of officers and members in the church, Campbell went far beyond the bare demands both of his doctrine of priesthood of believers and of the social contract. All such relationships were to be marked by "fraternal intercourse and mutual edification." Together the community of believers was to seek the discovery of the loftiest and most comprehensive principles which would excite to moral action. Since this was a task of officers and members working together, Campbell strongly stressed the importance of the participation of the total membership in the program of the church, and in the services of worship, ridiculing those assemblies in which all "save one consecrated tongue, are dumb in the Christian worship." Disagreeing with the maxim of Alexander Pope that

"that which is best administered is best," Campbell
aimed at more than mere efficiency of performance in
the organization of the church, granting that from the
standpoint of efficiency, the papal system was best. He
conceived the organization to be functional in the sense
of providing a medium through which the membership
could give expression to its religious life, rather than
one which sought "little thinking, much obeying, and
great efficiency." For this reason he felt that the organization should be set up in such a way as to stimulate both thought and action on the part of the mass.

At this point, Campbell's educational philosophy
merged with his political philosophy. As president of
Bethany College, as early as the year 1842, he had led
in the adoption of a program of student government. His
recommendation to the faculty at that time expressed
ideas of organization and government corresponding to
those which he urged for the church:

> ... We ... propose to the Students of this Institution, that
> they take a new degree in the department of self-government,
> and that they form themselves into a republic, in which they
> shall conform to the presiding spirit of all truly American In-
> stitutions. It is then suggested to them to meet, as the people
> do, in their primary capacity, and adopt a constitution, and
> divide the boarding house and precincts belonging to the Stu-
> dents into wards. So soon as they have resolved themselves
> into a sort of federal and state or direct government, they shall
> hold their elections, appoint their officers, enact their laws, hold
> their courts, and proceed to the execution of them.[22]

In harmony with this principle of self-determination,
Campbell, in his teaching, approached closely Wm. Mc-
Dougall's concept of the dual function of administration,
with the administrative group being: first, recipient of
the ideas of the group, the center toward which the creative thought of the mass flowed; second, executive, the

---

[22]*Millennial Harbinger,* 1842, p. 285.

arranging of those ideas into a pattern, and the return-
ing of this pattern to the group in the form of a program
of action. The congregation was thus to share in the
creation as well as the execution of the program. Insisting that the primitive church communicated in
prayers, in counsel, in labor, in giving and receiving,
Campbell affirmed:

> . . . There can be no Christian co-operation in one of these
> that does not suppose a co-operation in all. To pray for any
> thing for which we will not take counsel together, for which we
> will not jointly labor, for which we will not contribute with
> all our energies and means, is only mocking God and disappoint-
> ing ourselves.[23]

Affirming that Christianity taught the doctrine of personal liberty, freedom of choice, and personal responsibility, Campbell thus joined individual initiative with
co-operative action as the basic principle of procedure
in the church. The genius of government he held not to
reside in a mere appointment to office, of certain leaders,
but in an "intelligent, free and reflecting population."

The issue of all this was the advocacy by Campbell
of free discussion as the method by which the church
approach its task. He said:

> The spirit and soul of all reformations is free discussion.
> Every reformation in society has been the offspring of free in-
> vestigation.
>
> . . . .
>
> Along with this, and kindred to it, is the doctrine of equal
> authority in all persons—of equal rights to speak and hear on
> all subjects.[24]

There were occasions when Campbell affirmed that this
principle of free discussion took precedence over all
other claims in organizational and group life, even over

---

[23]*Ibid.*, 1834, p. 314.
[24]*Ibid.*, 1837, p. 577.

any priorities which might be claimed in the name of religion. Following is a typical utterance:

Neither the evidences of the gospel, nor the solemnities of religion; neither constitution of the church, nor the rights of its members; neither the divine right of bishops, nor the value of holy orders; neither the spirituality of the soul, nor the materiality of the body, can escape the ordeal of free and full discussion.[25]

Affirming his regard for the necessity and the utility of free discussion, Campbell said "if there be any doctrine too sacred to be examined, it is unnecessary to be believed."

Campbell thus appeared to seek for the congregation of believers the status of what McDougall calls the "deliberative group." Just as McDougall affirms that in a deliberative group it is possible for the group thought to result in a decision and an action "higher than that which its best minds, independently could have achieved," Campbell said that he had often been led, not only to reconsider, but to abandon some of his former conclusions "on suggestions and objections made by those whose education and capacity might be regarded as of a very humble rank." Such group action, he said, sought not simply the communication of knowledge nor the execution of a program but "the proper development and direction of the human powers."

On the other hand, Campbell made it clear that by "free discussion," he did not mean a method by which the members of the group could pool their common ignorance. He insisted that free discussion meant neither universal and eternal discussion, nor the discussion of every question propounded by every member of the church. To make it mean all topics of all persons at all times, he said, is "rather fanatical than enthusiastical; and directly tends to the annihilation, not of the wicked,

---

[25]*Ibid.*, 1845, p. 50.

but of the church itself.'' Free discussion meant rather
the marshalling of facts, joint consultation or counsel
in arriving at decisions, and conjoint purpose and co-
operation in carrying out the decisions made. The tendency of some to defeat the process of group thought by
using the deliberative assembly to parade their individualism was the occasion of a scathing satire on Campbell's part:

> . . . Of all the tyrants, political or ecclesiastical that have
> stained the historic page with their foul deeds of tyranny,
> anarchy, and misrule, save me from those fierce democrats
> whose shout in the day and whose song in the night, is—
>
> All men are born equal and free—
> In this blest land of liberty?
>
> I have had the misfortune to be acquainted with some few
> good brethren of this peculiar idiosyncrasy, whose prosing
> speeches about nothing would have tired the patience of the
> angel of Job; and whose generous democracy in a favorable soil
> would have flourished into a respectable tyranny. . . . When
> I have seen such spirits rise in a worshipping assembly, to
> ''occupy only a few moments'' with ''a very few practical re-
> marks,'' a chilliness has suddenly benumbed my soul, which,
> had they only imagined, might have instantly frozen the genial
> current of their eloquence, had it but a single element in its
> composition susceptible of any influence from without.[26]

Campbell accordingly set forth certain principles
which he felt would be conducive to the most effective
results in a process of group thinking. These principles
would not be out of place were they to appear in the
current writings of men like Harrison Elliott, Ordway
Tead, Emory Bogardus, and other writers dealing with
deliberative group action. Campbell's remarks on the
subject dealt with questions of convening, revolving, and
adjourning the assembly; with guiding principles for
the presiding officer; and with the decorum of the in-

---

[26]*Ibid.*, 1840, pp. 218-219.

dividual members of the group, including rules of order for the guidance of the group thought.

B. *A Conditional Democracy*

But it would be unwarranted to conclude that Campbell had achieved in his thinking what George Albert Coe calls the "deliberative religious group." The literalistic strain of his thought caused him to invoke too many restrictions for that. It would be more accurate to say that of the three types of religious assembly listed in Coe's category—the religious crowd, the sacerdotal group, and the deliberative group—Campbell's pattern would have resulted in a blending of the latter two. This was a natural issue of a part of his thought resting back on a presupposition demanding the acceptance of truth as a divine fiat, while another part rooted itself in the assumption of unfettered free investigation as the means of discovering truth. "A church is effective," he would have said, "when it adheres to the unchangeable specifications once for all given to the saints." "A church is effective," he would have uttered in the next breath, "when it invokes no restraint whatever on deliberative inquiry."

1. *Restrictions on Women*

The presence of this constant struggle between Campbell's literalism and his liberalism is seen in his attitude toward the place of women in the organization. On occasion he would assert that in Christ there is neither male nor female, and that both sexes are one in all moral, religious, and social privileges and enjoyments. In her book on his home life, Campbell's wife commented on the deference which he showed and the freedom which he allowed her in the home. Campbell also stressed the fact that since there is neither male nor female in Christ, should the circumstance require it, there was no law nor precedent which would condemn a "sister from immers-

ing another female.'' The following is typical of the
great tributes which he would at times pay to womanhood:

. . . God has given to woman the *affections* of the world. She
is sovereign in her husband's heart, and sovereign in the affections of her sons and daughters. And do not these fill the church
and fill the world? The mother's influence in the aggregate,
in church and state, in the family, the school, and the empire,
is really superior to that of the stronger sex. The great moral
heroes of the Bible, from the days of Eve to the conversion of
Saul of Tarsus, and from that to the present time, in the history
of the reformers of church and state, when properly contem-
plated, will appear to have been women, in their influence, direct
and indirect.[27]

On the other hand, there was the historical status of
woman in biblical times which bound his mind. In a day
when the spirit of democracy had led to movements advocating woman's rights, while Campbell was in the
van of progressive thinking on such issues as education,
slavery, and war, he was often reactionary regarding
the place of woman, not only in society, but in the church.
This judgment is forced upon the investigator, not only
by what Campbell advocated, but as well by the reasons
for his advocacy. At every point at which he sought
to restrict woman's freedom, the proof-text which he
sought was a biblical one. Insisting that her rightful
sphere was only ''housewide,'' he asserted that the female sex is ''constitutionally, legally, and religiously,
modest and retiring, in the presence of him whom God
made first.'' And his proof:

. . . The first great fact is, that Adam was first formed, then
Eve. Hence the man is not of the woman, but the woman is
of the man. He is first and she is second. He is senior and she
is junior. They are, therefore, neither equal in rank nor in age.

---

[27]*Ibid.*, 1855, p. 149.

Their office in the world is also unlike. . . . His lordship is earth wide, her queen ship is house wide.[28]

Campbell appealed to the words of the Apostle Paul in an attempt to disprove the claim of political and civil rights for women:

. . . Nor would an Apostle—who commanded and importuned them to be chaste, keepers at home, obedient to their own husbands; to adorn themselves with modest apparel, with good works, with a meek and quiet spirit; who commanded them to marry, to raise and educate children, and to teach their junior women to follow their example in similar pursuits—contradict himself, and stultify his own wisdom and discretion, by telling them, at the same time, that they had political or civil rights and duties, incompatible with these.[29]

In a long and controversial career, Campbell reserved some of his most vituperative language for those who dared to campaign for woman's civil rights:

It remained to the present age of progress—to the ultraists of the last half of the 19th century, in the extravagances of a moodish and fitful paroxysm for what they call equal rights, to perpetrate an inexpiable wrong and outrage against the dignity, the honor, and the happiness of woman, by alluring or dragging her from the nursery and the cradle . . . to legislative halls and political cabals, to wrangle and quarrel and brawl about political rights and wrongs.[30]

As to woman's place in the organization of the church, while Campbell was confronted with the historic fact of the existence of deaconesses in the New Testament church, he found there no justification for her occupying any public place of leadership in the church's services. His objection to woman occupying any such public leadership was based not on his functional principle, not on his judgment that she would not be as effective as men in these positions, but upon what he felt to be the literal

---

[28]*Ibid.*, 1854, p. 204.
[29]*Ibid.*, 1854, p. 205.
[30]*Ibid.*, 1855, p. 149.

biblical precedent and teaching. In an address on "Woman and Her Mission," he said:

. . . If Paul would not have a woman to pray *unveiled* in a Christian church, and if he made long hair a glory to her, because it veiled her beauty and protected her eyes from the gaze of staring sensualists, think you he would have sent her out on a missionary tour, or placed her in a rostrum, surrounded with ogling glasses in the hands, not of old men and women of dim vision, but in the hands of green striplings of pure impertinence! Be assured, not one word of such import ever fell from the lips of prophets or apostles.[31]

But Campbell did not stop simply at enjoining women from any public place of leadership in the organization. In spite of all that he had to say about the church as a deliberative group, he appealed to the divine fiat in support of his contention that woman should refrain from any participation in such deliberations other than by keeping silent:

With a superlative modesty and delicacy, he [Paul] inhibits them from asking a curious question, even in a religious assembly, and charges ministers of the church to cause their women— their wives and their daughters—to keep silence in the churches, alleging that to them "it was a shame," rather than a right, or an honor, "to speak in the church." He would have them to adorn themselves with modest apparel—to ask their husbands at home to instruct them more perfectly in the Oracles of God.

. . . .

Such are the Christian rights, duties, privileges and honors, of Christian women, in the judgment of great and good men, and of Heaven's own officials—apostles, prophets, pastors, and teachers.[32]

2. *Restrictions on Children and Novices*

Campbell tended to classify "novices" with children so far as their relationship to the church was concerned.

---

[31]*Ibid.*, 1856, p. 314.
[32]*Ibid.*, 1854, p. 206.

By the former term, he meant young people and adults who had only recently united with the church. His warnings against entrusting places of leadership to any such increased as he grew older. He constantly complained of "novices" entering the editorial field, and affirmed that the administrative affairs of the church were better entrusted to "experienced ministers of the word than to novices."

One ground of his insistence that many matters be decided by the "bishops" rather than the whole congregation was the fact that the church had many members in its ranks, including children who were "not always competent judges of either law or fact." On one occasion, he even questioned whether the votes of "babes in Christ" should be counted:

> . . . No community is composed only of wise and discreet and full-grown men. The Christian church engrosses old men, young men, and babes in Christ. Shall the voice of a babe be heard, and counted as a vote, in a case of discipline?[33]

Even on general items calling for a decision, Campbell insisted that in the event of a divided opinion, the "minors in age, experience, or numbers, should give place to the majors in age, experience or numbers."

3. Restrictions on the Uneducated

As in the case of his stand on universal education as a prerequisite to universal suffrage, Campbell abhorred the idea of freedom in the church without what he felt to be the qualifications necessary to the exercise of that freedom. He asserted that the age of "factious and ignorant majorities" was about to be identified with the "night ages of the world." He was wont to disdain the "common ignoramuses which constitute the majority," and while he fervently affirmed his faith in the

---

[33]*Christian System*, p. 88.

common judgment of the laity of the church, West properly observes:

> He knew them well, as did Voltaire, but was not one of them. At heart, he was an intellectual who preferred and favored the court of the learned, while he championed the rights of the deprived multitude.[34]

Campbell would have preferred that untutored minds be completely restricted from any place of leadership in the church, but since that seemed difficult, he sought to restrict their sphere of influence as much as possible. "Boys," he said, "and comparatively uneducated men, make better preachers than writers." He did not say to what extent the latter position was determined by his embarrassment over the number of young editors which had begun to compete with his *Millennial Harbinger*.

Campbell had some difficulty in adjusting his views on local autonomy, ordination by the local congregation, and democratic procedure in the decision of the congregation, with his own opinion of the uneducated mind. In one instance, he illustrated with a hypothetical case of a church of thirty members, only ten of whom were males. Of the males, only four were possessed of "common horse sense." But the thirty decided to ordain one of the members to "go into all the world and preach the gospel." Campbell inquired:

> . . . Now the question is, Are they to be condemned or justified who consider this man legitimately introduced into the world as a teacher of religion? Is any other society bound to credit his pretensions or to receive him *bona fide* as a legally authorized teacher of the Christian religion, and ruler in the christian church? Remember the question is not, Had the twenty females and nine males, by and with his own consent, a right to create, appoint, and ordain him a ruler and teacher over themselves: but whether they have reason or revelation on their side, when they introduce him to all the world, as a regularly

[34]Fred West, *Alexander Campbell and Natural Religion*, p. 71.

initiated minister, or ambassador, or teacher of and for Jesus Christ?[35]

None of Campbell's opponents in debate ever asked him a more challenging question than Campbell here propounded to himself. He never answered his own question, and in later years, apparently had forgotten it.

Thus, scorning mere efficiency of performance as the chief function of organization, Campbell conceived the membership of the church in dynamic terms. The membership was not only responsible for fulfilling the church's obligation in its social contract with the ministry, it was to share creatively in the building of the church program. Each member was to be functionally related to the total organization. The deliberative group was conceived as the medium by which the minds of the "brethren" were to be made articulate. The growth of the members in the process of this deliberative interaction was conceived as paramount to institutional efficiency of performance. At this point the "minds of the brethren" came close to rivaling the Bible in Campbell's thinking as the "voice of God."

We have noted specific limitations to this deliberative principle invoked by Campbell on women, novices, children, and the uneducated. His reasons for these limitations were strangely mixed. He objected to woman being as vocal as man in the church on what he conceived to be the grounds of biblical injunctions. He objected to the voice of a child, novice, or an illiterate neutralizing that of a mature, adult, male member on the grounds of common sense. The issue of his thinking was a conditional democracy in the administration of the internal program of the local congregation.

---

[35] *Christian Baptist*, V, 428-429.

CHAPTER FIVE

STRUCTURAL RELATION OF THE
LOCAL CHURCH TO THE WORLD CHURCH

. . . We never said a single word against system in any department of business, literature, morals, politics, or religion. Nor have we ever imagined that there is not a system of both religion and morals taught in the Holy Scriptures. But we are opposed to *human* systems of religious opinions, inferences, or articles of belief; and even to them only when made terms of union or of exclusion.[1]

No more difficult problem confronted Campbell than that of the structural relation of the local congregation to the world church. A large measure of his attention throughout a period of forty years was demanded by difficulties attending this task. No phase of his teaching has been more variously interpreted than his teaching on this point, and his Christian statesmanship has been nowhere more greatly praised or blamed.

Much of this variant interpretation and evaluation of Campbell rests on the fact that in none of his thought did he reflect greater change and growth than in his conception of the relation of the local congregation to the universal church. Most of the factions which have developed in the movement of which Campbell was the lead-

---

[1]*Millennial Harbinger*, 1831, p. 379.

ing spirit have arisen from conflicting views regarding his conception of supralocal church relationships.[2]

That such growth and change did take place is undeniable. In his chapter on "The Founding of a Brotherhood," Smith observes:

> Alexander Campbell . . . was eminently a practical man rather than a theorist. When he sensed the need for an organization, an institution, a magazine, he immediately set about supplying that need. So unusual was his constructive power, his executive ability, that he was remarkably successful in transforming his projects into actualities.[3]

But on the question of the specific nature of Campbell's change, and the grounds on which he changed, there is considerable disagreement. Smith is typical of most of Campbell's biographers when he attributes the change to a shift from a literalistic to a liberalistic approach:

> He had been insisting on the letter of the law. Now he turned his back on his literalistic "either-or" logic, and began to apply the *spirit* of the early Christians to the *life of today*. He would never run counter to the course outlined for church organization, for teaching the fundamental truths of the Christian religion, but he began to understand that in many ways literalism must yield to liberalism.[4]

---

[2]At least four "major" positions have been taken, the adherents of each quoting Campbell as authority. These are represented in general by four journalistic organs as follows: (1) the *Gospel Advocate* (Nashville, Tenn.), which, in general, opposes any supralocal church organization; (2) the *Christian Standard* (Cincinnati, Ohio), which advocates "independent" missionary, benevolent, and educational organizations, which are left "free" to serve where they will without accounting to anyone, and are to be supported by who will; (3) *The Christian-Evangelist* (St. Louis, Mo.), which holds to the principle of agencies under the control of a convention composed of and controlled by delegates from the local churches; (4) the *Scroll* (Chicago, Ill.), which feels that Campbell's objectives can best be achieved by an ecumenical emphasis, working through interdenominational agencies. There are several lesser factions, particularly among those allied with the first group, differing over the church's use of various media in meeting its functions, but all based on the principle of a scriptural "thus saith the Lord'" as an authority for such usage. These variant interpretations will be dealt with further in Chapter Six.

[3]Benjamin Lyon Smith, *Alexander Campbell* (St. Louis, Bethany Press, 1930), p. 177.

[4]*Ibid.*, p. 179.

While the record justifies the assertion of Campbell's growth, there is a question as to whether the attempt to attribute that growth to a shift from literalism to liberalism is based as much on the facts as on a desire to save Campbell from the charge of literalism. The sources quoted in the succeeding pages of this chapter reveal as clear a desire on the part of Campbell to justify his later position by an exact scriptural reference and precedent as he was in his earlier position.

1. *The Co-operation of Churches*

. . . Christians must regard the church, or body of Christ, as one community, though composed of many small communities, each of which is an organized member of this great national organization; which, under Christ, as the supreme and sole Head, King, Lord, and Lawgiver, has the conquest of the whole world in its prayers, aims, plans, and efforts. Hence there must be such an understanding and agreement between these particular congregations as will suffice to a recognition and approval of their several acts; so that the members or the measures of one community shall be treated with the respect due to them at home, in whatever community they may happen to be presented.[5]

The local congregation was to be related to all other congregations in working together for the larger interests of the kingdom, Campbell held, not by the coercion of any external ecclesiasticism, but by the impulsion of an inner spirit of co-operation and sense of unity of purpose. He arrived at this position by affirming (1) the autonomy of the local congregation; (2) the dangers of "independency"; (3) co-operation as the principle of Christian statesmanship.

A. *The Autonomy of the Local Congregation*

The church . . . a society of disciples . . . meeting together in one place, with its bishop or bishops, and deacon or deacons,

---

[5]*Christian System*, p. 76.

as the case may require, is perfectly independent of any tribunal on earth called ecclesiastical.[6]

The issue of Campbell's opposition to all forms of ecclesiastical control was his affirmation of the complete autonomy of the local congregation in respect to its own affairs. In the earlier days of his crusade against religious tyranny, this autonomy seemed to be complete, and the justification for it was what Campbell conceived to be the New Testament pattern. "An individual church or congregation of Christ's disciples is the only ecclesiastical body recognized in the New Testament." Campbell was as jealous and as zealous in guarding what he conceived to be the freedom of the individual congregation of believers as he was the freedom of the individual believer. His campaign against creeds was at once an attempt to free the living church from a dead church, to liberate the local church from an ecclesiastical hierarchy, and to emancipate the individual believer from priestly presumption. His opposition to the doctrine of apostolic succession was of a piece with the foregoing, and his denial of a "direct" call of the Holy Spirit to preach, apart from a social contract with the church, was an attempt to rid the church of what he considered to be the arrogance of the clergy. All this was in the direction of what he felt would be an untrammeled and unfettered freedom of inquiry, first, on the part of the individual believer, and second, on the part of the local congregation. The only restraint whatever allowed by him in his *Christian Baptist* days was his conception of what was "written" in the scriptures. The conflict of his literalistic approach to the scriptures with his reverence for free inquiry is nowhere more clearly evident. The two following statements rather uniquely point up this conflict:

---

[6]*Christian Baptist*, I, 70.

Weak minds are the slaves of old times, and of old customs. They need the crutches of antiquity, and human authority. But men of vigorous minds ask, *what is truth?* not *who* says it.[7]

I am opposed to all innovations. Innovations, with me, are not the creations of last year, last century, nor of the last millennium. Innovations are customs, usages, rites, doctrines that commenced one year after John wrote the word *amen* at the end of the Apocalypse.[8]

As if the issuing of these two statements from the same lips were not cause enough for amazement, the occasion of their saying is stranger still. If the popular idea of Campbell's earlier "literalism" and his later "liberalism" be accepted, we would at least expect to find the second statement in the *Christian Baptist,* and the first toward the end of his career. But the fact is that both statements were made not only when he was at the very peak of his power, but in the very same speech, in his debate with N. L. Rice. Here, again, that unconscious conflict in Campbell stands out, not as the upper and nether bases in the archway of his career, but as the parallel arms of that archway.

But if Campbell did not get away from his "literalism-liberalism," he at least did change in the area of his ecclesiastical atomism. At the time of his revolt from Baptist Associations he specifically rejected all forms of supralocal church gatherings which either legislated, decreed, ruled, directed, controlled, or assumed the character of a representative body in religious concerns. This rejection was categorical at the time, whether the gathering was composed of clergy or laity, or both, and whether it was called a session, a presbytery, a synod, a general assembly, a convention, a conference, an association, or an annual meeting.

It was this complete swing from the need of anything beyond the local church which caused Campbell tempo-

---

[7]*Campbell-Rice Debate,* p. 608.
[8]*Ibid.,* p. 609f.

rarily to deny the need of any missionary agencies, and to advocate that "having the record of God, and every member professing it, it becomes the duty and high privilege of every member to be a preacher of the gospel."

A study of Campbell's writings in the *Christian Baptist* leaves the distinct impression that he believed the local congregation could dispense with everything except a church paper. Since he was already the editor of such a paper, this is not too surprising, but not having as yet conceived the need of such a school as Bethany College, we find him declaring the local congregation free of the need of any kind of theological school:

. . . When the bishop rests from his labors, the church, of which he had the oversight, by his labors, and by the opportunity afforded all the members of exercising their faculties of communication and inquiry in the public assembly, finds within itself others educated and qualified to be appointed to the same good work. The church of the living God is thus independent of theological schools and colleges for its existence, enlargement, comfort and perfection; for it is itself put in possession of all the means of education and accomplishments, if these means be widely used.[9]

It was a simple solution. In his eagerness for the autonomy of the local congregation Campbell, at this time, would have freed it from all Christian history since the days of the apostles, from all Christian theology not expressed in exact biblical "pure speech," and from all Christian forces beyond the confines of the local group. A straight line was the shortest distance between two points, and to Campbell those two points were the final and complete revelation of God in the Bible at one end and the individual believer at the other. But Campbell himself was the mathematician who determined when the line was exactly straight.

[9]*Christian Baptist*, I, 72.

B. *The Dangers of Independency*

. . . Mobocracy may become as tyrannical as an unlimited monarchy. Both are to be eschewed for the same reasons. Louis XIV, though a persecuting tyrant, was no more to be feared than the organs of the popular assemblies in the "age of reason" and the "reign of terror."[10]

Campbell had no sooner sowed the wind of a loose autonomy than he began to reap the whirlwind of a rampant independency. Individual disciples who embraced his plea for religious liberty were too completely emancipated. Many soon became neither responsible nor accountable to the church as a whole. Entire congregations were led into error and factionalism by leaders who gloried in their irresponsibility. In fact, while Campbell gave as his reason for discontinuing the *Christian Baptist* the assertion that he did not want his movement to be labeled by that name, there is reason to believe that he was even more desirous of getting away from the implications of the extreme individualism of those days. Certainly, the selection of the title *Millennial Harbinger* could by no means of the imagination be construed as superior to that of *Christian Baptist* so far as names go. Then, too, there is the fact that immediately beginning with the publication of the *Millennial Harbinger* there was a swing from an emphasis on extreme individualism to an insistence on the need of co-operation. He soon began to flay what he called the little "independent popes" with as great abandon as he previously had the "ecclesiastical popes." In 1832 he wrote:

. . . It is not . . . of the wisdom which comes from above, nor of even human prudence, to countenance every one who wishes to be heard in the church or in society, or to employ all the members of the community either at one time, or in rotation, to preach, teach, or exhort.

. . . .

[10]*Millennial Harbinger*, 1838, p. 128.

We have, indeed, met with some very eager spirits, who, as you say, run wholly unsent and uncalled.[11]

Campbell's ingenuity was greatly taxed with the effort to bring into line those congregations which insisted on exercising their ''autonomy'' to the full. In the year 1845 he wrote:

. . . Let no one, then imagine that he is not as dictatorial and authoritative in doing wrong as in doing right—as dictatorial and self-willed in holding on to the present system, as he would be in insisting upon a new, and, in his judgment, a better one. I make this observation because I have frequently remarked how arbitrarily and tyrannically sometimes men act when they suppose themselves paragons of liberality, generosity, and the love of freedom. I have found sometimes the greatest tyrants among those who boast of the greatest republican liberality.[12]

The period of the early days of the *Millennial Harbinger* was comparable in the history of Disciples to the period of the Judges in Hebrew history. ''Every man did that which was right in his own eyes.'' W. T. Moore says of this time: ''In pleading for liberty the Disciples came perilously close to anarchy, and it required all the tact and ability of the leaders of the movement to bring order out of this confusion.''[13]

The first volume of the *Millennial Harbinger* was relatively quiet on the whole question of church organization, as if Campbell were allowing his readers time to forget some of the things he had said in the *Christian Baptist*. But the second volume began to ring with the plea for the co-operation of churches. And characteristically, he appealed to the New Testament and to reason as clearly in justification of this stand as he had previously when pleading for independency:

[11]*Ibid.*, 1832, pp. 501-502.
[12]*Ibid.*, 1845, p. 60.
[13]*History of the Disciples of Christ*, p. 312.

The churches in every county, have from scripture and reason, all authority to bring their combined energies upon their own vicinity first, and when all is done at home, they may, and ought to co-operate with their weaker neighbors in the same state, and so on increasing the circle of their co-operations, as they fill up the interior, with all light and goodness, until the knowledge of the glory of the Lord shall cover the whole earth.[14]

That Campbell became just as averse to an extreme independency as he was to an arrogant ecclesiasticism is revealed in his attempt to find a position which stood midway between the two. In 1836 he wrote in answer to one of his correspondents:

Allow me, then, to place before you a few of the extremes between which we have endeavored to stand:

Extremes

1. A domestic manufactured preacher.

   1. One especially called and sent by God alone.

2. Theological schools, with speculative, polemic, and pragmatic divinity.

   2. No literary or Bible schools for preachers.

3. Ecclesiastic synods, councils, conclaves, &c., of the clergy.

   3. No consultation or co-operation among the churches of Christ.

4. Hierarchs, or ecclesiastic potentates, in the form of popes, patriarchs, prelates, or other irresponsible masters.

   4. The wild congregational democracy of Cromwell's protectorship.

5. A fixed salary for those who deliver orations on the Sabbath.

   5. No remuneration whatever to those who daily "labor in word and doctrine."

6. Tithes and offerings to the clergy indispensable to membership in the true church.

   6. No use for money whatever in the christian church.

---

[14]*Millennial Harbinger,* 1831, p. 437.

7. Clerical lords over God's heritage, and austere dogmatic rabbis in the christian kingdom.

7. No rule or subordination in the church; no one having any authority whatever amongst the christian brethren.[15]

A variety of problems played a part in this swing of Campbell from his previous extreme independency. Reference has been made to his disappointment over the incompetent leadership which had sprung up under his "no clergy" program, and his swing to a "one-man" ministry. Note also has been taken of the personal visit he made to a church in Nashville, Tennessee, in order to stimulate the church to unseat a pastor whom he considered to be heretical. A third type of problem had to do with his growing conviction that great difficulties attended his absolute principle that the "brotherhood" was to be bound by the action of a single congregation, particularly as regards the ordination of an unqualified man for the ministry, and in regard to the action of disciplining a member. In 1840, answering a question regarding the method of disciplining a bishop for improper proceedings, he wrote:

. . . As the church of Christ in all the world is one church, made up of many independent congregations; when parties agree to refer a matter from one church to another, as to a committee from different congregations, there is no better way of settling difficulties in a free and voluntary one, than by such a reference.[16]

The following year, consequent on the action of a church in Pittsburgh, Pennsylvania, voting to withdraw fellowship from a minority group which he felt to be more truly in line with his teachings than the majority, Campbell came out with a long and vigorous article, "The Right of Appeal," in which he strongly condemned

---

[15]*Ibid.*, 1836, pp. 243f.
[16]*Ibid.*, 1840, p. 238.

the action of the Pittsburgh church, and pleaded for an appeal to a committee from neighboring churches.

Another type of problem which began to occasion alarm was the rapid growth of "general" agencies, such as church publications and church colleges, which came into being as private enterprises appealing to the denomination as a whole for support, but which were accountable to nobody except their founders. Campbell began to decry the multiplicity of such agencies, and his growing conviction that whatever concerned the welfare of the church as a whole should be accountable to the church as a whole was a large factor bearing upon the development of his conception of the co-operation of churches.

C. *Co-operation as Christian Statesmanship*

The independence of any community in Christ's Kingdom is not an independence of every other community in that kingdom, in whatever concerns the interests of that kingdom. This would, indeed, be a fatal error to the progress and prosperity of that kingdom. In what concerns every private community, it is, indeed, independent of, and irresponsible to any other; but it is both dependent on and responsible to every other community, in all that pertains to the interests, honor, and prosperity of all.[17]

For a time it appeared that Campbell, after having wandered into the far country of a wild independency, having almost squandered his movement in riotous factionalism, and having fed on the husks of a barren and incompetent local church leadership, must arise and go back to his early ecclesiastical house. But he escaped this dilemma by the development of two ideas. The first was the drawing of a distinction between what he considered to be eternally written and required and what he felt to be temporally expedient, a distinction expressed in his writings on the "law of expediency."

---

[17]*Ibid.*, 1850, p. 286.

The second was the distinction between the external control of the local church by a higher ecclesiasticism, and the control of a general agency through the internal spirit of co-operation of all local congregations in matters pertaining to the general good. With regard to the first distinction, he said: "Prudence, and not a divine oracle, led the Antiochan brethren to carry up this matter to the apostles and elders in Jerusalem. Consultative meetings in certain emergencies are still necessary."

Campbell thus drew a line between what he felt to be the content of the Christian faith, which was a matter of divine injunction, and the means of dispensing that faith, which he felt to be a matter of human expediency. But even these "expediencies" were not to be engaged in without regard to the scriptures. Where we do not have New Testament precept, he held, we have New Testament example:

. . . Not having the apostles and elders at Jerusalem as a court of appeal, we must appeal to their writings. These and our elders or men of experience are to preside over all our counsels and deliberations in the furtherance of the gospel, in the prevention of innovations, and in confirming the souls of the disciples when assailed by the craftiness of error and the policies of deceit.[18]

But there was a limit beyond which the New Testament example left the church to launch out to the solving of emergent problems, equipped only with human "prudence":

. . . We have a "distinct and comprehensible idea" of the ancient order of things in the New Testament, so far as it is essential to the perfection of church organization; and whatever is wanting to the mere rearing of the tabernacle is to be supplied, not by the traditions of the Fathers—their opinions, their authority or their facts; but to be supplied by, and re-

---

[18]*Ibid.*, 1847, p. 274.

garded as, the dictates of human prudence, varying its arrangements according to the ever-varying circumstances of society.[19]

Thus Campbell arrived at the definition of his "law of expediency":

. . . The law of expediency is the law of adopting the best present means of attaining any given end. But this is a matter which the wisdom and good sense of individuals and of communities must decide. This is not, this cannot be, a matter of standing revelation.[20]

The second major distinction which Campbell drew in arriving at his position regarding the structural relation of the local congregation to the world church was an issue of the question "Who shall ascertain and who shall interpret this law of expediency?" Such ascertainment was to be not by ecclesiastical degree, but by joint consultation and deliberation of the "messengers" of the several churches in a conventional gathering:

These [matters of prudence] are necessarily conventional and demand frequent changes and modifications of dispensation according to the ever varying circumstances and progress of human society. Hence, frequent conferences or conventions, sometimes called "ASSOCIATIONS," become expedient and necessary to give direction and energy to the instruments and means of social advancement.[21]

But in recognizing the common ground between the "Associations" which he had long ago repudiated and his "Conventions," Campbell made it clear that he was not sanctioning their right to exercise what he had previously considered to be an arrogant authority over the local congregation. The local congregation was still free to be bound or not to be bound by their decisions.

Thus, the same faith which Campbell posited in the "brethren" with regard to the administration of the

[19]*Ibid.*, 1843, p. 34.
[20]*Christian System*, p. 93.
[21]*Millennial Harbinger*, 1849, p. 271.

affairs of the local church was posited in the aggregate of the local churches in the administration of the larger affairs of the kingdom. Just as surely as all supra-local organizations were deterred from coercing the local congregation, so all local congregations were under an imperative to voluntarily combine their joint counsels in making plans for the general good. The very nature of the church demanded this. In discussing the "Body of Christ," he pointed out what he considered to be such necessity:

> This institution, called *the congregation of God,* is a great community of communities—not a community representative of communities, but a community composed of many particular communities, each of which is built on the same foundation, walks according to the same rules, enjoys the same charter, and is under the jurisdiction of no other community of Christians, but is to all other communities as an individual disciple is to every other individual disciple in any one particular community meeting in a given place.[22]

Campbell here laid the foundation of his conception of the relation of the local congregation to the world church, and this foundation was the same as that upon which the individual believer was related to the local church. Joint action was required, not by virtue of any authority having been vested in a specially called set of men, but by virtue of the nature of the Christian religion. Love was the very heart of his "law of expediency." All methods of procedure were to be settled according to the law of love and the will of the enlightened majority. In speaking of this principle of church polity, Kellems says:

> . . . Campbell falls back upon a principle which is uniquely his own, his unswerving faith in the correct judgements of the enlightened common mind. In a word, the majority of those who love the Lord must always decide such questions, and the minority, as in all social compacts must quietly bow to its will.[23]

---

[22]*Christian System,* p. 73.
[23]Kellems, *op. cit.,* p. 392.

It is important to note that, with Campbell, the necessity of co-operation arose from the nature of the Christian faith, but the means of co-operation were determined by the "law of expediency." In seeking to establish his principle that the churches were required to co-operate, he wrote innumerable articles in which he appealed to the New Testament scriptures for authority. The "first" Jerusalem conference was a favorite example to which he referred many times, of which the following is typical:

The Acts of the Apostles, from the establishment of the Jerusalem church, is one continuous scene of co-operation among all the churches, and of the necessity of a general understanding of this sort, as well as of the amenability of all public functionaries to the whole Christian community. Passing over minor instances, we have a most striking instance of this sort in the ready subordination of the Apostle Peter to all the congregations in Judea, Samaria, Galilee—indeed to all the churches of the circumcision, then the catholic church, on the imputation of departure from authority and precedent in making himself too familiar with certain Gentile families. In no wise complaining of over scrupulosity on the part of the brotherhood, nor pleading his high authority as the oldest and chief of the Apostles, he submitted to an investigation of his conduct before the brethren in Jerusalem immediately on his return from his tour from Joppa to Cesarea.

. . . .

Peter with the greatest equanimity and composure listened to the accusation and complaint, and not questioning for a moment the right of the church, with the consent and advice of its own elders, to investigate his conduct, to accuse, absolve, or censure, as the evidence should authorize, went into his own justification. . . . He was tried, and found fully justified and approbated in the whole transaction. . . . We rather wonder that a case so illustrious, so replete with instruction, and so much in the character of a grand precedent, should have been . . . of so little use to those who found their church polity on the New Testament.[24]

The interesting thing about this solution of Campbell's is the fact that he not only affirmed the "right" of the common mind to be expressed, both in the affairs of the local congregation and in supralocal affairs, but he affirmed the "rightness" of the decisions the common mind would make. Here is the ultimate of faith in the democratic principle.

In drawing the line between the "revealed" and the "expedient," Campbell came nearer to resolving the conflict in his thought resting on his basic presuppositions than at any other time. For him it was an adequate and a simple solution. That which was revealed was final and complete, and was to be technically and literally adhered to. That which was expedient was subject to change. In the former case, the Bible was the final and complete authority; in the latter case, human reason was final and complete, or to use his expression, "the voice of the people is the voice of God." Here he found a bridge between historic Protestantism and historic Roman Catholicism. In essence he said, in matters of revelation, the Bible is our authority, in matters of expediency, the church is our authority. But in the latter case, he stood with Protestantism in his conception of the priesthood of all believers, so that it was the whole church, not just its ecclesiastics, which was the final authority.

Whether Campbell's resolution of his problem was an adequate one is questioned on two grounds. One is the fact that, in affirming that a convention gathering of the "messengers" or the churches was to determine what was expedient, he had actually made the church the final authority over what is "revealed" as well as what is "expedient." When the church is granted the power

---

[24]*Millennial Harbinger*, 1842, pp. 133-137.

to determine the line of demarcation between the "re-vealed" and the "expedient," it is actually the final authority in both.

The second question regarding the adequacy of Camp-bell's solution is in regard to whether or not it wasn't too convenient for Campbell. The very fact that the margin between the "expedient" and the "revealed" shifted so greatly in his own thought from time to time, and that this shifting was always in accordance with the pragmatic principle involved in his definition of "expe-diency," that of "adopting the best present means of attaining any given end," raises the question as to whether Campbell was not "literal" when it was ad-vantageous for him to take refuge in "literalism," and "liberal" when it was advantageous for him to resort to "liberalism." In either case, he was basically prag-matic. The entire record suggests that he was theologi-cal in his thought when it was convenient to be, and he denied theology when it was more convenient to deny it than to engage in a speculative discussion of it; that he valiantly upheld the rights of the masses when it was convenient to his purposes, and he scorned the ig-norance of the masses when that ignorance obstructed his program; and that he was at once "literalist" and "liberalist" throughout his thought, according to which leg was nearest a solid rock in the stream of his career.

Perhaps this is too harsh, but not only does the record of Campbell's career suggest it, any attempt to evaluate his contribution demands it.

Feeling assured that he had marshalled sufficient New Testament authority to justify his affirmation of the necessity of co-operation, Campbell then proceeded to the task of achieving what he felt to be the more ex-pedient means of co-operation.

II. *The Media of Co-operation*

Need we not schools for the prophets, and conventional meetings, as committees of ways and means, to accomplish our mission as a people?[25]

Though he nowhere made a specific category of what he felt to be the means of co-operation, Campbell earnestly campaigned for specific media of co-operation, both within the religious movement of which he was the moving spirit, and between the churches of that movement and other Christian denominations. Once he had moved away from the extreme iconoclasm of his *Christian Baptist* days, he advocated, and practiced, fellowship in all the major interdenominational movements of his time. Thus, for convenience, the means of co-operation will be classified according to their denominational and their interdenominational characters.

A. *Denominational Agencies*

Some things begin by miracle; others by extraordinary effort. New societies occasionally originate by individual enterprise. But they cannot continue without conjoint counsel, co-operation, and government.[26]

Campbell's greater burden was the task of creating agencies for the expansion, strengthening, and perpetuation of the movement which had flourished under his leadership. For this reason, much of his mature leadership was devoted to the problem of rallying the aggregate of the local congregations of Disciples of Christ to the need of co-operative effort in developing agencies of denominational expansion, although he would not have used the term "denominational." He moved toward this objective by viewing the aggregate of the local congregations in the same setting as he did the individual local congregation, that of their social and geographical

[25]*Ibid.*, 1853, p. 109.
[26]*Ibid.*, p. 109.

milieu. For purposes of polity, he saw not an abstract church, but concrete churches:

... There is but one real Kingdom of Christ in the world, and that is equivalent to affirming that there is but one Church of Christ in the world. As to an invisible church in a visible world, schoolmen may debate about it till doom's day, but we know nothing of an invisible church in our portion of creation. . . .

. . . .

It is, then, a fixed fact in Christianity that Jesus Christ has but one church, or kingdom, in this world, and that this church is composed of all the communities properly called the Church of Christ.[27]

The first step, then, was for these congregations to recognize their social and geographical contexts, and to begin their program of co-operation by practicing fellowship with adjacent Christian communities.

1. *Regional Organizations*

Campbell was quick to call upon the scriptures in justification of a regional plan of organization of the churches:

... The churches had their angels, messengers, ministers, from its first organization. It had its Lukes, its Marks, its Barnabases, its Philips, its Timothies, its Tituses, . . .&c., employed as itinerants and local evangelists. It had its local heralds and its traveling heralds, sent out by one church, and by pluralities of churches and brethren. They had districts of churches, and provincial fields of labor. They had churches through all Judea, in Syria, in Galatia, Macedonia, Asia Minor; churches of the Gentiles, churches of the Jews, churches of the Samaritans— churches whose public character was known and appreciated throughout the world.

Districts intercommunicated with one another; not only churches in one and the same district, but churches in different districts.[28]

---

[27]*Ibid.*, p. 106.
[28]*Ibid.*, p. 302.

This regional plan was to include the total of local congregations in the region, and every individual congregation was under a moral and spiritual imperative to share in conjoint effort, counsel, and co-operation. In referring to Paul's exhortation to the churches of Galatia to make weekly contributions for the saints in Jerusalem, and to elect persons to carry it to Jerusalem, he says:

. . . A grand principle of co-operation is here clearly indicated, which, while demonstrating the individual independence of the Christian churches, as clearly indicates, not merely the propriety or the necessity, but the duty of conjoint effort and co-operation, in all that pertains to the general happiness and prosperity of the Christian paternity.[29]

The "church" district was to be commensurate with the geographical, or political district. That is, the "milieu" was to determine the size and extent of the district:

The churches were *districted* in the time of the Apostles. This is evident from the classifications so frequently mentioned in the Epistles. For example: "The churches of Galatia." . . . "The churches of Macedonia." . . . "The churches of Judea." . . . That they were so districted with a reference to some object, or for some cause, must be obvious. The question now is, For what cause were they so districted? This we answer in the form of a separate proposition—

The churches planted in those districts of country, because of some local and discriminating interest, as well as because of their co-operation for certain specified purposes, were denominated from the districts of country in which they lived.

That churches of certain districts had peculiar interests, arising from their own peculiar circumstances, is evinced on sundry occasions.[30]

As the churches of an area were under an obligation to co-operate, so the several areas, districts, or states were

[29]*Ibid.*, p. 303.
[30]*Ibid.*, 1831, p. 238.

under an obligation to co-operate together, and so on in an expanding circle, until provision was made for the entire needs of the kingdom:

But as we individually, or a particular church individually, cannot intercommunicate with all the churches in the world, we are not compelled to do so. But as far as we can intercommunicate with all the churches in a county, a province, a state, or an empire, in the fulfillment of our social duties, so far, and so far only, are we bound to do so. The measure of our duty and privilege is the opportunity vouchsafed to us.[31]

This regional organization of churches, according to Campbell, was to include all the factors essential to a "perfect system of co-operation." He enumerated these factors as follows:

1. Statistical knowledge. 2. Joint consultation or counsel; not *a council*, but *counsel*. 3. Co-operation, or working together by an executive board. 4. Ordinary or stated meetings in one place. 5. And occasional meetings extraordinary, on special emergencies. I do not mean ecclesiastical . . . tribunals; but deliberative, co-operative, and executive meetings.[32]

2. *Conventions*

In order to emphasize the nature of these "stated meetings in one place," Campbell designated them as "Conventions." Here, again, he made his appeal not only to "reason" but to scriptural precedent, referring to the "great convention in Jerusalem, when the Apostles, the elders, and the whole church in Jerusalem, assembled to decide an existing strife between Jewish and Gentile Christians." The local churches were represented at these "Conventions" by "messengers," for which Campbell again found New Testament precedent.

A historic event in Campbell's effort to develop intercongregational co-operation was an initial "Convention"

---

[31]*Ibid.,* 1853, p. 305.
[32]*Ibid.,* p. 307.

of churches, held at New Lisbon, Ohio, in August of 1831. This meeting, largely motivated by Mr. Campbell, made the following recommendations to the churches:

1. That the churches in each county . . . and all who publicly labor in the word and teaching, should meet annually in one central place for worship and edification, and to consult on the best means of promoting the cause in each county.

. . . .

3. That these county meetings shall have nothing to do with any church business, of any sort whatever; but shall spend the time in public worship and edification, in hearing reports from the churches, and those who labor in the word, of the success attendant on their operations, and to devise *ways and means* for giving greater publicity to the word in such places as may require their particular attention.

4. This arrangement is simply suggested to the consideration of the brethren, to be adopted, continued, or discontinued, as experience may dictate. But as experience is the great teacher of expediency, we would recommend that the experiment may be made, and that thus, until a better arrangement be discovered, correspondence between the brethren be kept up, and information on all subjects of general interest be communicated and received.[33]

But the exclusion of any church business, and the restriction of the "Convention" to "worship and edification, and the hearing of reports from the churches" was very soon found to be inadequate. While Campbell never ceased to caution that these "Conventions" and other "brotherhood agencies" were the media by which the churches co-operate, and therefore always responsible to and under the control of the local congregations, he soon found that such media clearly involved what is known as "church business." The most immediate business of the churches of a district he held to be the "conversion of their fellow citizens." That business, how-

---

[33]*Ibid.*, 1831, p. 446.

ever, was ultimately as broad as the needs of the kingdom of God itself.

In the beginning, these "Conventions" looked inward rather than outward. Their concern was largely with the needs of the local districts, rather than with providing avenues of fellowship for the churches of the district with the wider interests of the kingdom of God. For eighteen years these conventions developed along county, district, and state lines. Finally, in the year 1849, Campbell sounded the call for the first "general" convention:

I am of opinion that a Convention, or general meeting, of the churches of the Reformation is a very great desideratum. Nay, I will say further, that it is all important to the cause of reformation. I am also of opinion that Cincinnati is the proper place for holding such Convention. . . .[34]

This "General" convention was to be set up on the basis of delegated messengers from the churches, not "a Convention of Bookmakers or of Editors." These messengers were not to be "self-appointed," and Campbell stressed the value of representation from as many areas and churches as possible. Beyond, however, suggesting that in the event of certain churches being unable to send representatives, two or three churches, or even a district, might combine to send a delegate, no principle of representation received consideration. In fact, Campbell's idea, and the idea which was adopted by common practice among Disciples of Christ, was more that of a mass gathering than a convention. In all cases the total membership of the host church or churches, and surrounding churches, was urged to register. This was in keeping with Campbell's designation of the council at Jerusalem as a convention, "when the Apostles, the elders, and the whole church at Jerusalem, assembled to decide an existing strife between Jewish and Gentile Christians."

[34]*Ibid.*, 1849, pp. 475-476.

Campbell's plea for a "general" convention was answered in October, 1849, when the first General Convention of Disciples of Christ was held at Cincinnati, Ohio. This gathering was of great significance not only in that it permanently shaped the "convention" system for Disciples, but also because it placed the stamp of approval on certain other media of co-operation. These included one denominational society which Campbell had fostered, one which he had opposed (and which was later abandoned), and one interdenominational medium of co-operation.

3. *Missionary Societies*

The denominational medium of co-operation which received approval at the first General Convention of Disciples of Christ, and which had been fostered by Campbell, was the American Christian Missionary Society. This step marked the completion of one of the most drastic changes in Campbell's conception of church polity.

Despite Campbell's insistent denial that he had changed his views regarding such agencies as missionary societies, certain facts speak for themselves. In the fifth issue of the first volume of the *Christian Baptist,* he wrote:

. . . The missionary work was done. The gospel had been preached to all nations before the end of the apostolic age. The bible, then, gives us no idea of a missionary without the power of working miracles. . . . From these plain and obvious facts . . ., it is evident that it is a capital mistake to suppose that missionaries in heathen lands, without the power of working miracles, can succeed in establishing the christian religion. If it was necessary for the first missionaries to possess them, it is as necessary for those of our time who go to pagan lands, to possess them.

. . . .

Is, then, the attempt to convert the heathen by means of modern missionaries, an unauthorized and hopeless one? It seems to be unauthorized, and, if so, then it is a hopeless one.[35]

In the last issue of the *Christian Baptist* he had begun to ameliorate his absolutist position against missionaries somewhat, but still held to the idea of "lay" missionaries:

I know from a little experience, and from some observation, as well as from what the Acts of the Apostles teach, that the most efficient system, ever yet adopted, was that of the founder of the christian institution of making every man and woman in the ranks *a preacher* in the ancient import of that term. Every church on his plan, was a theological school—every christian a missionary; and every day's behavior, a sermon, either in word or deed.[36]

Three years later, in the third issue of the *Millennial Harbinger,* although not yet crusading for the missionary cause, Campbell's language had taken on quite a different tone:

We have given, we think, sufficient evidence, in fact, and not merely in speech, that we are friendly to all *co-operations of Christians* for the promulgation of the gospel, and the advancement of human happiness by all lawful means; and I have no hesitation in saying, that if all was done at home which our means could effect, we would unite with the whole church of God in any evangelical mission to lands and tribes where the name of the Lord has not been named.[37]

In the light of his earlier opposition to missionary agencies, Campbell was cautious in his swing toward them. During the next decade, other than an occasional mention that some effective means of co-operating in the missionary cause needed to be devised by Disciples of Christ, he wrote little on the subject directly. Indirectly, however, he wrote a great deal. He advocated

[35]*Christian Baptist*, I, 15.
[36]*Ibid.,* VII, 640.
[37]*Millennial Harbinger,* 1832, p. 616.

the work of "evangelists," an office which he equated in function with that of the "missionary." Even as early as the year 1831 he stressed the need of this type of "home" missions:

. . . The churches in each county should, therefore, form an intimate acquaintance with one another, and co-operate first in all means necessary to the conversion of the county in which they are located, and of which they are a part. For example, the churches in this county of Brooke, now amounting to six, besides those on the line, partly in Brooke, Washington, Pa., and Ohio, Va. ought to unite their energies for the conversion of their fellow citizens.[38]

In the year 1840 Campbell began a series of articles on the theme "The Duty and the Means of Supporting Evangelists." In this series, he not only advocated the desirability of the churches of an area, in a county or district, co-operating to secure the work of an evangelist for the purpose of planting new churches, but he stressed the need of the evangelist being fully sustained by such churches, and characteristically appealed to the New Testament in support of his position. In the months prior to the holding of the first "General Convention" in Cincinnati, he became more direct in his appeal for the need of missionaries:

The public interests of the aggregate Christian community in every one nation, province or empire, as much require public agents, whether called evangelists, messengers, delegates, or classified under one all-comprehending designation and denomination, missionaries, or "messengers of the churches," as do the private interests of every particular community require its own special and particular agents or officers.[39]

Campbell finally threw the entire weight of his influence in favor of organized missionary effort, through the medium of an agency responsible to the local congre-

---

[38]*Ibid.*, 1831, p. 436.
[39]*Ibid.*, 1849, p. 269.

gations via their "General Convention," by accepting
the presidency of the American Christian Missionary Society set up by the Cincinnati Convention. The function
of this society was stated in the second article of its constitution: "The object of this Society shall be to promote the spread of the gospel in destitute places of our
own and foreign lands."

Campbell expressed his gratification at the action of
the Cincinnati Convention, and sounded the keynote of
a long series of articles and addresses advocating the
cause of organized missions in the first issue of the
Millennial Harbinger in the year 1850:

> . . . It is the glory, and I trust it will be long regarded as
> the glory, of the first convention ever assembled of our brethren,
> that then and there they unanimously resolved, in the name
> of the Lord, to institute, to organize, and put into operation, a
> society for spreading salvation and civilization over all lands,
> as far as the Lord will give them the means and the oppor-
> tunity.[40]

Characteristic of his insistence on "starting at Jerusalem," Campbell made the rather grandiose gesture of
delegating the first missionary of Disciples to, of all
places, the city of Jerusalem.[41] His second venture in
foreign missionary endeavor, however, was prophetic of
a modern missionary trend. That was the commission-
ing not of a trained Caucasian, but a colored Christian
minister, an emancipated slave, as a missionary to
Africa. On the occasion of his recommendation of this
undertaking, Campbell said:

> It is not for me, nor for any one to choose, but for us all
> to unite, to select, to contribute, and to co-operate in the large
> field of our fallen humanity.

. . . .

[40]*Ibid.*, 1850, p. 76.
[41]The man sent on this mission, doomed from the beginning to failure,
was Campbell's son-in-law, Dr. John T. Barclay. *Millennial Harbinger,*
1850, p. 87.

We have recently had emancipated from slavery, through the
benevolence of brethren in Kentucky, a colored brother, a gifted
preacher of the gospel. . . . Knowing him so well and so long
as I do, I conceive it my duty, before sitting down, to offer
the following resolution, viz: *That Brother Ephraim A. Smith
be requested to report, at proper intervals, to the Corresponding
Secretary of this Board, whatever he may deem important on
the condition and prospects of Liberia in particular, and of
Africa in general, with special reference to the location of a
missionary station in Africa, and that the prayers of the brethren, not only of this organization, but of all the brethren every-
where, be offered to the throne of grace for his safe-keeping and
protection.*[42]

This venture had quite a different influence than the previous one, with the result that Africa has always loomed
large in the missionary endeavor of Disciples of Christ.

Although in his declining years Campbell found it incumbent on him to relinquish other offices which he held
in various agencies of the brotherhood, he never severed
his relationship with the American Christian Missionary
Society. Richardson states that during his closing years
he donated to the Society his interest in the hymnbook
from which he had long derived a considerable portion
of his income.

4. *Religious Periodicals*

The fact that Campbell himself was an editor and
publisher of a religious periodical for a period of forty-
one years speaks strongly enough regarding his faith
in this medium of Christian service. He wrote more
than once of the power of the pen. On the other hand,
beyond the consistency of his faith in the power of the
pen, the only consistency to be found in his attitude regarding this method of church co-operation is the fact
that he was pragmatically consistent. At any given point
in his career, his attitude toward such publications ap-

---

[42]*Ibid.*, 1853, p. 614f.

pears to have been influenced by factors not altogether free from personal considerations.

It must be remembered that the movement which he led was largely generated and shaped by two factors: the popularity of his religious editorials in the *Christian Baptist* and the *Millennial Harbinger,* and his effectiveness in public debate. In religious journalism he was both the spearhead and the peer among Disciples of Christ, if not of the entire country in his day. Few things stand out more clearly in his career than his jealousy of this position. Any hint of any other arrangement he treated with great sensitiveness as an affront to his person. This fact is essential to an adequate understanding of his conflicting attitudes toward a central publication society for the brotherhood.

For a period of years he was alone as the editor of a religious periodical among Disciples of Christ. But the very success of his own venture inspired many of his followers to seek to emulate him. At first he looked with favor on these new ventures, as marking the growth of his movement. But two factors caused him to look with growing disfavor on this spread of religious publications: the threat of rivalry in popularity on the part of some, and the threat of what he considered to be heresy on the part of others.

In the year 1841 he made a proposal favoring a central organ for Disciples of Christ, with the clear implication of himself as the publisher, but whose pages would be open to "all our scribes":

True, indeed, all our scribes might be heard once-a-week in one large sheet, and the proceeds of their labors might go to the education and support of Evangelists. Soon as our College will be in operation we may, perhaps, propose one large weekly sheet devoted to Religion, Literature, and the Chronicles Ecclesiastic and National of the Age; in which a score of writers and their periodicals might be merged, and the brethren and the world have a great deal more for two or three dollars per annum, than from a cohort of pamphlets and monthlies. All our scribes could then deliver themselves free from cost and risque; and if the brotherhood will risque all the expenses, they should have all the profits sacred to their own disposal.[43]

While the article clearly suggested a central religious periodical to be representative of Disciples of Christ, to be owned by them, and whose profits would go to the support of their work, there is one noticeable omission. There is no suggestion of its being controlled by them. While in the case of all other media of co-operation Campbell clearly stressed the need of all agencies being responsible to the "brethren" through their conventions, the implication here is that "all our scribes" would be under the control of the editor, but there is no suggestion of anybody to control the editor.

But the fact that Campbell considered himself excepted from the control of the brethren as a religious journalist does not mean that he did not believe in such control.[44] Later in the same year in which he wrote the previous article, he again called attention to this need:

. . . In a more advanced state of intelligence the time will come, I doubt not, when every community will be as cautious and careful in the selection of its public instructors of the type as of the tongue; and when no one shall so interpret the doctrine of equal rights as to plead that all men have the same right to become what God has never made them, of equal age, intelligence, capacity, and talent—of equal ability to enlighten the public, and direct the energies and action of a great community.[45]

By the year 1852 the crop of irresponsible scribes had got so out of hand that Campbell became vigorous in his denunciation of them:

---

[43]*Millennial Harbinger*, 1841, p. 230.

[44]It is interesting to note that this proposal, never realized by Campbell, and later opposed by him when initiated by others who failed to enlist him at the head, was exactly the basis upon which R. A. Long, a lumberman of Kansas City, Mo., made the gift of the Christian Board of Publication, St. Louis, Mo., to Disciples of Christ.

[45]*Millennial Harbinger*, 1841, p. 324.

As a community we have been the most reckless in choosing our editors, our scribes, our elders and our preachers. I know that in all revolutions, reformations and changes in society— political, ecclesiastical, or moral, this is an accident or contingency always inevitable. Time, however, that great teacher and revolutionist; in other words, human experience, will, in the long run, correct and redress these wrongs and aberrations.

We have had a brood of periodicals, the most voluntary and irresponsible that I have ever known. We have editors just out of the shell of conversion; a youth converted this year, the next a *preacher*; the next a *scribe*, then an *editor!!* What a brilliant climax![46]

This multiplicity of irresponsible religious journals prompted Campbell to again propose the idea of a central publishing house, this time with three journals, a weekly, a monthly, and a quarterly. He insisted that such a program of co-operation "ably conducted, well-sustained, and widely circulated, with reputable contributors from all the land" would be vastly preferable to the readings of "diluted ideas in Homeopathic doses, as we now have them dispensed in invisible pills, in the ratio of one to a gallon of water."

Later in the same year, in a direct attack upon *The Christian Magazine,* published at Nashville, Tenn., and upon the views of its editor, Elder Ferguson, Campbell was unequivocal in his condemnation of "independent" religious journals:

. . . We must have reviews. While we have so many voluntary, and only partially educated scribes and irresponsible editors, we must have reviews.

.   .   .   .

The oracles, public declarations, or printed exhibitions of principles, either moral or religious, according to the experience and action of all communities, *neither are, nor should be, of voluntary and individual creation.*[47]

---

[46]*Ibid.,* 1852, p. 390.
[47]*Ibid.,* pp. 493-496.

But when, in the following year of 1853 the General Convention of Disciples authorized the creation of a "Christian Publication Society," with headquarters at Cincinnati, Ohio, and under a different management than that of Campbell, it occasioned Campbell's bitter condemnation. He was not content to attack it on the grounds that while it was authorized by the convention, the delegates sent to the convention had not been authorized to so act by the local congregations; he pursued his opposition to the point of attacking it for doing the very thing which he himself had previously suggested, viz., directing the proceeds to the support of activities of Disciples of Christ:

As for the Christian Publication Society . . .

1. *As a community* have we, at any specific meeting, *called for the purpose,* decided that such an institution is demanded by our own wants?

2. Is it intended to publish books for gratuitous distribution?

3. If not, can we, without an act of incorporation, institute such a manufactory, and conduct its pecuniary affairs?

4. Under what authority can the Christian Church engage in the manufactory or scale shop, without secularizing it more or less?

5. Can the Christian communities engage in any manufactory or commercial institutions, for the purpose of raising funds to pay preachers, in whole or in part, for their evangelical labors?[48]

The following year Campbell personally declared that Disciples of Christ had no organized Christian publication society:

Because there never were delegates elected by the churches, and sent, instructed by the churches to get up such an institution, from any State or Territory in the Union, so far as I have any documentary evidence.[49]

This was an amazing example of the sheer pragmatism of Campbell's platform of "scripture and reason," for

---

[48]*Ibid.,* 1853, p. 690.
[49]*Ibid.,* 1854, p. 470.

the American Christian Missionary Society, of which
he had accepted the presidency, could have been abolished on exactly the same grounds. Yet, the weight of
his opposition prevailed, and two years later he triumphantly announced that at the anniversary meeting
of the Societies in Cincinnati the Publication Society had
been dissolved, and the "Missionary Society made, what
it ought to be, the Central Point of our concentrated ac-
tivity and liberality as a people."

This ended any possibility of a central publishing
house for Disciples of Christ in Campbell's lifetime, but,
as if he had not already been inconsistent enough, two
years later Campbell advocated a central journal for
Disciples for each state in the union:

> . . . Every State in the Union in which our brotherhood are
> in possession of the talent and the means to sustain an accept-
> able weekly visiter in the form of a weekly paper, devoted to the
> cause we plead, ought to avail itself of its service in visiting
> every family in the State. Our theory has been one good week-
> ly, one good monthly, and one good quarterly Review for every
> State, provided it has the men and the means adequate to the
> demand. If not, one of each for all the United States.[50]

Campbell's judgment thus expressed itself in favor of
religious periodicals as a medium of co-operation on the
same grounds of responsibility to the local congregations
as other media, but his personal sensitivity prompted
him to block the realization of such a proposal. Smith
quotes W. K. Pendleton, Campbell's son-in-law, and his
successor as editor of the *Millennial Harbinger,* as
authority for the statement that Campbell opposed the
publication society because he considered it a slight on
his own work of publication.

5. *Church Colleges*

The history of Campbell's attitude toward the Christian college parallels the history of his attitude toward

---

[50] *Ibid.,* 1858, p. 393.

missionary organization. In the second volume of the *Christian Baptist,* he said:

> One of the greatest blemishes in the character, and one of the greatest defects in the system of most of our literary institutions, is that they are religiously sectarian, and politically aristocratic in their constitution and administration.[51]

But his objection, at this time, to the church college, was not only on the ground that it was sectarian. He appealed to "reason and revelation" in support of the position that men could not make a young man a teacher of Christianity by means of purposeful teaching. "To train any young man, purposely to make him a teacher of christianity, I am always ready to show, to be ridiculous and absurd; contrary to reason and revelation."

As early as the year 1833, however, he had adjusted his position to the point where he commended the effort of a "Brother Bennett" to start a Christian college in Illinois. But in this first utterance of approval of the Christian college, he indicated his belief that the college should be responsible "to the brethren," by chiding the founder for not proceeding by getting the consent of the churches in advance:

> ... It will no doubt be a question with some of them whether you ought not first to have had the concurrence of the Christian church, or "commonwealth of Christ," for whose "benefit" this institution is said to have been got up, before you proceeded in the affair.[52]

In the year 1837 he not only commended the founding of Georgetown College by "brethren and friends of the reformation," but appealed for the support of the community at large "whose interest it is to sustain a college of this independent and truly catholic nature."

Foreseeing the need of a trained leadership if his movement were to survive, Campbell interested some of

---

[51]*Christian Baptist,* II, 152.
[52]*Millennial Harbinger,* 1833, p. 190.

his friends in the securing of a charter for Bethany College to be located on grounds which he donated, located at Bethany, Va. (now West Virginia). The first meeting of the board of trustees was held in May, 1840, and at the second meeting held in September of the same year, Alexander Campbell was elected president of the institution, and instructed to prepare a course of study for the school.

From the day of the inauguration of Bethany College, Campbell vigorously promoted the cause of the church college. A letter to a co-worker in 1850 is typical of his expression in this connection:

Beloved Brother Coleman:

. . . .

Bethany College has paramount claims on me and on all the friends of the cause to which I have consecrated my life. To further it abroad and build it up at home, in raising up men for the field when I shall be absent from this planet, seems to me a paramount duty.[53]

From the beginning, the Bible was an integral part of this curriculum, and Campbell strongly indicated

two erroneous opinions very generally cherished and propagated in Christendom. These are: 1st. *That religious instruction is necessarily sectarian.* 2d. *That morality can be taught as well without religious instruction as with it.*

These I regard as false and injurious opinions, and, therefore, to be repudiated by all sound reasoners.[54]

He further held that neither religion nor moral science can be taught effectively without the teaching of the Bible.

While Bethany College was designed to provide a literary education for all students, it had as a particular goal the training of a Christian ministry. Campbell

[53]*Memoirs of Alexander Campbell,* II, p. 591.
[54]*Millennial Harbinger,* 1850, p. 123.

urged each church, not only to seek out some worthy young man as a prospective student, but to "prepare him for the work, then send him to the field, and support him in it."

While Campbell generally encouraged a growing interest in a trained leadership among Disciples, he complained of the independency of some college movements, and pleaded for more co-operation and order in the planning of an educational strategy:

. . . We are glad to see a spirit, a public spirit abroad, in favor of colleges, as well as of churches. But there is no State co-operation, no general concentration of mind, of counsel, or of effort, as yet exhibited in these great and most important undertakings.

. . . .

Miracles have their day and cease. . . . Individual enterprize has also its day and ceases.

We need general consultation for great general purposes; special consultation for special purposes.

To illustrate this: there are, I believe, three chartered colleges in the great State of Illinois, under the proposed or actual superintendence of our brethren.[55]

Campbell condemned the tendency of churches in a circumscribed area getting up a college, then appealing to the whole brotherhood for support. "Every county has a right to have a college if it propose to build one. But it has no right to call upon another county to assist it."

Yet, in this, as in his journalistic endeavors, Campbell assumed a primacy in that he took the right of Bethany College to appeal to the entire "brotherhood" for support as an accomplished fact. He further assumed that Bethany had a unique mission among Disciples of Christ:

---

[55]*Ibid.*, 1855, p. 579.

. . . It should be made perfectly able to meet the wants of
the whole brotherhood, so far as any one great institution could
accomplish this, and that, consequently, all should proportion-
ally contribute to that end.[56]

Campbell thereby sponsored a campaign for the permanent endowment of Bethany College, and allocated
goals to the several states, and as a stimulant toward an
increased interest, awarded scholarships to be determined by the states of Virginia, Indiana, Illinois, and
Ohio at their annual conventions, and to be awarded to
"one young brother from each of the above States . . .
who has given proof of ability to speak to edification."

But even with the assumption of the right of Bethany
to appeal to the entire "brotherhood," the campaign for
the endowment of the school was a long and arduous one.
The "brethren" were slow to forget Campbell's youth-
ful stand against a paid and a trained ministry. Campbell himself made gifts to the school and, according to
Richardson, bequeathed to it his valuable library plus
a sum of $10,000 in his will. It was not until two months
before Campbell's death that the future of the school,
and with it possibly the whole Disciple struggle for an
educated ministry, was assured through a pledge of
$50,000 by T. W. Phillips, of Newcastle, Pa. Regard-
ing this gift, W. K. Pendleton wrote:

Dear Brother Allen: Your communication of last month,
reporting a part of the liberal contributions which have been
recently made to Bethany College, has doubtless gratified many
of her friends—none perhaps more than the great and good
man who, in the prime of his life, gave so much of the anxiety
of his noble Christian heart to the founding of this institution.
You and I know how earnestly he has looked forward to this
day, and with what unfaltering faith he has cherished the
hope that his brethren would not let this begun work fail for
the want of their support. We have seen how the announce-

---

[56]*Ibid.*, 1852, p. 113.

ment of your success thus far has brought the silent tears of gratitude to his eyes. It has seemed that God was allowing him to see the fruit of his labors, that his heart might be satisfied before it should be still in death. The donation of the noble Brother Phillips, of *fifty thousand dollars,* has impressed him with a sense of confidence and gratitude, as though it had been a personal favor to himself.[57]

The interest of T. W. Phillips, Sr., in Bethany College initiated a dynasty in the training of Christian leaders for Disciples of Christ. This support has now reached to the fourth generation of this family, and at least half a dozen Disciple colleges have been substantially strengthened as a result, and training provided an untold number of Christian leaders. This story is an epic in itself.

6. *Benevolent Homes*

Whether from lack of need, or lack of interest, little attention was given among Disciples of Christ of Campbell's day to the matter of homes for the orphan and the aged. Yet, in what few references Campbell did make to this type of co-operation, he pronounced himself completely in favor of it. The following is expressive of his attitude: "We have always and uniformly borne our testimony in favor of temperance, righteousness, benevolence, and the co-operation of all christians and christian churches in the grand enterprize of converting the world."

The only recorded movements for the establishment of orphanages under Disciple sponsorship received not only Campbell's approval, but his financial support. One of these was the establishment of an orphanage for girls, the other of one for boys:

We feel that this Male Orphan School, projected by Bro. Scott, is, in this great category of good works, full of promise

---

[57]*Ibid.,* 1866, p. 36.

of a rich harvest of glory to God and happiness to man.

. . . .

As my wife took some stock in the Female Orphan Asylum at Midway, I feel disposed to be one of fifty to purchase the site, and to give $500 to endow the Male Orphan Asylum. I will bind myself, or my heirs, when *forty-nine* shares, of $500 each, are paid, to pay to each $500.[58]

In a sweeping statement in which he listed the media of co-operation which he believed should be under a "general superintendency" of the churches, Campbell listed "moral agencies of every sort":

. . . The public press, evangelical missions, domestic and foreign bible translations, religious tracts, and moral agencies of every sort necessary or favorable to the prosperity of the churches of Christ and to the conversion of the world, Jew and Gentile, are probably the objects which might advantageously claim a sort of general superintendency, either by committees raised for the purpose or at the general annual meetings of these local or state associations.[59]

B. *Interdenominational Agencies*

While Campbell's major attention after the fourth decade of the 19th century was devoted toward the stabilizing of the movement of which he was the moving spirit, and many of his specific writings convey the impression that he almost equated his movement with the kingdom of God, there is sufficient data to show that he never lost his interest in the ecumenical church. It is not to be denied that his career as a whole fell considerably short of the grand concept expressed in his debate with N. L. Rice when he stated that he wanted to invoke no test of fellowship which would exclude one follower whom Christ would admit. Yet those occasions on which he evidenced a narrower, more exclusive spirit, are better understood in the light of the continuing

---

[58]*Ibid.*, 1855, pp. 162-163.
[59]*Ibid.*, 1849, p. 273.

contradictions evidenced throughout his thought than
as an indication that he had departed from his ecumenical views. When it is remembered that at times he
started his premises on the presupposition of the literally
fixed and unalterably authoritative language of scripture, and at others as an ecumenical Christian on the
presupposition of the priority of a relentless spirit of
free inquiry, but that, wherever he began, he had an
extreme method of treating each theme as if it were
the one of major importance in Christendom, his apparently irreconcilable positions are better understood.
With the deep faith he had in certain principles of democracy as being indispensable to the effective structure
of the church, it is not surprising to find him devoting
the great bulk of his writings to the development of a
structure which would stabilize the movement which he
led.   But that no more excludes his faith and interest
in an ecumenical church than his tenacious insistence on
immersion as a prerequisite to participation in the ordinances of the church excluded his desire to have fellowship with all Pedobaptist congregations.

That, despite much of his language, Campbell did not
equate his movement with the total kingdom of God,
or even with the universal church, is seen not only in
such utterances as those found in his debate with Rice,
but also in his consistent advocacy of two current interdenominational media of co-operation—the Sunday
School Union and the American Bible Union.

While it is true that in the *Christian Baptist* he in-
dicted such organizations as the Sunday school along
with missionary and other church-related organizations,
he specifically stated as the ground of his objection to
the Sunday school the fact that it was a separate organization from the church rather than on the ground of
its function:

> . . . I never had but one objection to the *administration* of
> the system—never one to the system itself. That objection was

simply to the sectarian abuse whenever any bias was given either in the Sunday School itself or in the tracts or little volumes presented as premiums, by which it seems to me that there was an unfair advantage taken in making an institution peculiarly catholic, sectarian, and partial.[60]

As early as the third volume of the *Millennial Harbinger*, however, recognizing that the Sunday school as a separate organization seemed to be here to stay, he began to look upon it with favor:

We have given, we think, sufficient evidence, in fact, and not merely in speech, that we are friendly to all *co-operations of Christians* for the promulgation of the gospel. . . . Many of our brethren contribute to . . . Sunday Schools, with all their imperfections. Let every man, we say, be fully persuaded in his own mind, and act consistently.[61]

Campbell believed that education, including the teaching of the Bible, was a task of the state. But in lieu of this work being done by the state, he advocated the support of Sunday schools:

. . . If I had a thousand votes in the State they should all go for *universal education* at public expense. I would make the literary and moral education of every child born on the territory of the commonwealth the first and paramount duty of the State. I would in the mean time, in the absence of that provision, encourage Sunday schools, private schools, public schools, and church schools, where they could be patronized. I go for schools of every sort so long as there is one of my neighbor's children uneducated.[62]

He believed that the work of the Sunday school transcended all sectarian considerations, and was a concern of the whole community:

. . . In the absence of a practical and actually existing scheme of universal education, adapted to the genius of human nature in all its intellectual and moral characteristics, the Sunday

---

[60]*Ibid.*, 1847, p. 200.
[61]*Ibid.*, 1832, p. 616.
[62]*Ibid.*, 1838, p. 422.

School system is one of transcendant importance, having claims upon every friend of God and man in the whole community. Every human being has an abiding and paramount interest in the religious and moral character of the society in which he lives. . . . I therefore . . . address myself to, the selfishness of man in enforcing the claims of the Sunday School system, as, in the present order and state of society, of great—indeed, of indispensable importance. . . . The Sunday School institution stands pre-eminently deserving the attention and co-operation of all good men.[63]

Campbell further approved the action of the first General Convention of Disciples of Christ in sponsoring the Sunday school movement, and making provision for Sunday school literature. But perhaps the most complete evidence of his faith in the Sunday school as an interdenominational medium of co-operation was when, in writing to Elder A. W. Corey, he stated that Disciples of Christ probably could do more good by uniting with Sunday School Unions than in getting up schools of their own:

Our brethren, as the burned child dreads the fire, dread sectarianism. But this is, I doubt not, carried too far—especially when it prevents them from co-operating in teaching, or in sending their children to teach, or to be taught, in Sunday Schools. I doubt not that our brethren in all places will see it a duty they owe to themselves, to the church, and to the world, either to have in every church a Sunday School of their own, or to unite with the Sunday School Union in their truly benevolent and catholic institution. Indeed, in a majority of cases they can both do, and enjoy more good in uniting their efforts with the Union Schools, than in getting up schools of their own. I hold it to be rather cowardice than faith to keep away from Sunday School co-operation.[64]

The other interdenominational medium of co-operation which Campbell especially espoused was the American Bible Union. His support of this work began long before

---

[63]*Ibid.*, 1847, p. 200.
[64]*Ibid.*, p. 201.

he advocated even any denominational media of co-operation, and his devotion to its cause never wavered. Even when attacking other church-related organizations in the *Christian Baptist*, he looked with favor on this work: "With regard to bible societies, they are the most specious and plausible of all the institutions of this age. No man who loves the bible can refrain from rejoicing at its increasing circulation."

Campbell expressed the conviction that the church is itself a Bible Society. He early took an active interest in the work of the American Bible Union, and was an early advocate of an American Revision. While he insisted that violence had been done the scriptural meaning of *baptizo* in that the King James Version had simply anglicized the word when they should have translated it "immerse," he disagreed with those co-workers of his who held that this was ground for refusing to support the work of the American Bible Union:

> . . . All the immersionists in America, either are, or will be Bible Union men, despite of all opposition.

. . . .

> I stand strong in the faith of the American Bible Union, and I will give it my suffrage and my aid so long as it faithfully carries out its own maganimous principles. We want, at present, no other Bible Society, than it.[65]

When a group of Disciples in Cincinnati set up to organize a denominational Bible Society, designed to propagate a translation more acceptable to themselves, Campbell vigorously opposed it, and called upon all Disciples to co-operate in the interdenominational, or nondenominational, American Bible Union:

> . . . As to a Bible Society, unless as a monied institution, *we, as a people,* never needed any, how specious soever a Bible Society may stand before us on its own merit. We never had

---

[65]*Ibid.,* 1854, pp. 543f.

a Bible manufactory, so far as I am informed, but were retailers
of the Bibles manufactured by the common Bible Societies of our
country. We were only Bible Society shop-keepers and retailers,
with the additional expenditure of store rooms, clerks, committees, and agents.

. . . .

And why not co-operate cheerfully, liberally, generously, with
them [the American Bible Union], not only or merely in the
work and expenses of the revision, but in making the Bible
Union association the receptacle of every dollar we give for
Bible purposes?[66]

When the Cincinnati Convention of 1849 set up a
denominational "American Christian Bible Society,"
Campbell continued to voice his opposition, until the
year 1857, when he triumphantly announced the dis-
solution of the Society.

While the specific media of co-operation, denominational and interdenominational, which Campbell expressly advocated, centered in those agencies discussed
above, the principle which guided him provided for
emergent needs not necessarily evident in his day. The
following article, written in the year 1835, is reflective
of his position:

Co-operation among christian churches in all the affairs of
the common salvation, is not only inscribed on every page of
apostolic history, but is itself of the very essence of the christian
institution.

. . . .

So perfect is the union, communion, and co-operation under
Christ the living head, that if one member suffer, is honored or
dishonored, all members sympathize with it.

. . . .

Should anyone ask how far this co-operation is to be carried
out, we would answer in general terms, To the utmost bounds

[66]*Ibid.*, pp. 542f.

of every obligation arising from the love of Christ to the church, and from his general philanthropy exhibited in his tasting death for all. In its details it comprehends all that can be done for the purity, peace, and the prosperity of the Israel of God, and for the salvation of all the ends of the earth.[67]

In the light of the emphasis which has been placed upon Campbell as the apostle of Christian union, it is amazing that so little has been said about his emphasis upon co-operation. A survey of his voluminous writings reveals that all he had to say upon the subject of union amounts to only a fraction of what he had to say on the subject of the co-operation of churches, including congregational, denominational, and interdenominational co-operation.

[67]*Ibid.*, 1835, pp. 120-121.

CHAPTER SIX

THE FUNCTION OF THE CHURCH

Order, fully defined, is not simply method, nor simply arrangement, though sometimes so used; but arrangement with reference to design. It is *rational arrangement.* That arrangement may be *rational,* there must be some end in view; and the arrangement must be made in reference to that precise object: therefore, the best order is only another name for the most rational arrangement.[1]

In all the voluminous writings of Campbell on the subject of the church, specific articles dealing with the function of the church are scant. Yet, throughout his writings he took that function for granted. His editorials on church organization dripped with allusions to the church's function.

Further, he held that all arrangement is "arrangement with reference to design." It was characteristic of him to inquire into the purpose of a thing. In his debate with Robert Owen he held that the very existence of a society involved the existence of a social compact:

I am yet at a loss to know what Mr. Owen means by *society.* A society without a social compact, to me is unintelligible. Society is not a number of persons covering a certain piece of ground like the trees in our forests. They must congregate upon some stipulations, express or implied. These stipulations are to be performed, and consequently, responsibility and account-

---

[1]*Millennial Harbinger,* 1835, p. 484.

ablity forces itself upon Mr. Owen in defiance of the powers of his imagination. . . . In entering into society man surrenders a part of his natural liberty for other benefits, which he could not enjoy as a hermit. This surrender he must never recall, nor those benefits must he withhold; they are, therefore, under continual obligations to each other.[2]

Campbell's very approach to the structure of the church was a functional approach. He held that the existence of an organization in the church was for the purpose of aiding the church in fulfilling its functions.

. . . When Jesus ascended up on high, having received his mediatorial position and appointment, he also immediately received and vouchsafed *gifts*—that is, *officers*—for the church. "He gave some apostles, some prophets, some evangelists, some pastors and teachers," for the work of the Christian ministry, for the edifying, or the building up, this great temple "for an habitation of God through the Spirit." These are as much fixtures in Christ's church as our animal organs are divine fixtures in the human body, without which it could not live, much less fulfill its mission in this world. Organs are, indeed, essential to the growth and action of every body—vegetable, animal, political, ecclesiastic or religious. Hence, in all conventions of the people literary, moral, or religious, the first act is organization. Then the body is created, lives, moves, acts, and enters upon its mission.[3]

Using the analogy of the human body, Campbell pointed out that the function of the church organization is to provide expression for the church as a whole in its functioning:

. . . The animal body has in its head, or government, four distinct functions. It has the functionaries of seeing, of hearing, of smelling, and of tasting, for the whole personality. These control all its animal energies necessary to the prosperity, the safety, and the happiness of the whole corporation. Paul goes farther in this figure than we need to go. He makes every

---

[2]*Campbell-Owen Debate*, pp. 392-393.
[3]*Millennial Harbinger*, 1855, p. 373.

member of the body an officer. He has commissioned and uncommissioned officers. And out of all churches he makes one church.[4]

But it would be a serious mistake to understand Campbell as subscribing to that "functional" approach to the church which would look upon it simply as a sort of sociological tool by which man gets what he wants, or by which certain biological hungers are met. The function of the church he held to be not simply utilitarian. It has a divine reference. It is twofold, yet it is one. The breath of the church's function inhales the divine purpose and exhales the needs of humanity. In the mind of Campbell no line of demarcation is made between the two. In meeting the needs of humanity, the church is making itself the instrument of the divine purpose, and conversely, the church must commit itself to the divine purpose if it is to meet the needs of humanity.

In arriving at a clearer conception of what was included in Campbell's understanding of the function of the church, attention may be directed to the way in which he conceived the church as having multiple functions woven into this grand twofold, yet single, function. His writings suggest, first, general functions of the church in the world; more particular functions of the local congregation in the community which it serves, and yet more specialized functions in relation to the members of its own spiritual community.

1. *The Church's Function in Relation to All Humanity*

In the first volume of the *Christian Baptist* Campbell gave voice to a conception of the function of the church in relation to all humanity which he either took for granted, or to which he made allusions, throughout his

[4]*Ibid.*, p. 382.

writings. Referring to the New Testament church, he said:

> They viewed the church of Jesus Christ as the scheme of Heaven to ameliorate the world; as members of it, they considered themselves bound to do all they could for the glory of God and the good of men.[5]

This dual task of working for the "glory of God and the good of man" was conjoined over and over again by Campbell, and with many varied expressions. Whatever the particular functions of the church, they are but tributaries emptying into the Ohio and the Missouri of these two streams, which, together, blend into the Mississippi of the program of the kingdom of God:

> . . . Be it remembered, that as the seas and oceans are made up of drops of water,—so the history of the church and of mankind, is composed of the biography of individuals, and of the records of innumerable small communities, which in their aggregate, develope human nature, and unfold the providence of God to mankind.[6]

It is interesting to note that in this statement the goal to "develope human nature, and unfold the providence of God" is made common both to the church and to the history of mankind, implying an identity of goals for both.

More specifically, this task of the church involves the "converting of the world," which in turn includes Bible distribution and evangelical labor. The means of this was keynoted in a question which he put to the convention of Disciples of Christ of Great Britain in the year 1848: "By what ways and means may the gospel be effectually published in this land?" This preaching of the gospel and the converting of the world was "planned and ordered by the will of heaven." The

---

[5]*Christian Baptist*, I, 6.
[6]*Millennial Harbinger*, 1834, p. 506.

church is thus essentially a missionary, evangelical, and converting institution. Included in this converting function is the task of "Christianizing Pagandom." No area of the earth is to be left untouched, and no fragment of the church can be indifferent to this basic function. In short, the whole world is the field of the whole church:

> The churches in a country, a province, or a State, may, indeed, by their joint consultation, contributions and co-operation, do much to evangelize their respective districts. But the world is the field of the whole church, and the whole church ought, as far as in its power, to co-operate in the great cause of sending the gospel to all nations. She fails in her duties to her Lord, and in the fulfillment of her mission into the world, unless she puts forth her whole power, according to her means, in this transcendent enterprize.[7]

Every member of the church is embraced in this commission, and every creature in the world is the object of its philanthropy. Those members who cannot go into the farthest evangelical fields in person are under an imperative to send those who can go. All proper auxiliary societies of the church owe their existence to this need of diffusing Christian knowledge, and for carrying out more effectively this grand intention of converting the world.

And what is this "gospel" whose preaching is a function of the church? It is the "gospel of the grace of God, as delivered to us by the Lord Jesus Christ in person, and by his divinely constituted apostles, prophets, evangelists." The preaching of the gospel consists in the declaration of facts, and the proving of them. And what are these facts? They are a "history of the life of Jesus Christ, his sayings and doings, his death, burial and resurrection as attested by the Prophets, and witnessed by the Apostles." They consist of the

---

[7] *Ibid.*, 1851, p. 605.

. . . Original gospel, with its evidences, and with all the claims upon the understanding, the conscience, and the heart of every alien, every sinner, of every rebel, to whom they can gain access. Being a matter of fact, a matter of faith, and not a doctrine, not a philosophy, not a theory, not a speculation, it is to be simply stated, or as Paul said, *declared*, with all earnestness, and sincerity as a positive message sent from the Lord Jesus Christ, emanating from the everlasting philanthropy of his Father and our Father, from his God and our God.[8]

The conversion process which is the object of the preaching of this gospel includes, according to Campbell, the reception and the acknowledgment of Jesus as the Lord Messiah, the Savior of the world, the putting of oneself under his guidance and the guidance of the divine word, and the taking to heart of the extension of the knowledge of his name. But, in keeping with his conception of the twofold function of the church, this object has a human as well as a divine reference, and includes the adoption of a virtuous and godly life, and the illumination and reformation of the world. It includes the "advancement of human happiness by all lawful means." It is, in fact, the "drama of redemption." It comprehends "all that can be done for the purity, peace, and prosperity of the Israel of God, and for the salvation of all the ends of the earth." The supreme task of the church is therefore to put forth all its energies, and all its means of doing good "while ever there is good to be done, at home or abroad, until the knowledge of the glory of God cover the whole earth as the waters cover the bosom of the ocean." The church, then, with Christ as its head, has "the conquest of the whole earth in its prayers, aims, plans, and efforts."

In the mind of Campbell, the procedure by which the church approaches the fulfilling of its function in the world is both clear and simple:

---

[8]*Ibid.*, 1865, p. 515.

There is, first, the oral preaching of the gospel to the world. In the second place, there is the planting of churches by the labors of evangelists, and setting them in order. In the third place, there is the edification of the church by its eldership— the elders, pastors, and teachers. In the fourth place, there are the means of doing this in the way of translating, printing, and circulating of the Holy Oracles.

In the fifth place, there is the erection of church houses, usually called meeting-houses, or Christian synagogues. In the sixth place, there are public conventional meetings, at certain times and places, for the consummation of these great works. . . . All these are enjoined upon us, either in the form of precepts, of precedents, or of suggestions by the authorized ambassadors of Christ.[9]

This procedure pointed to more particular applications of the church's function in the local communities where the "churches" were established.

2. *The Church's Function in Relation to the Community*

Just how far Campbell believed that the church's task of "glorifying God" is commensurate with its task of "unfolding the nature of man" is seen in gleaning his references to the function of the church in the community. The church must adapt its program to meet the "exigencies of the times." In relating the church to the community Campbell would include in its functions all that worked for the total well-being of humanity, never forgetting that this is at once God's purpose and program.

The divine and human references of the church's function wedded together in divorceless union true morality and true religion:

. . . In spite of scepticism, deism, atheism, or pantheism, there is an inseparable connexion between true morality and true religion. It is religion, the religion of the Bible, as we all agree,

[9]*Ibid.*, 1851, pp. 508-509.

that suggests the master motives and controlling impulses to
morality. It is the belief of the Self-Existent, of the Eternal
Majesty, whose omniscient eye pierces night and day, earth and
sky, time and eternity. . . . Apart from this belief, morality is
mere policy or public utility, or the hypocrisy of a polite education.[10]

The common function of introducing a "purer, a
brighter, and a happier day on our country and the
world" belongs to all sects of the church, and, Campbell
said, challenges them to recognize the existence of a
common religion in our culture:

Can we not have a common religion and free ourselves from
this incubus that paralyzes every effort to introduce a purer, a
brighter, and a happier day on our country and the world?
Protestants will all say, We may—we can—we ought. Let them
say, We will—we shall; and it is done. Meanwhile let the
simple facts, without the theories of religious belief—let the
belief of God, of Christ, of immortality, of eternal life and
eternal death, without any partizan theory—let temperance,
righteousness, benevolence, and judgment to come, without
metaphysics, be inculcated on one—on all, by every parent,
guardian, teacher, and in every school, and college, and university in our land; and we may have—nay, we shall have, quite
another and a better state of things.[11]

Campbell even went so far as to say that this common
Christianity embraces everything elementary with regard to piety and morality, and on which all good men
in all denominations are agreed:

It is also becoming more and more evident, that, notwith-
standing all our sectarian differences, we yet have something
called a *common* Christianity;—that there are certain great
fundamental matters—indeed, every thing elementary, in what
is properly called piety and morality—in which all good men of
all denominations are agreed; and that these great common
principles and views form a common ground on which all

[10]*Ibid.*, 1836, p. 597.
[11]*Ibid.*, p. 597.

Christian people can unite, harmonize, and co-operate in one great system of moral and Christian education.[12]

So far as the community is concerned, the dual task of glorifying God and redeeming mankind requires the church to function in two pre-eminent ways: it serves as the spokesman of God, and it stands as the critic of the institutions of society. With regard to the first, its claim to divine sanction rests not on ecclesiastic preference, but is an expression, with Campbell, of his faith in the rightness of the decisions of the enlightened Christian mind: "The voice of the whole church is the voice of God—because it is the voice of reason and of truth."

The function of the church as a critic of the social institutions is best seen in the way in which Campbell himself criticized those institutions in the name of the church. No institution, not even the church itself, was immune.

In its function of "unfolding human nature," the church commands every man to think, to act, and to feel for himself. It is, therefore, the only perfect cradle of human liberty on the earth, the only proper school of equal rights, and is, therefore, necessarily, a critic of our political and economic institutions. In founding a new kingdom, with its converting program, Jesus "establishes the doctrine of personal liberty, of freedom of choice, and of personal responsibility, by commanding every man to judge, reason, and act for himself." The church prescribes the only rational foundation of liberty ever submitted to the human understanding.

But Campbell would have the church articulate its criticism of our social institutions not only vocally, but supremely by its example. In this way he saw the church as the vanguard of civilization's struggle for racial equality and understanding:

---

[12]*Ibid.*, 1841, p. 445.

. . . We have learned from the holy Apostles, and even reason enlightened by the lamp of Heaven, teaches us, that "in Christ Jesus there is neither Greek nor Jew, circumcision nor uncircumcision, Barbarian, Scythian, bond nor free;" and we may add, neither black nor white; "but Christ is all in all." In political society, ranks, and classes and casts are necessary, and may be necessary to the good order and government of the world; but if there be on earth a spot of ground, on which all ranks and degrees of men, all classes and casts of society should feel, confess, and exhibit that they stand on equal ground—it is in the temple of God.[13]

Campbell believed that as the church comes to a more thorough understanding of its mission and message it will set itself more completely to the task of solving the racial problems of society.

As critic of the social institutions of mankind, Campbell held that it is a function of the church to contrast its gospel with the genius of war. This criticism must not be content with negative declarations, but must be ready with a positive program designed to secure peace. Campbell advocated the settling of international disputes by arbitration, and called upon Christian nations and Christian states to adopt such measures.

But Campbell portrayed the role of the church as critic of social institutions most clearly in its opposition to those forces which make for the decadence of the family, and in its advocacy of an adequate program of education. With regard to the former, he wrote:

We have nominal Christian parents with almost Pagan families in all churches of the land. We mean that there are many professed Christian parents who almost wholly neglect their families, and suffer them to grow up without religious or moral culture. . . . We want, and must have, a radical and thorough reformation in family religion and family education.[14]

---

[13]*Ibid.*, 1835, p. 17.
[14]*Ibid.*, 1837, p. 538.

With regard to education, Campbell believed it not
only to be a function of the church to criticize what he
felt to be a woefully inadequate curriculum in the public
schools, but a common function in which all sects should
pool their efforts. He held that until we can secure
universal education "we shall be wanting in the grand
elements of a Christian community." But he felt that
one of the chief contributions of the church is to supply
that element of the curriculum which is indispensable
to any proper education. In pleading for the Bible as
an essential element of the educational curriculum,
Campbell came as near gathering into one sentence the
various "goods" for which the church strives as he
did at any time, and here, only by implication:

A school or a college without the Bible, we may safely
alledge, is rather heathenish than either Christian or philosophical. It is not in accordance with the wants of society,
with the genius of human nature, with the interest of the State,
with the progress of civilization, with the advancement of the
church, with the glory of God, or with the happiness of man.[15]

But while Campbell conceived the church as having
a general function in glorifying God by working for
the good of all humanity, and more particular functions
in the community as it serves as the spokesman of God
and the critic of the social institutions, he saw it as a
community within a community, and, as such, saw it as
having certain specialized functions in relation to the
members of its own body.

3. *The Church's Function in Relation to its Own Members*

In addition to its functions in the community and in
the world, the church, said Campbell, is charged with
"its own discipline and the oversight of its members."
Its individual members and congregations are thus "sub-

---

[15]*Ibid.*, 1850, p. 174.

ject to the call of one another,'' and should therefore be
"subordinate to one another in everything that the common interests of the whole community may require.''

The church, for the sake of all its other functions,
has an institutional one, "the necessity of connected and
concentrated action in the advancement of the Kingdom,''
and "the spreading of the knowledge of truth.'' This
includes the functions of "preaching, baptizing, and
teaching.'' It necessarily also includes the creation of
officers and workers to direct the church in its varied
functions, the "choosing and setting apart of qualified
persons for all its peculiar services, necessary to its own
edification and comfort, as well as to its usefulness in
the world.'' It includes the planting of new churches,
and "the better supplying of young and infant communities with help—with more adequate assistance.''
It embraces "general and organized co-operation in all
the ways and means of more energetically and system-
atically preaching the gospel and edifying the church.''
It means the extension of the bulwarks of the church,
from city to city, and from country to country. It means
devotion to "the honor, dignity, and influence of Christianity in the world.'' It involves joint action in "the
dissemination and support of the gospel, and mutual
encouragement of one another in the work of the Lord.''

The institutional function of the church, said Campbell,
is preventive as well as projective. It involves "the prevention of innovations, and confirming the souls of the
disciples when assailed by the craftiness of error and
the policies of deceit.'' It includes "the curbing of error-
ists, factionists, and party men.''

But the church's function in relation to itself is more
than institutional. It has the function of supplying its
members with special privileges, the imparting to them
of special blessings. It is to bring its message to bear
upon them "in its sublime and glorious doctrine and
bearings, and thus the members are still educating or

building up in the most holy faith." It is to provide an avenue whereby they can "worship God through the one Mediator." It is to be an "ecclesia," where an organized body of Christians may meet "in one place, for Christian doctrine or learning, for mutual edification, social worship, and spiritual enjoyment." Its function is to create a "spiritual community—a community of persons intelligent, believing, loving, fearing and serving God in the hope of eternal life." It is to help Christians "in a church capacity" to "move in all spiritual and moral good." In order more effectively to do this, the church is to function as a "Missionary, Temperance, Bible, Education, and Philanthropic Society."

But fundamental to this entire function of "growing in grace," the church, believed Campbell, is to provide and to be a fellowship. It is to "dispense the supper as well as pray for all men." But this is simply a symbol of that more thoroughgoing fellowship afforded by the church for its members:

> . . . *What is the central idea of communion?* Is it *faith?* Is it *doctrine?* Is it *philosophy?* Is it *ecclesiastical polity?* Or is it all these together? These, indeed, are of transcendent importance to any other questions connected with church polity or church institutions.
>
> .   .   .   .
>
> *Koinoonia* is the Greek word represented in the Christian Scriptures by the words *communion, contribution, communication, distribution,* or *fellowship.* . . . There is, evangellically contemplated, the same communion in each and every one of these Divine institutions;—in prayer, in confessing our sins, in praise, in thanksgiving, in sanctifying the Lord's day, and in eating the Lord's supper. We commune in each and every one of these. These one and all being equally Divine institutions, are equally means of our growth in grace.[16]

The apex of this fellowship Campbell held to be fellowship with the divine. One of his indictments against

---

[16]*Ibid.*, 1863, pp. 206-207.

written creeds was that they would not permit the church to "receive into communion all whom God would receive into heaven," and he affirmed that "God loves his children more than our creeds, and man was not made for the Bible, but the Bible for man."

But even this aspect of the "fellowship" is at its richest when the "brethren" have fellowship together and with God in the working out of his purposes, when the members of Christ's body, from areas large and small "like springs in the desert, rivulets and streams, flow together, and carry on their broad bosom the ark of salvation to the rescue of a world sinking to ruin, in ignorance, guilt, and bondage."

The most glorious aspect of the church's specialized functions in relation to its members Campbell held to be the creative. Desiring to govern human action without letter, motivating its members to "serve in newness of spirit, and not in the oldness of the letter," its congregations are designed as "schools of moral excellence." Its genius is in presenting to the human mind the loftiest and most comprehensive principles which can incite to moral action:

. . . Christianity discovers principles of action which no political, moral, or religious relations hitherto known, could originate. These new relations, and these new principles of action, are stronger than death, more triumphant than the grave, and lasting as eternity. The discovery of a new, gracious, spiritual, and eternal relation, and correspondent principles of action, moral and religious, is the basis of that association called the christian church or congregation.[17]

The person of Christ and the principle of love are, according to Campbell, integral to this creative function of the church:

All the principles of obedience, all the principles of action, how numerous soever we may suppose them, are reducible to

[17]*Christian Baptist*, VI, 501.

one great principle, sometimes called the new commandment. . . .
The Christian institution creates in the heart of man this love.
It gives it birth and being. It is a love of a higher order, of a
sublimer genius, than any former age or economy could produce.[18]

But that principle of love is given meaning, and is
made concrete in a Person, the Person of Jesus Christ.
The noble function of the church is to impel men to
respond to such a principle and to such a Person:

. . . This is the grandeur of the christian scheme, that it sets
men in love with such principles and such a person; that it
makes virtue and goodness almost as necessary as the Pagan's
fate, and yet as free and easy as the action of the heart or the
labor of the lungs.[19]

It is this function of the church which most clearly reveals the indispensability of its work, according to Campbell:

. . . The gospel—yes, the gospel, the proclamation of God's
philanthropy, as it was uttered by the Apostles on Pentecost,
or in any one of their converting discourses, would have been,
and still is, alone sufficient to produce those principles in the
heart which issue in all holiness and in all morality.[20]

Surveying, then, the general function of the church
in glorifying God and working for the good of all humanity; the particular functions of serving as God's
spokesman and as a critic of the social institutions; and
the specialized functions of perpetuating its institutions,
and of helping its members to ''grow in grace,'' Campbell affirmed that if the church had not been hindered
by its own strife and by a narrow spirit

. . . the glorious gospel of the blessed God would long since
have permeated the whole human race, gladdened every land,
visited every domicil of man, and elevated, adorned, beautified,

---

[18]*Ibid.*, VII, 655.
[19]*Ibid.*, p. 656.
[20]*Ibid.*, p. 658.

and beatified all the families and tribes of humanity, and would thus have made the wilderness and the solitary places glad; and have caused the broad moral deserts of the earth to rejoice, and to blossom as the rose.[21]

Conclusion

Considering the conflicts revealed in Campbell's thought regarding the nature of truth, the surprising thing is to find so much of his educational philosophy in harmony with the more valid principles of religious education today. To speak of his "educational philosophy" is acceptable, for he never admitted a dichotomy between "education" and "religious education." To him any program of education worthy of the name necessarily included religion as an integral factor in the curriculum. The weaknesses which he saw in a schizophrenic educational system split into so-called "religious" and "secular" personalities were not simply passing problems of the early nineteenth century. Thoughtful students of our times see in them some of the chief limitations to our twentieth-century culture. They see the need of helping the pupil, in the words of Stewart Cole, to "bring his various discoveries about life into a cosmic perspective of life."[22]

Campbell not only joins with our contemporary leaders in his recognition of this need. He *is* our contemporary in his recognition of many of the problems attendant upon the achievement of this ideal. He recognized and stressed the existence of a common religion in our culture. He approached T. G. Soares' dream of a community-centered system of education[23] in the urgency with which he stressed the importance of nursery and adult schools, and in his conception of the "life-centered" nature of effective education, as well as in

[21]*Millennial Harbinger*, 1857, pp. 253-254.
[22]*See* Stewart Cole, *Liberal Education in a Democracy*, p. 230.
[23]*See* T. G. Soares, *Religious Education*, pp. 150-180.

his insistence on looking on the Sunday school as a concern of the entire community.

While formulating no "theory of identical elements," his insistence that it is an error to suppose that in "cultivating the intellect we are cultivating the moral sentiments and feelings" was prophetic of E. L. Thorndike's experiments in the transfer of training. His conception of the nature of personality as being "insatiable for knowledge, fellowship, happiness, and growth" is not inconsistent with F. H. Allport's definition,[24] and his understanding of the function of education as being that of developing man's free powers for more effective functioning in his relations to both God and man is supported by Hugh Hartshorne's figure of the levels of functioning from the automatic to the infinite.[25]

Campbell's conception of Christian nurture was for the most part in harmony with Bushnell's theory,[26] which in turn has been validated by history and by modern educational psychology. His position was a protest against the same theological extremes which aroused Bushnell's protest, and he was just as suspicious of the "conversionist" theory of inducting children into the Christian faith. On the other hand he was equally suspicious of any precommitment of the child's faith, and thus he was led into a divergence from Bushnell's view. Perhaps the most satisfactory solution is the practical one which some communions have found—one in which the child grows up in the matrix of the family life as a Christian, not knowing himself to be anything else, and yet in which provision is made for a focal point of decision at which time he can consciously and publicly organize his life around his basic loyalty to God.

But the instance of Campbell's divergence from Bushnell's theory of Christian nurture was one of the few

---

[24]See F. H. Allport, *Social Psychology*, p. 100.
[25]See Hugh Hartshorne, *Character in Human Relations*, pp. 241-246.
[26]See Horace Bushnell, *Christian Nurture*, pp. 136ff.

occasions on which he permitted the legalistic strain of his theology to intrude into his educational philosophy. The result is that, on the whole, he is to be found at his best in his educational philosophy. Here his creative conception of the validity of free inquiry for the most part predominated, and blended with just enough of his authoritarianism to lead him to hold to the principle of growth guided by constant divine values, and thus to escape the static nature of a pure transmissive education on the one hand and the academic anarchy of certain extreme emphases of some "progressive" educators on the other. While holding that it is always detrimental to the ascertainment of truth to allow our "previous conclusions to assume the position of fixed and fundamental truths, to which nothing is to be at any time added," he at the same time never swerved from his belief that there is an indispensable content of Christian faith to be shared.

It was Campbell's educational method which suggested his approach to the major problems to which he gave his attention. In his insistence on the need of universal education as a precondition to universal suffrage he struck a chord which we may not theoretically embrace but which we must practically endorse. His educational approach to the problem of international peace, his advocacy of an international court of arbitration, and, more especially, of a Christian Internationalism, was prophetic of the birth of both the United Nations and the World Council of Churches. To what extent the acceptance of his proposals for the gradual emancipation of slaves might have averted a tragic conflict between the States is somewhat hypothetical, but there can be no question as to his approach to the problem being an educational one.

It is not surprising, therefore, to note that Campbell's educational method sounded his approach to the struc-

ture and function of the church, and that, in turn, his conception of the structure and function of the church
should have an important bearing on the church's educational program.

To begin with, attention is drawn to the fact that a
basic ground of his objection to what he considered
to be the tyranny of ecclesiasticism was what he felt such
tyranny did to the principles of personality and of
growth. It is also important to note that he enlarged
the tyrannies he opposed to include far more than an
ecclesiastical structure, that, in fact, they came to include all the pedagogical techniques by which some men's
minds are held in subjection to others. The fact that,
at this point, he subjected himself to the criticism of
sinning against his own ideal points not so much to
limitation in that ideal as to a limitation in himself as
a person.

It would, of course, be both naive and presumptuous
to suggest that any of the educational positions of
Campbell delineated above represent a distinctive "contribution." Too many factors are usually present in
the changing trends of our culture to justify such a
claim, and too many others have shared, at least in part,
his views. Some, like Bushnell, have, at given points,
gone further in impelling others to share their views.
It would be more acceptable to say that Campbell, as
the most influential figure in America's largest indigenous religious movement, has made an impact rather
than a distinctive contribution. And that impact is perhaps most strongly felt in his attempt to conceive a
church structure which scorns the techniques by which
some men's minds are held in subjection to others. This
impact holds in spite of the fact that the very groups
most influenced by Campbell have violated his principles
of freedom just as surely as did he; for amidst all
the perversions of his principles of freedom there has
never ceased to exist that resurgent quest for a type of

religious assembly which is enriched by the free interplay of minds and hearts, the minds and hearts of the
"brethren," which conceive the church essentially as a
fellowship, and in which the Christian principle of love
impels toward co-operative action with all other Christians while scorning ecclesiastic coercion. This conception of the creative function of the deliberative group,
of the educational value of the participation of the congregation in the creation as well as the execution of the
program, and of the conjoining of individual initiative
with co-operative action as the basic principle of procedure in the church's organizational life is in accord
with acceptable educational practice, and approaches
Coe's "deliberative religious group."[27]

Further, Campbell sounded the advance for religious
education in some of the educational strategies which
he suggested for the church. In insisting on the church
taking an account of the social context in which it exists
he heralded the work of men like Kincheloe,[28] Leiffer,[29]
and others. His proposal to send an American Negro
Christian as a missionary to Africa was a forerunner of
the present trend of placing an increasing responsibility
on Christian nationals in the mission field. His conception of the call to the ministry as being in the nature
of a social contract with the church, functionally understood, has received increasing support. His suggestion
of the value of using religious case histories is one
which commends itself to us as meritorious for our
times. But the one point at which he might have made
an indispensable contribution to religious education was
one on which he unfortunately changed his strategy.
That was when he conceived of the church as a unit, and
advocated a unified program in which the church, as a

[27]See Geo. A. Coe, *The Psychology of Religion*, pp. 130-134.
[28]See S. C. Kincheloe, *The American City and Its Church*.
[29]See M. H. Leiffer, *City and Church in Transition*.

church, perform the functions of the Sunday school, the Missionary Society, and so forth, only to abandon this position later on practical grounds. While his desire to co-operate with existing agencies was commendable, it is quite possible that if he had clung to his original insight regarding a unified church program, he might have made a greater contribution to the religious world than in some of the other ways by which he so earnestly sought to make a contribution. The current struggle to overcome a fractured church program, the so-called horizontal type of church organization, might have been advanced by many decades, and Alexander Campbell might be better known to us as the forerunner of the modern religious education movement than as a theological iconoclast.

Seldom has a religious communion more thoroughly adopted the personality of its chief religious leader than have Disciples of Christ. Disciples of Christ today bear the stamp of Campbell's personality, including his strength, his weaknesses, and his contradictions. Even at the level of the specific techniques of organization which he espoused, the best Christian statesmanship among Disciples is as marked for its inability to devise an adequate principle of conventional representation and a satisfactory philosophy of ministerial ordination as it is for its ability to share in the development of an ecumenical Christianity and to achieve the reality of an individual religious organization which is both creative and dynamic.

Perhaps the first task of Disciples of Christ should be that of getting over their "Campbell consciousness," of shaking off the Campbell personality, by actually getting to know Campbell and themselves objectively and critically. This would include an abandonment of the tendency to approach Campbell from the standpoint of either praise or blame, and the replacing of this tendency with an attempt to understand him, to become aware of his limitations, and to share his insights.

Such a venture would necessarily include a recognition on the part of the divergent groups, particularly the four major divergent groups, that none of them has an exclusive right to claim Campbell as an authority. It would involve a recognition, in short, of the fact that all of them have a right to claim Campbell as an authority, for Campbell was at times just as inconsistent in his thought as they are divergent in theirs. It would be difficult for the *Gospel Advocate* to voice any more bitter opposition to supralocal church organization than did Campbell in the days of the *Christian Baptist*. While it is true that Campbell later sought earnestly to lead his group away from such ecclesiastical atomism, it is just as true that there is no record of his having ever retracted his opposition to instrumental music in services of worship, or to ornate edifices of worship. The *Christian Standard* would have real difficulty finding authority in Campbell for the support of independent missionary, benevolent, and educational organizations, or even of independent religious journals. Perhaps no greater violence could be done to Campbell than to represent him as favoring any religious enterprise or group which is not accountable to the brethren through their conventions. On the other hand, it is also evident that the authoritarian view of the scriptures entertained by the *Christian Standard* and the independent groups which it espouses is a view for which they have as much authority in Campbell as any other which can be credited to him. *The Christian-Evangelist,* and with it the bulk of Disciples, can find authority in Campbell for every medium of co-operation which they support, either by overt act or in principle. This applies to both denominational and interdenominational media of co-operation. They, too, can find in Campbell as much authority for a progressive conception of revelation, and for an open-minded spirit of inquiry, as the independents can find for an authoritarian view of the scriptures. On the other hand, the attempt to maintain that this attitude represents the mature Campbell, implying that all other representations of him were outgrown, is itself a misrepresentation of Campbell. *The Scroll* can find abundant support in Campbell for an ecumenical view of Christianity, and for a spirit of free inquiry. But to disguise Campbell as an apostle of the enlightenment is the sheerest kind of rationalization, suggestive of George Tyrrell's comment on Harnack's Jesus: "The Jesus Harnack sees is the visage of a red-faced German liberal peering at him from the bottom of a deep well." Neither can we find in Campbell authority for an indifference to denominational media of co-operation. The church Campbell saw was never an abstraction. He saw concrete local congregations, and he saw the aggregate of those congregations comprising the church of Christ on earth. He saw no loyalty to the church in general without that loyalty being expressed through a church in particular. The co-operation which he urged was one which exhausted itself neither at the top nor at the bottom, but one which was commensurate with the whole range of the kingdom of God on earth.

A long step toward understanding will be taken when it is recognized that the attempt to "save" Campbell from his contradictions by relegating those contradictions to different periods of his life is itself Campbellian in its desire for too simple a solution. Incompatible statements reflecting his attitude toward the clergy, the redeemed status of unimmersed persons, the missionary cause and the agencies for its accomplishment, the nature of revelation and truth, the word "Christology," the problem of human slavery, Christian nurture and infant dedication, whether Christianity is under "law" or "principle," the status of womanhood in the church, and the literal or liberal interpretation of the scriptures are found concurrently in too great abundance in Campbell's thought to justify this commonly accepted solution. Ecumenical and liberal statements in his earlier writings are matched by equally arbitrary, legalistic, and literal statements in his age of "maturity."

A more valid approach to Campbell must recognize this basic conflict in his thought, and, recognizing it, see Campbell as a symbol of transition from an authoritarian to a creative conception of Christianity. It must grasp the fact that although Campbell himself did not succeed in reconciling his scriptural with his rational norm of truth, he refused to relinquish either norm, and ultimately to be true to Campbell demands that we come to a conception of revelation that does not outrage reason, and to a conception of reason which is at home in the same universe with revelation. It must mean that, whereas Campbell relied now on the norm of scripture, now on the norm of reason, we must rely ever on both norms, and that the two be not at variance.

The second major task confronting Disciples of Christ is the recognition of the fact that many of the issues which gave impetus to the polemic career of Campbell are no longer relevant to our contemporary scene. To exhaust our energies with timeworn "pleas" which no longer apply is as ridiculous and futile as to combat atomic bombs by the beating of tom-toms.

Campbell confronted a denominational scene so intense that one sect of Presbyterians could charge his father, Thomas Campbell, with heresy for offering communion to another sect of Presbyterians. The historic plea for Christian unity was an issue of this condition. But Dis-

ciples of Christ of today are in the anomalous situation
of retreading the ancient fabric of the Campbells' message and rolling it past Presbyterians (as well as Methodists, Congregationalists, and so forth) who have not
only practiced union by forming mergers while Disciples
of Christ have practiced division by pulling apart, but
whose leaders are fully alive to the message and problems of union. For Disciples of Christ to plead as a
pattern for union a basis which has not been adequate to
hold their own factions together is both irrelevant and
ridiculous in the light of the historic situation of great
mergers between the "sects."

Campbell viewed an ecclesiastical world so jealous of
its orthodoxies that its written creeds were rigid tests
of fellowship. Much of Campbell's career was a protest
against any and all tyrannies by which men sought to
shut their fellow men out from Christ. Today Disciples
of Christ are in the embarrassing situation of attacking
the creeds of denominations which for the most part long
ago either ceased to use them as tests of fellowship, or
accepted the principle of private interpretation in regard
to the meaning of the creeds, while in danger themselves
of having embraced an oral creed which is frequently
made a rigid test of fellowship.

The extreme Calvinism of Campbell's day insisted on
looking on the infant child as so depraved by original
sin that he was in need of the rite of baptism in order
to escape the fires of hell. Campbell joined his voice
with Bushnell's position by further objecting to a parent's usurpation of the child's volitional right of decision. But both Campbell and Disciples of Christ continued to covertly practice what Bushnell overtly pleaded,
unwilling to admit that the alternative was a "neutral"
theory of education, that we must either share our faith
or withhold it. Disciples of Christ today face pedobaptist groups which for the most part no longer view infant
baptism in the light of extreme Calvinistic theology, but

as an overt act of dedication—the kind of dedication which all Disciples of Christ believe and seek to practice, either overtly or covertly.[30]

Campbell rebelled against a theology which held that there are no means of grace, that God saves whom he will, and whom he will he destroys. The call to the ministry was either by apostolic succession or by a direct operation of the Holy Spirit. Campbell conceived the ministry as functional, the call to the ministry as in the nature of a social contract, and ordination as a seal that the minister had already been called. Disciples of Christ today face a scene in which even those groups which continue to embrace the doctrine of apostolic succession have so enlarged their conception of the functional nature of the office of the ministry that they are usually far more careful to insure the selection of men qualified to fulfill their part of the social contract than are a group of Disciples who have as yet discovered no satisfactory general principle of ordination.

Along with his literalistic approach to the scriptures Campbell advocated principles of biblical interpretation, which, if adopted, must inevitably lead to an intelligent biblical criticism. Since his day many advances have been made in the field of biblical criticism, advances which have not only changed but have enlarged our understanding and appreciation of the scriptures. But for a Disciple today to wed himself to his slogans ("Where the Bible speaks we speak"; "No book but the Bible"; "Call Bible things by Bible names") frequently puts him

[30]The overt act of infant dedication is growing as a practice in many churches of Disciples of Christ.

in the position of knowing more Bible and less truth than his contemporaries.

This is a part of the changed scene which makes many of the original "pleas" of Disciples of Christ irrelevant today. To continue to stick our heads in these nineteenth-century sands is to lead an ostrichlike existence. All of which leads to the question, "Whither the Disciples?" This question suggests the third major implication for Disciples of Christ growing out of Campbell's conception of the structure and function of the church. That implication is the task of seeking to share those insights of Campbell which have permanent validity, which are pertinent to an emergent Christianity. This is not to suggest that the insights discussed above have no permanent validity so much as to affirm that no longer are some of them revelant issues. But there are other issues which are not only relevant, but, if anything, more pertinent, to our contemporary scene than to the situation pictured in Campbell's day.

Disciples of Christ need no greater sense of ambassadorship than that which they can find in three emphases which are as strong as any to be found in Campbell—much stronger than some others which have been given greater prominence. Those emphases are (1) ecumenicity, (2) co-operation, and (3) creative democracy.

It must be recognized that Campbell's belief in Christian union was rooted in his conception of the ecumenical nature of Christianity, not vice versa. To preach a kind of Christian union which would restrict Christianity to an exclusive pattern is the worst kind of violence to this ecumenical concept. To be true to Campbell is to be true to Campbell at his best. And Campbell was at his best when he protested any proscription which would shut out any brother whom Christ would receive, when, in his defense against N. L. Rice, he said: "The gentleman complains that our foundation is too broad—too liberal. It is indeed broad, liberal, and strong. If it were not so, it would not be a Christian foundation."

In a world which has shrunk to a neighborhood, an ecumenical Christianity is equipped to make a world impact unprecedented in history. And Disciples of Christ, with their historic concern for union, are peculiarly situated to seize this profound insight of their foremost religious founder, and to consecrate themselves to the enrichment of emergent ecumenical movements, to lose their platform of union in order to find an ecumenical reality.

Campbell was pre-eminently a practical man. While he believed in, and pleaded for, union, he was confronted with a picture of division. Therefore, as a first step toward the goal in which he believed, he embraced the strategy of co-operation. And because he believed in taking the first step first, he had infinitely more to say about co-operation than he did about union. Further, while he believed that the genius of Christianity jealously sheltered the liberty of individuals, congregations, and communions, he further believed that the very nature of that liberty impelled individuals, congregations, and communions to co-operate freely and fully with all other Christians, individually and collectively, in the promotion of all good. To practice denominational isolationism is the greatest violence to this principle, and from such isolationism to preach union is unthinkable. Those Disciples who share Campbell's profound insight into the Christian principle of co-operative action have every reason to justify their existence as a body, and to contribute to the correlate goal of an ecumenical church.

If there is any one of the insights of Campbell for which Disciples are more peculiarly adapted by genius and by history than any other, it is that insight which conceived each individual collection of Christians, or "ecclesia," as most ideally constituted when enriched by the free interplay of each mind and heart in the group.

In discussing the possible outcomes of the collective action of individuals, Dr. McDougall adduces data to support his claim that the resultant action of individuals so congregated may be, on the one hand, less intelligent and less desirable than that of the least intelligent member acting as an individual, and on the other, more intelligent and more desirable than the individual action of the best and most intelligent member. In further delineating those essential factors which best insure the most desirable outcome of group action, he lists factors which are likely to be found in the religious deliberative group.[31]

Disciples of Christ are not only among those religious groups which have the opportunity of insuring the incorporation of those factors contributing to the most desirable type of group action; they are, in a way, the religious counterpart of the American political quest for a democratic way of life. Owing their very charter

---

[31]*See* Wm. McDougall, *The Group Mind,* Part I.

to the "religious declaration of independence," developing along the American frontier and emerging as the most prominent of the indigenous religious movements of America, it is tragic that they have permitted certain ancient shibboleths to becloud the grand advantage of their position. If Disciples of Christ would concentrate on the educational possibilities of a local church organization so structured as to stimulate and elicit the creative participation of the most humble part in the functioning of the whole, they would justify the faith of Campbell not only in the right of each member to so participate, but in the rightness of the outcome of such participation; they would demonstrate the ultimate of faith in democracy; they would sound the most desirable educational approach to their task; and they would have found not only a plea, but a program.

BIBLIOGRAPHY

I. *Primary Sources*

A. *Books*

Campbell, Alexander. *Christian Baptism, with Its Antecedents and Consequents.* Bethany, Va., Printed and Published by Alexander Campbell, 1851, 444 pp.

Campbell, Alexander. *The Christian System in Reference to the Union of Christians and a Restoration of Primitive Christianity, as Plead in the Current Reformation.* 3rd edition, Pittsburgh, Published by Forrester & Campbell, 1840, 354 pp.

Campbell, Alexander. *The Christian Preacher's Companion, or, the Gospel Facts Sustained by the Testimony of Unbelieving Jews and Pagans.* Centreville, Ky., Published for R. B. Neal, 1891, 160 pp.

Campbell, Alexander, and Rice, N. L. *A Debate Between Rev. A. Campbell and Rev. N. L. Rice, on the Action, Subject, Design and Administrator of Christian Baptism; Also, on the Character of Spiritual Influence in Conversion and Sanctification, and on the Expediency and Tendency of Ecclesiastic Creeds, as Terms of Union and Communion.* Lexington, Ky., A. T. Skillman & Son, 1844, 912 pp.

Campbell, Alexander, and Walker, John. *A Debate on Christian Baptism, Between Mr. John Walker, A Minister of the Secession, and Alexander Campbell, to Which Is Added a Large Appendix (Second Edition Enlarged).* Pittsburgh, Published by Eichbaum and Johnston, 1822, 292 pp.

Campbell, Alexander, and Maccalla, W. L. *A Debate on Christian Baptism, Between The Rev. W. L. Maccalla and Alexander Campbell, in Which Are Interspersed and to Which Are Added Animadversions on Different Treatises on the*

Same Subject Written by Dr. J. Mason, Dr. S. Ralston, Rev. E. Pond, Rev. J. P. Campbell, Rector Armstrong, and the Rev. J. Walker. Buffalo, Va., Published by Campbell & Sala, 1824, 420 pp.

Campbell, Alexander, and Owen, Robert. *Debate on the Evidences of Christianity Containing an Examination of the "Social System," and of All the Systems of Scepticism of Ancient and Modern Times; Between Robert Owen, of New Lanark, Scotland, and Alexander Campbell, of Bethany, Virginia, with an Appendix by the Parties.* Bethany, Va., Printed and Published by Alexander Campbell, 1829, 2 vols. in one.

Campbell, Alexander, and Skinner, D. *A Discussion of the Doctrines of Endless Misery and Universal Salvation in an Epistolary Correspondence Between Alexander Campbell of Bethany, and Dolphus Skinner, of Utica, N. Y.* Utica, N. Y., C. C. P. Grosh, Printer, 1840, 436 pp.

Campbell, Alexander. *Letters to a Skeptic, Reprinted from the Christian Baptist.* Cincinnati, H. S. Bosworth, Publisher, 1859, 57 pp.

Campbell, Alexander. *Memoirs of Elder Thomas Campbell, Together with a Brief Memoir of Mrs. Jane Campbell.* Cincinnati, Published by H. S. Bosworth, 1861, 319 pp.

Campbell, Alexander. *Popular Lectures and Addresses.* Philadelphia, James Challen & Son, 1863, 647 pp.

Campbell, Alexander, and Purcell, J. B. *A Debate on the Roman Catholic Religion* (First Published in 1837). Cincinnati, Chase & Hall, Publishers, 1875, 360 pp.

Campbell, Alexander. *The Sacred Writings of the Apostles and Evangelists of Jesus Christ, Commonly Styled the New Testament. Translated from the Original Greek, by Doctors George Campbell, James Macknight, and Phillip Doddridge, with Prefaces, Various Emendations, and an Appendix by Alexander Campbell.* Stereotyped from the Third Edition, Revised. Bethany, Va., by A. Campbell, 1833, 336 pp.

Campbell, Selina Huntington. *Home Life and Reminiscences of Alexander Campbell by His Wife.* St. Louis, John Burns, Publisher, 1882, 503 pp.

B. *Periodicals*

Campbell, Alexander, Ed. *The Christian Baptist.* Published Monthly, Edited by Alexander Campbell, Vol. I—Vol. VII. (Years 1823-1830.) Bethany, Printed by A. Campbell, at the Bethany Printing Office, 1823-1830.

Campbell, Alexander, Ed. *The Christian Baptist,* Edited by Alexander Campbell. Seven Volumes in One, Revised by D. S. Burnet, from the Second Edition, with Mr. Campbell's Last Corrections (Thirteenth Edition). Cincinnati, Published by H. S. Bosworth, 1867, 670 pp.

Campbell, Alexander, Ed. *The Millennial Harbinger,* Vol. I— Vol. XXXV. (Years 1830-1864.) Bethany, Printed and Published by the Editor, 1830-1864.

Pendleton, W. K., Ed. *The Millennial Harbinger.* Vol. XXXVI-Vol. XLI. (Years 1865-1870). Bethany, Printed and Published by W. K. Pendleton, 1865-1870.

II. *Secondary Sources*

A. *Books*

Abbott, B. A. *The Disciples, an Interpretation.* St. Louis, The Bethany Press, 1924, 271 pp.

Ainslie, Peter. *The Message of the Disciples for the Union of the Church, Including Their Origin and History.* New York, Fleming H. Revell Company, 1913, 212 pp.

Athearn, C. R. *The Religious Education of Alexander Campbell, Morning Star of the Coming Reformation.* St. Louis, The Bethany Press, 1928, 204 pp.

Baxter, William. *Life of Elder Walter Scott.* (The Walter Scott Centennial Edition, Abridged by B. A. Abbott.) St. Louis, The Bethany Press, 1926, 215 pp.

Billington, R. A. *The Protestant Crusade, 1800-1860; A Study of the Origins of American Nativism.* New York, The Macmillan Co., 1938, 514 pp.

Bogardus, Emory Stephen. *Leaders and Leadership.* New York–London, D. Appleton-Century Co., 1934, 325 pp.

Brown, William Adams. *Church and State in Contemporary America.* New York, Charles Scribner's Sons, 1936, 360 pp.

Brown, William Adams. *The Church, Catholic and Protestant.* New York, Charles Scribner's Sons, 1935, 421 pp.

Brown, William Adams. *The Church in America.* New York, The Macmillan Co., 1922, 378 pp.

Bushnell, Horace. *Christian Nurture.* New York, Charles Scribner, 1864, 407 pp.

Davis, M. M. *How the Disciples Began and Grew, A Short History of the Christian Church.* Cincinnati, The Standard Publishing Co., 1915, 244 pp.

DeGroot, A. T. *The Grounds of Divisions Among the Disciples of Christ.* Chicago, Privately Printed, 1940, 228 pp.

DeGroot, A. T. (And E. E. Dowling.) *The Literature of the Disciples of Christ.* Advance, Indiana, Hustler Print, 1933, 78 pp.

Egbert, James. *Alexander Campbell and Christian Liberty, A Centennial Volume on His Controlling Ideas—Enforced by His Own Words.* St. Louis, Christian Publishing Co., 1909, 344 pp.

Elliott, Harrison Sacket. *The Process of Group Thinking.* New York, Association Press, 1928, 229 pp.

Ferguson, C. W. *The Confusion of Tongues, A Review of Modern Isms.* Garden City, New York, Doubleday, Doran and Company, 1928, 464 pp.

Fortune, A. W. *The Disciples in Kentucky.* St. Louis, Published by the Convention of the Christian Churches in Kentucky, Christian Board of Publication, 1932, 415 pp.

Garrison, J. H. *Memories and Experiences, A Brief Story of a Long Life—An Autobiography.* St. Louis, Christian Board of Publication, 1926, 269 pp.

Garrison, J. H., Ed. *The Reformation of the Nineteenth Century; A Series of Historical Sketches Dealing with the Rise and Progress of the Religious Movement Inaugurated by Thomas and Alexander Campbell from Its Origin to the Close of the Nineteenth Century.* St. Louis, Christian Publishing Co., 1901, 514 pp.

Garrison, W. E. *Religion Follows the Frontier—A History of the Disciples of Christ.* New York and London, Harper and Brothers, Publishers, 1931, 317 pp.

Garrison, W. E. *Alexander Campbell's Theology, Its Sources and Historical Setting.* St. Louis, Christian Publishing Co., 1900, 302 pp.

Garrison, W. E. *An American Religious Movement; A Brief History of the Disciples of Christ.* St. Louis, Christian Board of Publication, 1945, 167 pp.

Garrison, W. E. *The Sources of Alexander Campbell's Theology.* St. Louis, Christian Publishing Co., 1900, 302 pp.

Gates, Errett. *The Disciples of Christ (The Story of the Churches).* New York, The Baker and Taylor Co., 1905, 346 pp.

Gates, Errett. *The Early Relation and Separation of Baptists and Disciples.* Chicago, The Christian Century Co., 1904, 124 pp.

Grafton, T. W. *Alexander Campbell, Leader of the Great Reformation of the Nineteenth Century.* St. Louis, Christian Publishing Co., 1897, 234 pp.

Haley, J. J. *Debates That Made History; The Story of Alexander Campbell's Debates with Rev. John Walker, Rev. W. L. Maccalla, Mr. Robert Owen, Bishop Purcell, and Rev. Nathan L. Rice.* St. Louis, Christian Board of Publication, 1920, 249 pp.

Hartshorne, Hugh. *Character in Human Relations.* New York, C. Scribner's Sons, 1932, 367 pp.

Hayden, A. S. *Early History of the Disciples in the Western Reserve, Ohio, with Biographical Sketches of the Principal Agents in Their Religious Movement.* Cincinnati, Chase and Hall, Publishers, 1875, 476 pp.

Kellems, Jesse R. *Alexander Campbell and the Disciples.* New York, Richard R. Smith, Inc., 1930, 409 pp.

Kershner, F. D. *How to Promote Christian Union, an Historical and Practical Handbook.* Cincinnati, The Standard Publishing Co., 1916, 235 pp.

Kincheloe, Samuel Clarence. *The American City and Its Church.* New York, Friendship Press, 1938, 177 pp.

Longan, G. W. *Origin of the Disciples of Christ, A Review of Prof. W. H. Whitsitt's Volume Entitled "Origin of the Disciples of Christ." To Which Is Added an Appendix*

Containing Extracts from Reviews of Prof. Whitsitt's Book by Baptist Writers. St. Louis, Christian Publishing Co., 1889, 195 pp.

Lunger, Harold L., *The Political Ethics of Alexander Campbell.* St. Louis, The Bethany Press, 1954, 304 pp.

McDougall, Wm. *The Group Mind.* New York, G. P. Putnam's Sons, 1920, 418 pp.

McLean, Archibald. *Alexander Campbell as a Preacher: A Study.* New York, Fleming H. Revell Co., 1908, 46 pp.

Moore, W. T. *A Comprehensive History of the Disciples of Christ, Being an Account of a Century's Effort to Restore Primitive Christianity in Its Faith, Doctrine and Life.* New York, Fleming H. Revell Co., 1909, 830 pp.

Morrill, M. T. *A History of the Christian Denomination in America, 1794-1911 A.D.* Dayton, Ohio, The Christian Publishing Association, 1912, 407 pp.

Pigors, Paul John William. *Leadership or Domination.* Boston and New York: Houghton-Mifflin Co., 1935, 354 pp.

Richardson, Robert. *Memoirs of Alexander Campbell, Embracing a View of the Origin, Progress and Principles of the Religious Reformation Which He Advocated,* Cincinnati, Standard Publishing Co., 1913, 2 vols.

Smith, Benjamin L. *Alexander Campbell.* St. Louis, The Bethany Press, 1930, 399 pp.

Sweet, William Warren, *Makers of Christianity, from John Cotton to Lyman Abbott.* New York, Henry Holt and Co., 1937.

Sweet, William Warren, *The Story of Religion in America.* New York and London, Harper & Brothers, Publishers, 1930, 542 pp.

Tead, Ordway. *The Art of Leadership.* New York, McGraw-Hill Book Co., 1935, 308 pp.

Tyler, B. B. *A History of the Disciples of Christ* (The American Church History Series). New York, The Christian Literature Co., 1894, 164 pp.

Walker, Williston. *A History of the Christian Church.* New York, Charles Scribner's Sons, 1940, 624 pp.

Ware, Charles C. *Barton Warren Stone, Pathfinder of Christian Union, A Story of His Life and Times.* St. Louis, The Bethany Press, 1932, 357 pp.

Welshimer, P. H. *Concerning the Disciples; A Brief Resume of the Movement to Restore the New Testament Church.* Cincinnati, The Standard Publishing Co., 1935, 205 pp.

West, Robert Frederick. *Alexander Campbell and Natural Religion.* New Haven, Yale University Press, 1948, 250 pp.

Whitsitt, W. H. *Origin of the Disciples of Christ (Campbellites), A Contribution to the Centennial Anniversary of the Birth of Alexander Campbell* (Fourth Edition). Louisville, Charles T. Dearing, 1899, 112 pp.

Willett, Herbert L. (And Others.) *Progress, Anniversary Volume of the Campbell Institute on the Completion of Twenty Years of History.* Chicago, The Christian Century Press, 1917, 329 pp.

B. *Periodicals*

The Christian-Evangelist (National Weekly of Disciples of Christ), St. Louis, Christian Board of Publication.

The Christian Standard (Devoted to the Restoration of Primitive Christianity). Cincinnati, The Christian Standard Publishing Co.

The Harbinger and Discipliana (Quarterly publication of the Disciples of Christ Historical Society), Canton, Mo., and Nashville, Tenn.

The Gospel Advocate (An Independent Weekly Representing the Churches of Christ). Nashville, Tenn., The Gospel Advocate.

The Scroll. Chicago, Published Monthly by the Campbell Institute.

INDEX

A

American Bible Society, 133, 219, 221ff.

American Christian Missionary Society, 203, 205ff., 212

Apostolic succession, 21f., 34, 50ff., 112, 134, 140, 250

Appomatox Decrees, 44

B

Baptism. *See* Immersion

Baptist, 32f., 40ff., 50, 66, 96, 99, 126, 161

Bethany College. *See* Church colleges

Bible, as a textbook, 19, 26ff., 96, 214, 220, 235; authority of, 19, 29, 40, 45, 54f., 75ff., 84, 112, 122f., 150f., 195, 248; interpretation of, 70, 250; revision of, 130, 222

Bishops, 20ff. *See also* Elders

Bushnell, Horace, 94f., 105f., 241ff., 249

C

Campbell, Alexander, apostle of freedom, 24f., 57ff., 78, 89-115; conflicting statements, 15, 52f., 56, 59f., 62f., 72f., 80ff., 107, 144, 151, 173f., 183f., 195, 211f., 219f., 247f.; contributions of, 240-254; debates, 14, 58f., 114; educational philosophy, 92ff., 114, 168-173, 177ff., 235, 240ff.; gift of satire, 30, 47; political philosophy, 97ff., 169-179

Campbell, Thomas, 15ff., 32, 40, 55, 248

Children in the church, 61, 105ff., 129, 133, 176f., 248

Christ, divinity of, 69; lordship of, 18, 75-90, 119. *See also* Christology

Christian Baptist, 12, 15, 41, 52, 89, 113, 117, 126, 138, 150, 183ff., 203, 208, 213, 219, 227, 246

Christian dispensations, 75ff., 82, 86

Christian nurture, 94ff., 105ff.

Christian unity, 13, 54f., 121f., 224, 232, 248f., 251f.

Christianity, a liberal institution, 58f., 88f., 106, 123f., 223f., 238ff.

Christocracy, 75-86, 92

Christology, 80ff.

Church, as a fellowship, 86ff., 131f., 154, 168-173, 235-240, 244, 253; authority of, 19f., 137-149, 154-159, 193ff., 233; functions of, 120, 225-254; nature of, 35, 116-124, 193, 198, 234; ordinances of, 124-130

Church auxiliaries, 45, 71-74, 120f.

Church colleges, 70, 96f., 169, 185, 212-217

Church courts and councils, 23, 44f., 52, 64-67, 122, 131

Church membership, 129-134, 167-179

Church of England, 25, 33ff.

Church officers, 20-22, 37f., 48ff., 84, 112-115, 135-149. *See also* Deacons and Elders

Clergy, greed of, 49f., 148f.; power of, 45-53, 64, 105; reformation of, 29f. *See also* Ministry and Preachers